STARK RAVING RULERS

TWENTY MINOR DESPOTS OF [THE TWENTY-FI]RST CENTURY

SEAN MONCRIEFF

POOLBEG

Published 2004 by Poolbeg Press Ltd.
123 Grange Hill, Baldoyle,
Dublin 13, Ireland
Email: poolbeg@poolbeg.com

1 3 5 7 9 10 8 6 4 2

A catalogue record for this book is available from the British Library.

ISBN 1-84223-210-X

Typeset by Patricia Hope in Sabon 10.5/13.75
Printed by Cox & Wyman, Reading, Berkshire

www.poolbeg.com

Contents

FOREWORD

First, a definition: by 'Despot' I mean an individual or party who continues to rule their country by autocratic means – either by rigging elections or not having any at all; who forbids freedom of the press and who employs the state security forces for political purposes.

They are *minor* because – unlike Stalin or Hitler – they have not achieved the dizzy heights of mass murder. Apart from China, Despotism is more a cottage industry these days: if your country is small, unimportant and unnoticed, you're more likely to get away with it.

To paraphrase the cliché, once you look for twenty despots, many more come along. Some may quibble with my choices, and certainly there are dozens of countries not mentioned here who endure autocratic governments and a lack of democracy. Today there are still *billions* of people on this planet who have no control over their political future, who can be harassed, starved, tortured and killed for simply getting in the way. People die horrible deaths in countries most of us have never heard of.

So this book does not claim to be an exhaustive survey. It is, rather, a representative sample of oppression in the twenty-first century. Despite the fall of the Eastern Bloc and talk of the 'international community', things haven't got any better, just different.

Of course, from the relative comfort of the West, it's easy to criticise. Part of the problem is that many of these countries have had Western-style democracy grafted upon them when perhaps some other system might have suited better, at least initially. Definitions of 'freedom' differ in different parts of the world, according to the local traditions and immediate need. Yet right is right and wrong is wrong, and it is a patronising cop-out to let some murderous dictator off the hook just because the 'culture' is different to ours.

However, it's only fair to point out that not all the despots profiled here are particularly evil or vicious: a small number have used their absolute power to benefit their citizens. Sometimes, dictatorship works. Sort of.

Some of the facts I report here may be proven to be incorrect. It is in the nature of dictatorships to be secretive, so in a small amount of cases, exhaustive fact-checking proved difficult.

If I have misrepresented any of the murderers, thieves and madmen profiled here, then I extend my profound apologies. I'll just have to live with the guilt.

PRESIDENT ALEXANDER GRIGORYEVICH LUKASHENKO

of the Republic of Belarus

Now here's a funny one: funny unusual rather than funny ha-ha. More than a decade after the demise of the USSR, Belarus is a little taste of Soviet Russia: in fact, it's more Soviet Russia than Soviet Russia ever was. Belarus is a country with its own language and culture, yet has a leader who still yearns to give away its sovereignty.

And that leader, President AG Lukashenko, (as the fawning official biography calls him), is the funniest thing of all: a gruff, bluff, plain-speaking man who has no time for intellectuals or namby-pamby liberals; who can spend several hours telling you what a plain-speaking man he is. He is a man with a genuine support base in his country, yet who still feels the need to fix elections and suppress political rivals. He is a man who repeatedly accuses the US of interfering in the electoral processes of his country: and he's right, the US *does* interfere. In the last truly authoritarian state in Europe, here is an old-style socialist who sports a moustache and comb-over which makes him a double for Adolph Hitler.

3

Low self-esteem: that could be at the heart of both Belarus and its leader. Deep in his psyche, AG may fear that he doesn't really deserve to be president; deep in its psyche, Belarus may fear that it doesn't deserve to be a country.

Part of the problem is that Belarus – often referred to as White Russia – always seemed to belong to someone else. First settled in the fifth century by a mixture of Baltic and Slavic tribes, it became part of Russia in the twelfth century, then two hundred years later was absorbed into the Grand Duchy of Lithuania, which in turn became part of Poland. Poland and Russia then spent the next two hundred years knocking the hell out of one another, a lot of which took place in and around Belarus. Didn't do much for tourism.

Finally, in the eighteenth century, after Napoleon had been and gone, it became part of Russia again.

But people just couldn't get enough of having wars there, so Belarus was devastated by World War I, and following swiftly on from that, the Soviet-Polish war of 1919-20. When the war finished, Belarus had been split in half: the western section remained with Poland while what was left became the Byelorussian Soviet Socialist Republic, or Byelorussia.

Naturally, when World War II broke out, the various armies couldn't wait to get into Byelorussia. The Russians used the hostilities as an opportunity to snatch back the piece of Byelorussia that the Poles had grabbed. But they didn't keep it for long. Nazi Germany invaded in 1941, remaining there for three years. Byelorussia's Jewish population of some 2.2 million – there since the fourteenth century – was annihilated.

The Soviet army took back control in 1944 – including most of the western section grabbed from the Poles. The country had been flattened. Two years later, both Ukraine and Byelorussia became founder members of the United Nations: the only two Soviet republics allowed their own representation at the UN. This, however, was not an indication of any greater independence from Moscow's rule. To allay Stalin's fears that the UN would not be dominated by Western powers, Churchill and Roosevelt had suggested that Ukraine and Byelorussia be given their own seats at the UN – thus assuring the USSR of three votes in the general assembly.

In fact, Byelorussia spent the next twenty years having the *Byelo* part gently expunged from its consciousness. As the country was rebuilt, Russians held all of the key posts while the Byelorussian language was effectively banned. Apparently, Kruschev felt that Communism would work much better if everyone spoke Russian.

And it worked too: today in Belarus, most people speak Russian as a first language, while back then, even Communism seemed to be having a positive effect. Byelorussia became one of the most prosperous parts of the USSR – and thus in far less need of oppressing. Yes, their culture was being diluted by a totalitarian regime, but – relatively speaking – this was one of the happiest periods in Byelorussian history, and at least partially explains why AG Lukashenko retains popular support.

But that prosperity received something of a dent in April 1986 when an explosion blew the steel and concrete lid off reactor number four at the Chernobyl Nuclear Power Plant. Located in neighbouring Ukraine, the fall-out poisoned the land for hundreds of miles around, including large swathes of Byelorussia, which to this day remains rank with contamination. It is estimated that one-third of the country's agricultural land is unusable; or more precisely, shouldn't be used. But we'll get to that.

Thus the Byelorussian economy was already looking a

bit dodgy when the USSR broke up in 1991. But, having no choice, the Byelorussian Supreme Soviet voted to declare independence and change the name of the country to Belarus. Only one deputy voted against the dissolution of the USSR: AG Lukashenko. And a fat lot of good it did him.

No USSR, but the Belarus' Supreme Soviet still fancied a little bit of communism and installed Stanislau Shushkevich, a moderate reformer, as its leader. But you know the way it is when you're a *moderate* reformer: you're a bit too much of that, a bit too little of the other. By trying to please everyone, poor old Stanislau managed to satisfy no one, in the process making an even bigger mess of the economy. In 1994, he was ousted after a vote of no confidence.

Running desperately short of ideas, the old guard commies who still dominated the Supreme Soviet decided to give democracy a try. It could work. They knocked up a new constitution, placing legislative power in the hands of a new 260-member Supreme Council. Later that same year, elections to the Council and for the presidency took place. AG Lukashenko was elected with over eighty per cent of the vote: all this 'reform' wasn't working for the public either, many of whom – especially in rural areas – yearned for the more prosperous USSR days. However, reformers took a majority of seats in the new Supreme Council.

And let's be clear: it was a *bona fide* electoral win. Almost uniquely among our despots, AG started with a genuine mandate. He just never felt the need to get another one.

So who is he? He was born in 1954 in the rural Vitensk region of Belarus. Not the ritziest of addresses, and not the most comfortable of childhoods either: to use the old-fashioned parlance, AG was illegitimate, putting him and his scandalously unmarried mother in the firing line for plenty of tut-tutting and childhood taunts. Enough perhaps to place a fine big chip on the young AG's shoulder.

He did the usual couple of stints in the army and ended up managing a state farm. For fun he liked to play the accordion and ice hockey. Big, manly pursuits.

But as is often the way in communist countries, work and politics are inextricably linked: AG obviously pleased his betters so much that they encouraged him to run for election to the Supreme Soviet. He was elected in 1990 and quickly made a name for himself, booming his disapproval while a member of the modestly titled Supreme Council Committee on Fighting Corruption. To quote again from the official biography: 'A.G. Lukashenko follows the sober way of life; he denounces idlers, traitors, drunkards, those who do not keep their word'.

It is an image he has maintained to perfection. He likes to be called *Batka* (father), just like Stalin was, and loves being photographed astride a tractor, chatting to salt-of-the-earth workers or playing sport. Particularly sport: he was even chairman of the Belarusian Olympic committee, despite a rule which forbids political officials from holding such an office. On another occasion, he refused to meet an official from the Council of Europe on the grounds that he had a football match to attend. "Fifty thousand fans are waiting for me," he said. "I cannot let them down." AG loves sport. And he loves annoying foreign diplomats even more. One of his first acts as president was to congratulate the military for shooting down two US balloonists who had strayed into Belarusian airspace.

It was the kind of thing that worked a treat with the plain folks during the 1994 presidential elections. Perhaps he was the man to put things back the way they were in the good old USSR days. Which was exactly what AG intended to do.

However, while denouncing and being sober were obviously big passions of his, he didn't seem overly keen on his wife. He met Galina, the mother of his two sons, while at college. Apparently, he used to buy her flowers and even wrote poetry. Yet after the presidential election, AG and his sons moved to the capital, Minsk, while Galina remained behind in the tiny village of Ryzhkovich, 150 miles down the road, close to the state farm AG used to run.

In a typically frank statement in 1997, AG declared that 'wives have no business in the affairs of state officials', adding that he had no need of 'advisers in the form of his wife and children'.

However, it is an open secret in Belarus that Galina isn't all alone in Ryzhkovich, where her income is said to be just $16 a month. She is in the constant company of two secret police guards. Rather than divorce his wife, AG just had her arrested.

But hey: even a guy as sober as AG gets lonely. At first, he was constantly seen in the company of an attractive brunette named Irina Abelskaya, officially described as the president's personal doctor. You can insert the 'prescription' and 'treatment' jokes yourself. Later on, Irina turned blond, and gave birth to a baby boy.

AG has also been linked to a beauty queen, Lika Yalinskaya, and a little-known singer, Irina Dorofeyeva, who became considerably better known when state TV and radio suddenly started playing her songs.

But back to the politics. As soon as he was in power, AG declared he was having none of this reform nonsense. Price controls were reintroduced, exchange regulations reimposed and privatisation halted. The economy went back to being centrally planned, just like in the good old days. Today, ninety-five per cent of the economy is in the hands of the state.

The difference was that in the good old days, Belarus had the USSR to buy its products, and the USSR to buy cheap gas from. In the good old days, a third of its land hadn't been poisoned by Chernobyl.

Or, at least, that's what the namby-pamby liberals were saying. AG was having none of it, and declared that it was his intention to forge closer links with Russia: to eventually merge the two countries into one state.

Yet not everyone was thrilled with this prescription: certainly not the Belarusian nationalists who began protesting in the streets. Even the Supreme Council started to get a bit shirty, squabbling with the president over the distribution of power. And despite rolling back the economic reforms, the financial lot of the ordinary citizen was not getting any better.

AG listened to the whingeing for a couple of years, then got sick of it. In 1995 and 1996, he called two snap referenda. Both of them were passed, but in both cases foreign electoral monitors reported irregularities. The referenda were subsequently judged by a Belarusian court as non-binding since they violated the 1994 constitution. All of which was ignored, naturally. The new 1996 constitution increased AG's term of office from five to seven years and gave him new sweeping powers: Commander-in-Chief of the armed forces, head of the powerful Security Council and the ability to dissolve the parliament. Which he swiftly did, replacing it with a new two-tier House of Representatives. There were fresh elections to the new Palata Predstavitely, but again there were widespread allegations of vote-rigging, tampering with the electoral lists and barring opposition candidates on technicalities. In effect, the new parliament was hand-picked by AG.

With a suitably supportive parliament, AG then went about devising a set of guidelines for Belarusian 'development' until 2000: a five-year plan. Just like they used to have in the USSR.

But you'll always have the knockers. The international community condemned the elections, while the International Monetary Fund suspended lending any more dosh to Belarus until market reforms were put in place. Since 1999 (when AG's original term of office was due to expire), many countries have refused to recognise him as the legitimate head of state. Protests in Minsk in that year were met with widespread arrests. Many opposition leaders had to leave the country, and quick. Other political opponents received prison sentences on trumped-up charges (usually 'corruption' of some kind). There are continuing allegations of torture in Belarusian prisons.

Afterwards, a presidential decree required all associations to re-register with the state. Any that the President didn't like the look of were simply not re-registered, effectively barring them from political activity. When the Belarusian Congress of Trade Unions complained, it had its bank account frozen.

At this stage AG was seemingly obsessed with the notion that everything would be OK once there was political union between Russia and Belarus: an aim now enshrined in his 1996 constitution. Russian was made the second official language. In 1997 he evicted all foreign aid organisations and even banned the Belarusian flag, considering it dangerously nationalistic.

At international soccer matches, Belarusian fans are regularly arrested for wearing red and white: the national colours of their country.

But why was AG so keen on a merger with Russia? One explanation is that he genuinely thought it would help Belarus; another is that he is plain bonkers, while a third theory has it that this was as much to do with ambition for himself as for his country. A new union would enable him to pursue a political ambition perhaps secretly fostered years ago: president of the USSR. Or close enough.

Yet if it did happen, it was never going to be a union of equals. Belarus' GDP equalled just three per cent of Russia's, while AG's already poor reputation overseas didn't make him the sort of friend the Russian leadership really needed.

Nonetheless, they were polite when AG came to call, which was often. Like a woman dealing with an over-keen suitor, they smiled and nodded, though not too enthusiastically. In 1997 they signed an agreement which vaguely aspired to union. They began making arrangements for economic and monetary merger. Yet the progress was slow. Given his track record with women, the Russians weren't entirely keen on getting into bed with him.

Even if the Russians had been keen, AG wasn't making it easy for them. With a travel ban slapped on him by the EU and the US, he sought the affections of other countries: like China, Iran, Libya and Iraq. Not a smart move. Especially Iraq. In the For-Us-Or-Against-Us mood after September 11th, AG fell firmly into the latter category. In the run-up to the Gulf War, the US accused Belarus of helping Iraq develop Weapons of Mass Destruction, an accusation not helped by an intercepted shipment of military uniforms from Belarus to Iraq. During the war, Belarus was mentioned as a possible bolt-hole for Saddam if he fled the country. Bet he wishes he was there now.

AG denied the WMD accusations, but no one paid any attention. Apart from running an undemocratic regime, he seemed to have gone out of his way to snub western countries and their diplomats: the state media constantly pumps out a message of how Belarus is surrounded by hostile nations, while AG himself seems to delight in delivering petty slights to his western neighbours. In 1998 he effectively evicted six ambassadors from their residences on the grounds that the sewers had to be fixed. By a wild coincidence, they happened to be Britain, the US and France, Greece, Italy

11

and Germany: all countries that had criticised his regime. No doubt, the bug-sweepers were out in force when they returned.

Belarus posed no strategic threat to the US, but by not making the right noises about the War on Terror, it was now on the Baddies List. Colin Powell branded him the 'lone remaining outlaw in Europe'. He had to go. So to get rid of him, the Americans mobilised one of their best secret weapons: Michael Kozak.

Kozak became the American ambassador to Belarus in 2000, and for a very specific reason: he was a specialist in attempting to influence the outcome of foreign elections, through the use of something far more deadly than covert operations. He used marketing. He'd done it before in Serbia and Nicaragua. Basically the drill was to make contact with opposition groups, help organise them into a viable political force, and then give them huge piles of cash to make their political dreams a reality.

Under American law, this is illegal: US aid money may not go to foreign political parties. So instead they gave the cash to individuals who just happened to have a great deal of party political machinery around them. It quacked, but it wasn't quite a duck. The duck was given about $50 million, and was named Vladimir Goncharik, who the Yanks hoped would take out AG in the 2001 presidential elections.

Ambassador Kozak started with students. He imported student leaders from Serbia – hugely influential in the fall of Slobodan Milosevic – to advise Belarusian students how to organise themselves. As a result, Zubr (Bison) was established: a movement of guerrilla-style protestors who used tee-shirts, stickers and websites to promote their message. Over a period of months they plastered Minsk with pictures of a crazed-looking AG over the slogan 'It's time to get rid of him'.

Next, the American produced doctored opinion polls to give the impression that AG was fast losing support while Goncharik – who previously had a very low public profile – was becoming wildly popular. In truth, secret polls had revealed that there wasn't any opposition leader who could mount a credible challenge to AG: partially because of AG's propaganda machine (his picture is everywhere), and partially because the opposition groups spent so much time fighting with each other.

Then came the propaganda. Some of it was outright lies: that AG had banned the speaking of Belarusian; that he persecuted Jews and Catholics. However, some of it was far more credible. In 1999, an opposition leader named Viktor Gonchar, along with several other politicians and journalists, disappeared. The two state prosecutors originally tasked with investigating these disappearances suddenly found the need to flee Belarus, and were eventually granted asylum in the US.

They claimed that Gonchar and the others had been killed by a hush-hush military unit called Almaz, used to 'control' criminals and political dissidents. They claimed that the men had been shot with a pistol usually used for the execution of death row prisoners and then were buried in a secret plot within a cemetery in Minsk, specially reserved for such extra-judicial killings. Or murders, as they are commonly known. The prosecutors produced detailed times, dates and paperwork which directly implicated the Belarusian leadership. Some weeks later, the Belarusian public executioner, now hiding in Germany, produced corroborating evidence.

Naturally, AG denied the accusations, claiming that this was just part of a conspiracy to oust him from power. He advised the US 'to mind its own business and not meddle in things it does not understand'. And yes, the accusations were part of a conspiracy to oust him from power. But they had the distinct ring of truth. Soon after, the paramilitary commander who is the head of Almaz was given a promotion.

But sensing that these accusations might do some damage, AG delivered a storming public speech. Declaring that "I am not afraid of anyone", he publicly threatened to have both the Prime Minister and the Mayor of Minsk arrested if they gave any hint of disloyalty: "I will defend myself. How? There are interior ministry troops, of course. There is the Special Tasks Brigade. There are the Alfa and Almaz special units. This brigade will defend the President. They will never surrender."

You mention those killings again, and you could become one of them.

AG was a bit rattled. But not *too* rattled. Let's not forget that this is a totalitarian regime where the independent media, such as it was, was routinely harassed and suppressed, where the former Soviet secret police, the KGB, is still called the KGB and can bug, raid or arrest anyone it likes. The president was still very much in control.

And he was clever too: in secret, the US had offered to stop meddling, to give military and financial aid if he would promise fair elections. He had agreed, but had done nothing. In 2000, the year that Michael Kozak began his 'democracy building', parliamentary elections saw pro-AG candidates win a landslide victory: 107 of the 110 seats on offer.

Not that surprising, because, as usual, most of the opposition candidates had been disqualified from taking part on various technicalities: out of 565, only 54 didn't support the president. Prior to the poll, they hadn't been given equal access to state media, (contrary to the government's own guidelines), plus there were police raids on the headquarters of opposition parties. And just to be sure, ballot boxes were stuffed and voter registration lists tampered with. A normal election in Belarus.

There were the usual complaints, but AG dismissed his political opponents as a 'handful of windbags' funded by the west.

So you can guess what happened in the following year's presidential campaign. All those funny stickers put up by the students had been very quickly taken down again by the KGB. Lukashenko got 75 per cent of the vote. The Minsk ambassador for the OSCE, which monitors election for fairness, described the Lukashenko regime as one of 'decadence and dictatorship'. AG threatened to expel him and the US ambassador as spies, while hinting that he might also hold a referendum to enable him to run for a third term as President.

Belarus television showed riot police preparing to beat anyone senseless who tried protesting the result. In Minsk, there was a small explosion behind the US embassy. No one was hurt, but the message was clear. Months later, the US ambassador was replaced.

No doubt about it: AG had won a hands-down victory over the Yanks. Yet in reality, the real losers were the Belarusian people. Despite the fact that Lukashenko, like Mussolini, makes the trains run on time, he has completely failed to improve the lot of his people: half of them live below the poverty line.

In the one-third of Belarus blighted by the fallout from the Chernobyl disaster – where the level of radioactive caesium 137 is forty times higher than it should be, where milk and crops are poisoned – farmers are forced to continue working the land. They are forced to feed contaminated food and milk to their children. And it is done not out of cruelty, but because there is no other option. It has caused massive health problems. Alcoholism is rife.

And in the short term at least, there seems to be no solution to these problems. The International Monetary Fund still refuses to lend Belarus money until it undertakes market reforms – which stubborn, no-nonsense AG refuses to do. Also, it's now official that Russia isn't going to come to the rescue.

In 2002, after years of giving the notion polite lip-service, Russia declared that it has no interest in a political union. The best it offered was to make Belarus its 90th region. Not only that: President Putin was even a bit cruel: "who wants to be friends and live together with someone weak?"

The Americans had won after all. When it came down to either being pals with Washington or Minsk, there was really no contest.

Not surprisingly, AG fumed. "Belarus is an independent state with all the attributes of sovereignty. We're not going to be the north-western edge of any country."

Yet, given that Lukashenko had put so much store in this plan, it must have been devastating news. It was a political humiliation handed out by the country which Belarus had so publicly hero-worshipped. Once again, a knock to the self-esteem: AG Lukashenko and his little empire were not quite good enough.

With hardly any friends abroad, the enmity of the US and EU, a starving population and a growing opposition movement, poor old AG isn't going to get any more secure. In 2003, he decreed that the heads of businesses, unions or any other organisations were not allowed to call themselves 'President'; that honour being reserved for AG alone. (The idea was borrowed from Uganda's Idi Amin: another dictator of dubious sanity.)

Things aren't going to change in Belarus, because bluff, no-nonsense AG Lukashenko isn't going to change; he's incapable. There's a joke that he once visited one of the areas invisibly poisoned by Chernobyl: where cancer rates are stratospheric, where children are regularly born with horrible deformities. Standing in the middle of some idyllic countryside, he took a long look around, then declared: "I can't see anything wrong."

SULTAN HAJI HASSANAL BOLKIAH MU'IZZADDIN WADDAULAH

of the Sultanate of Negara Brunei Darussalam

Yep, the smaller the country the bigger the name. And Brunei (let's be informal) is small: it consists of two disconnected strips of land on the island of Borneo, which, if you didn't know, is in south-east Asia and is the third largest island in the world. Being so big, the neighbouring states of Malaysia and Indonesia also own bits of Borneo; much larger bits: the Malaysian section completely surrounds the tiny Sultanate.

Yet despite its Danny DeVito size, Brunei has the economic muscle of an Arnold Schwarzenegger: it's jam-packed full of oil and gas. It is the third-largest oil producer in south-east Asia and the fourth-largest producer of liquefied natural gas on the planet. About ninety-five per cent of Brunei's exports are taken care of by the Brunei Shell Petroleum Company, which is why it is often referred to by those crazy guys in the international banking community as the 'Shellfare State'.

Which proves that even bad jokes can contain a large

element of truth. With a population of just 340 000, residents of Brunei are not subject to tax *of any kind*. Only companies in Brunei pay income tax, which is the lowest in the region. Added to that, education and healthcare are both completely free, while food and housing are subsidised.

It's warm. It has beaches and rainforests. It is relatively unspoiled by tourism. Let's go live there now.

Only snag is: in its 1 500-year history, Brunei has only ever had one election, and the result of that was ignored. Brunei is an absolute monarchy, with the monarch ruling by decree. You do what the Sultan says.

But let's be fair: Sultan Bolkiah has used surprisingly large amounts of the oil money to benefit his people, who have the largest per capita income in south-east Asia. And in return, there has been virtually no (public) resistance to his rule. He regularly travels around his Kingdom and is almost always warmly welcomed; he doesn't even need bodyguards. So, in some respects, Bolkiah is no dope. (In other respects he is, while his brother is a total eejit. But we'll get to that later.) From an early stage, he seemed to decide that the best way to win over his subjects was to make life so nice for them they couldn't be bothered to agitate for democracy.

That, and bend the rules of the constitution a little. Well, a lot actually.

Plus a little religious brainwashing.

And total control of the media.

But no one seems to mind. Really.

After all, Sultan Bolkiah is no fly-by-night dictator who happened to get lucky: he is descended from a line of Sultans which stretches back to when God was a boy: a trading kingdom existed at the mouth of the Brunei river as far back as the seventh or eight century AD, when it did regular business with the Chinese and the Arabs, selling spices, silk, textiles, camphor and the saliva of the swift bird, which apparently is the key ingredient of bird's nest soup. Yuk.

The Kingdom shrank and swelled a few times, depending on how various wars were going, but its golden age was the fifteenth century to the seventeenth century, when it controlled all of Borneo, most of the Philippines and even Manila. Because of all this travelling, modern Brunei has something of an ethnically mixed population. The majority are Malay, but there is a large Chinese community as well as a few native tribes, (who until relatively recently used to go in for such jolly pastimes as headhunting.) And as we shall see, some of the Brunei are more equal than others.

The Sultanate went into a bit of a decline after the seventeenth century, mostly due to internal squabbles over royal succession. By the nineteenth, Brunei had shrunk in size and become a haven for pirates.

Then, in 1839, the British adventurer, James Brooke arrived, just in time for the start of an uprising. Being an adventurer, and being part of the British empire, he naturally sided with the monarch and helped put the rebellion down.

Good thing too: because this helped start a relationship between Brunei and Britain that was to last until today. It also helped maintain the Sultanate while other countries in the region were torn apart and re-drawn by the colonising powers. Everyone was happy with this arrangement, more or less. The British North Borneo Company expanded its influence over the island and made lots of money, while the Sultan (now backed up by British troops) stayed in charge.

In 1888, Brunei became a British protectorate – a move which shielded it from being absorbed into the fledgling Malaysian confederacy. The Sultan maintained internal control of the country, but gave that up in 1906 when executive power was transferred to the British. Still, this arrangement protected the ruling dynasty. And apart from a brief visit from the Japanese during World War Two, things remained like this until 1959.

That was the year that the Brits decided that it might be better to let Johnny Foreigner run his own blasted show. A new constitution was written which declared Brunei a self-governing state, while foreign affairs, security and defence remained the responsibility of the United Kingdom. It was a helpful new arrangement, probably not unrelated to the fact that Shell (a British company) was now helping Brunei to suck millions of barrels of oil out of the ground.

Funny thing though: the Sultan of the time was named Omar – Bolkiah's daddy – and he didn't seem at all keen on his new-found political power. Perhaps he lacked self-confidence. Or perhaps he was bone idle. Whatever the reason, two minutes after the new constitution was signed, he started making noises about amalgamating Brunei into Malaysia – something which previous Sultans had tried to avoid.

Naturally, there were ructions. The people weren't thrilled. Concerned that an unstable country isn't a good oil-producing country, Britain pressured Omar into having elections, which he did in 1962. The Partai Rakyat Brunei (Brunei People's Party) won a convincing victory. Unfortunately for Omar though, the PRB were dead against becoming part of Malaysia.

But it was their first-ever election, so perhaps Omar didn't quite understand how it was supposed to work. He completely ignored the result, and declared the amalgamation would go ahead anyway. So the PRB staged an armed rebellion.

Luckily, there were enough British troops there to quickly crush it. This did give Omar some pause for thought. He changed his mind, and announced that Brunei would remain independent. However, because of the worrying outbreak of violence, he also announced that the constitution was suspended and he would continue to rule by decree. The constitution remains suspended to this day.

In 1967, Bolkiah took over as the 29th Sultan of Brunei. He was but twenty-three years of age and had just finished his stint at Sandhurst Military Academy in the UK where he left with the rank of Captain and a love of playing polo.

Daddy stayed on as Minister for Defence while Bolkiah learned the ropes, a process which seemed to take the best part of ten years. In 1979 Brunei signed yet another friendship agreement with the UK – ensuring that British troops would remain there – while it achieved full independence in 1984.

Politically, virtually nothing had changed. Although Brunei has an independent court system based on the British model (and Islamic courts which can rule on issues of religious and family law), the government of the Sultanate was left to a series of committees, all of them appointed by the Sultan and most of them made up of his relations and members of the nobility. (Brunei has an hereditary nobility with the title Pengiran.) A glutton for work, Bolkiah is Prime Minister, Minister for Defence and Minister for Finance. His brother Mohamed is Minister for Foreign Affairs.

There was no political freedom, but the oil cash had been rolling in – and Bolkiah had been spending. By 1984, Brunei had the second-highest per capita income *in the world*.

Apart from the houses, the hospitals, the cheap food, the

universities and schools (if a university course is not available at home, the government pays for students to study overseas), Bolkiah also built roads: in Brunei, there is virtually no public transport, because there's no need. Everyone has one or two cars, and naturally, petrol is dirt cheap. Because Brunei was importing 90 per cent of its food, (only five per cent of Brunei is cultivated), the Sultan bought a cattle farm in Australia. It is 2,262 square miles – bigger than Brunei itself. Employment (at least for Malays) is virtually guaranteed in Brunei's sprawling civil service.

Hey: the boy was doing good, so quite understandably, he decided to splash out on a few treats for himself. After independence, he ordered 2 000 luxury limos and also became the world's biggest customer for Rolls Royce cars. On his daughter's 18th birthday, he bought her an Airbus. He built the Omar Ali Saifuddin mosque – one of the largest in the world, and then turned his attention to having a nice place to live.

He built himself a palace. A palace with 1 788 rooms, 1 000 closets, 257 toilets, 18 elevators, over 2 000 phones, 564 chandeliers, more than 50 000 light bulbs, a banquet hall that can seat 4 000, a mosque and a heliport. It is bigger than the Vatican, and naturally, the biggest in the world.

He also made a few investments. He has bought hotels, offices, buildings, race horses, factories. To show what a sweet guy he is, he gave $1 million to the United Nation's Children Fund; in the late 1980s – after meeting a nice man called Oliver North – he reportedly gave $10 million to the rebel group, the Contras, who at the time (with some US help) were trying to topple the democratically elected government of Nicaragua. (Bolkiah subsequently claimed that he thought the money was for medical supplies – a claim which showed a startling naivety).

Charities and sharp businessmen from all over the planet flocked to get a bit of the Sultan's action. Sometimes the deals were legitimate and he made money, sometimes not. But it didn't seem to matter because no matter how much he spent, the richer he seemed to get: thanks to huge increases in the price of oil in the 1970s, the Sultan had inherited $40 billion when his father died in 1986. And the fortune had increased to a whopping $67 billion by 1990: he was now officially the Richest Man in the World. Cool.

But it wasn't to last, of course. If Bolkiah could be a bit wide-eyed going into business deals, this was nothing compared to his younger brother, Jefri; known familiarly in Brunei as PJ.

PJ was originally Minister for Finance in Brunei and head of the Brunei Investment Agency. In such a position, he had access to almost limitless funds. And given that the sign on the door said 'Investment', PJ did just that. He set up the Amedeo Development Corporation, and started developing. He built VIP houses and luxury hotels. After a trip to Disneyland, PJ decided to construct a Brunei version, the Jerudong Park which, apart from being spectacularly lavish, didn't charge an entrance fee, (bit of a flaw in the business plan there). He bought hotels, office buildings and the posh London jewellers Asprey & Garrard, whose customers included Princess Diana and Posh Spice.

Along the way, Jefri also picked up a few trinkets for himself. Turned out that Jefri had an almost obsessive need to buy stuff; stuff he would usually never use.

But, the problem was that PJ was a completely rubbish businessman. So after a financial slump in Asia in the mid-1990s, Sultan Bolkiah had a closer look at the books: to discover that something in the neighbourhood of $12 billion was missing from the nation's coffers. Almost all of

PJ's investments had lost money, and it seemed that every time he ran into a bit of financial trouble, the young prince had helped himself.

The Sultan wasn't too pleased, to put it mildly. He sacked PJ as Minister (taking over the job himself) and wound up Amedeo. He then took Jefri to court. This was an unprecedented move. For the first time in their history, members of the Brunei Royal family were washing some of their extremely filthy laundry in public.

But it proved a bit too filthy for the Sultan. Even on the first day, Jefri made tabloid headlines by admitting he had recently spent £1 200 sterling on bed sheets. For the secretive Bolkiah, this was over-sharing. So the Sultan withdrew the case. He settled on a personal allowance for PJ of just $300 000 a month, (tough, when you have four wives and thirty-five kids to look after) and further ordered Jefri to auction his personal goods to meet some of the debts.

The auction took place in August 2001 and lasted for a week. PJ's goodies filled twenty-eight warehouses. In no particular order, here are some of toys he had amassed:

100 chandeliers
An Apache attack helicopter simulator
Gold-plated toilet brush holders
Hundreds of fridges
Several giant marble Jacuzzis.
Thousands of pieces of jewellery
(from Asprey's in London)
Two Fire Engines
200 tons of Burmese teak
A wood-turning machine
Seventeen aircraft

Six fork-lift trucks
7 000 tons of marble
An extensive art collection, including works by
Renoir and Modigliani
A yacht, named 'Tits'
Two smaller boats named 'Nipple 1' and 'Nipple 2'
A Formula One racing car
A recording studio
A fleet of luxury cars, many of which could not start.
(They had never been driven.)

For his part, Jefri claimed that his downfall was the result of shadowy forces plotting against him. He moved to London and hasn't been back since.

It wasn't a happy time for Sultan Bolkiah, and not just because of the family rifts it created: it announced to the world that the days of Brunei's spectacular wealth were over; that one day, the money would be gone altogether. From being the richest man in the world in 1990, Bolkiah is now way down the list – 29th – with a fortune estimated at being below $10 billion dollars.

Not bad all the same, but something of a worry when the source of that wealth could be about to run out: according to some estimates, Brunei's oil might last only for another ten or eleven years. Already, production has been cut back to extend the life of the reserves. And when the money goes, so too does the main source of Bolkiah's power. Already, Brunei's national economic growth has slowed to about two per cent a year, which isn't very much. There have been attempts to diversify the economy, but so far this has consisted more of talking about it than doing anything. As seventy per cent of Brunei is covered in rainforest, this could be harvested as a valuable resource.

Yet it seems as if the Sultan hasn't even bought a saw, preferring to launch more searches for oil. So far, nothing.

The thing is: the people of Brunei might not be so keen on the way things are when the lolly starts to run out.

Particularly the Chinese, who make up about sixteen per cent of the population. Despite the fact that people of Chinese origin have lived in Brunei for over a thousand years – and despite the fact that many of them are extremely successful in business – they have never been granted full citizenship, mainly due to a paranoid notion of preserving Brunei ethnic purity. (Until 2002, children could inherit citizenship from their fathers, but not their mothers, thus discouraging Brunei men from marrying inferior outlanders.) These 'foreigners' are allowed international certificates of identity so they may travel abroad, but essentially they are stateless, and denied certain privileges of citizenship, including the right to own land.

There is a procedure by which they can apply for a passport, but it involves taking a complicated Malay language exam which even most Malays wouldn't pass.

More recently, there have even been moves to introduce an employment quota system for some of Brunei's larger companies (like our friends in Shell), which would favour Malays. Given that so many Chinese have generated wealth for the country, while many Malays have just lived off it, they are almost certain not to be too thrilled.

Not that they are going to say it in public. Not yet, anyway. The media in Brunei is either wholly owned or directly controlled by the Sultan. They are all encouraged to report 'positive' stories and journalists can be jailed for publishing 'false' news. Foreign media can be – and have been – quickly taken off the shelves if they print anything remotely critical of the Brunei or its ruler.

In recent years, what was censorship has now turned into outright propaganda, with Brunei's radio and TV being used to promote a concept called Melayu Islam Berja (MIB) or Malay Islamic Monarchy. Basically, MIB is a quasi-philosophy which states that Brunei should develop into a fully Islamic state – with the Sultan firmly at the head of religious belief and practice. As such, it promotes Bolkiah from being a mere Sultan and into something closer to a prophet. Don't forget his long lineage: one of Bolkiah's ancestors, the third Sultan, was named Sharif Ali and was said to be a descendant of the Prophet Mohammed – making Bolkiah a descendant of Mohammed. Oh, fancy.

MIB has been taught in schools and universities for more than a decade now, securely brainwashing an entire generation.

Yes, as with many despots around the world, Bolkiah seems to have got a bit up himself. The signs have always been there: a palace that's big enough for the United Nations, all that money, a lineage going back to the Prophet. When Bolkiah gave an interview to the *Sunday Telegraph* in 1988, the journalist had to spend two days being briefed on protocol before being allowed to meet the Sultan. The tips he was given included keeping his hands folded in his lap at all times (difficult if you want to take notes), and under no circumstances to cross his legs, as this would be taken as a sign of disrespect.

Then again, for the Sultan to appear more godly to his people is a shrewd move, as Brunei is already a deeply religious country. Sunni Muslim, the people address each other using formal titles. Most women wear the traditional tudong, while men wear the songkok, a Malay cap. Alcohol is banned. McDonald's is limited to serving egg sandwiches. Although the remit of the Islamic courts is limited, they regularly order offenders to be caned and are rather keen on publicly shaming the guilty. If you are caught in bed with someone to whom you are not married, your naked photo will be printed in the local press.

However, while the Sultan publicly parades his religiosity, his private life may be a different matter. Apart from the Prince Jefri scandal, Bolkiah's two other major public embarrassments have both had to do with women. Back in the early 1990s, when fun-loving playboy Jefri was still in favour, seven American women arrived in Brunei for some modelling and promotional work – for which they were to be generously paid $127 000 each. Among them was Shannon Marketic, a 27-year old former Miss USA and devout Christian.

Their employers, it turned out, were Jefri and Bolkiah. According to Marketic, the women were brought to the Sultan's gigantic palace, but were not asked to do any modelling or promoting. Instead, they were 'expected to engage in various sexual acts'.

Marketic went home to Los Angeles, where she launched a $90 million lawsuit against the Sultan. According to the papers she filed, it was a regular occurrence for Bolkiah to import high-class hookers from the United States for six-week stints.

The case, however, didn't succeed: a US district judge found that the Sultan's status as a head of state entitled him to 'sovereign immunity'.

Embarrassment number two was a little closer to home, and involved the Sultan's wife. Or more precisely, wife number two. (Under Brunei law, men are allowed up to four wives. It's bit like a duty-free allowance). Bolkiah was first married at the tender age of nineteen to his first cousin, Anak Hajjah Saleha. In a privately-published biography of the Sultan, she was described as a "sweet bedimpled soulful-eyed lass of 16."

But twenty years and six kids later, Anak wasn't as well, bedimpled, as she used to be: a fact which many Brunei citizens (who like their Royal family perfect) and Bolkiah noticed. So on a Royal Brunei Airlines flight one day (this is the official account) he saw Mariam Bell, a half-Brunei, quarter-Japanese, quarter-English beauty. Despite her non-noble birth and flagrantly half-foreign ethnicity, the Sultan married her.

It was like a fairy tale: in fact, it probably *is* a fairy tale. This is a multi-billionaire who owns a fleet of private airplanes. What would he be doing on a commercial jet?

Whatever the circumstances of their meeting, Mariam and Bolkiah got hitched. She provided four kids. In government and business offices all over Brunei, her picture was hung alongside that of the Sultan and his first wife.

But then in February of 2003, it was suddenly announced that Bolkiah was divorcing Mariam. Overnight, all those portraits had to come down. Most Brunei citizens were shocked. Subsequently, some felt sympathy for Mariam, both for the abruptness of the announcement and the fact that, in recent years, she too had put on a little weight. Others were glad she was gone, and for almost exactly the same reason: because she had put on a little weight. In Brunei, putting on weight is a big deal.

No reason was given for the split, though there were rumours that the couple had been unhappy for some time; there were whispers of Mariam being involved with someone else.

Whatever the reason, a divorce was the last thing the Sultan needed, especially at a time when he was trying to distract the populace from a possible economic crisis. When he wanted to appear more godly, he was suddenly annoyingly mortal.

And the kids probably aren't going to help any either. Bolkiah's eldest son, al-Muhtadee Billah, has already been named Crown Prince, making him next in line to the throne when the Sultan decides to call it a day. However, there are rumours that the unmarried Billah is thinking of getting hitched to a woman of non-noble birth – a union which the palace would very much disapprove of.

For Sultan Bolkiah, it's all about maintaining power. During that *Sunday Telegraph* interview, he claimed that the Brunei people 'showed no signs of wanting to change a system that had worked well since time immemorial'. Not if they know what's good for them. In 1985, as a piece of window dressing, two political parties were permitted to come into being. One was banned three years later while the other – after constant harassment – has become inactive.

For years Bolkiah ruled by showering gifts on his subjects. Now he's trying to maintain their attention by pretending to be a religious figure. But if neither of these works, there's always the Despot's last line of defence: good old-fashioned oppression.

He hasn't used it much (yet), but the Sultan has in reserve a nifty little law called the Internal Security Act, (ISA). Under the terms of the ISA, the Sultan can arrest anyone he likes for two years if he thinks they are a threat to national security. And he can renew this two-year detention indefinitely.

So far, the ISA has been used only a handful of times, mostly on Christian missionaries. All were eventually released, but only after signing statements regretting their 'crimes' and agreeing to Islamic 're-education' sessions.

But if any serious political opposition springs up, the ISA

will be there to get rid of it. And don't think that Sultan Haji Hassanal Bolkiah Mu'izzaddin Waddaulah might be too nice to take such drastic steps. Remember the Brunei People's Party? After the election result in 1962 was ignored and the BPP made a ham-fisted attempt at revolution, all its leaders were arrested without trial. Forty years later, they are still in prison waiting for one.

PRESIDENT PAUL BIYA

of the Republic of Cameroon

There are three reasons why you may have already heard of Cameroon:

1. *Football.* In the 1990 World Cup finals, the Cameroon team made something of a splash by taking out supposedly superior opposition such as Argentina, Romania and Columbia. They got as far as the quarter finals. It was especially remarkable as their star player was one Roger Milla, who attracted a lot of attention both for his ability to score goals and the rather suggestive dance he would do afterwards. At the time Milla was in his early forties and originally hadn't been a member of the Cameroon squad, being too old. But he had been included at the insistence of the President, Paul Biya. Later on, Biya made Milla a 'roving ambassador' for football, essentially using him to meddle in subsequent football controversies in Cameroon.

2. *Freaks of nature.* On August 21, 1986, Nyos, a volcanic crater lake in Cameroon, 'exploded', releasing lethal clouds

of carbon dioxide and sulphur dioxide. The gas killed virtually every living thing within a ten-mile radius. The official death toll was 1 700, though some locals believe it could have been closer to 3 000: survivors were not allowed back to bury their dead or collect belongings. To this day, scientists aren't sure exactly what caused the explosion, though it was probably to do with a build-up of gas below the ground. However, many locals believe that the President, Paul Biya, was paid by Western governments to test a bomb that would kill people but leave buildings intact. That's just how much they love him.

3. *Iraq.* By pure coincidence, Cameroon happened to be one of the non-permanent members sitting on the UN Security Council in March 2003, when the US and UK were about to go to war against Iraq. An attempt by George Bush and Tony Blair to get the Security Council to approve the action suddenly meant that Paul Biya was, for the month of March, flavour of the month while they tried to woo his vote. Biya certainly liked the idea of all the US dollars his support for the war would bring, but also didn't want to give *le hump* to the French, who were against it, and with whom Cameroon has long colonial ties. Curiously, Roger Milla was wheeled out as government spokesman on the issue. He told the world's press: "We will not sell our souls." In the end, Roger and Paul were saved the agony of soul-selling when the US and Britain withdrew their draft resolution (believing it would be defeated), and went to war anyway.

And then everyone went back to ignoring Cameroon. Even at the time of the UN vote, many western newspapers took a bit of a *Camerwhere?* attitude towards it, as if it was slightly beneath the likes of Tony Blair to suddenly have to suck up to some tinpot president he obviously hadn't heard of before.

But such is international politics: it is *always, always* about self-interest. If your country isn't a threat to anyone, or seen to be helping another threatening country, then you will be ignored. If you have something other countries want, such as oil or a strategic location, then you will be courted. Cameroon has some oil, but not enough for any important countries to be that bothered about. And it's in West Africa, which ain't strategic. In the international 'community', no one cares about West Africa.

In truth, apart from Cameroonians, no one ever has. The country is an artificial creation and even its name is a mistake. People have lived there since the first century, and today an estimated 200 distinct ethnic groups live in the region, speaking 24 major African languages. Tribes such as the Bantu and the Kirdi would regard themselves as being completely foreign to each other, yet thanks to the gift of colonialism and the utter indifference of the rest of us, they are forced to share the same citizenship. Small hunting bands of pygmies – the original inhabitants of central Africa – still dwell in the remote southern forests, completely unaware that they live in a 'country' at all.

Contact with Europe was first made in the 15th century, with the arrival of the Portuguese. Having found what they thought were shrimps (camarões) in the main river, they named it Rio dos Camarões, or Cameroon. Later on they discovered that the shrimps were actually crayfish, but the name stuck anyway.

Having no *camarões* to harvest, the Portuguese opted to grab some of the people instead. A large-scale slave trade ensued, and soon the Spanish, Dutch, French, and English were all joining in. Oh, happy days.

A couple of hundred years later and the Germans were

in charge. They gave it the more Kraut-sounding name of Kamerun and made it a protectorate in 1884. And being Germans, they couldn't help but develop plantations and build roads and bridges. But after Germany's ass-kicking in World War I, Cameroon was taken off them and divided between Britain and France under a League of Nations – and later a United Nations – mandate.

Suddenly one 'country' became two 'countries', each heavily influenced by their colonial masters. To add to all the tribal divisions, Cameroon developed two distinct cultures: Anglophone, fish-and-chip-eating in the west, and Francophone, snail-eating in the east. Everyone was confused.

But in the way of such things, independence inevitably rolled around. The French half got it in 1960. Just to confuse things further, the British section was divided in two the following year: the northern part of west Cameroon joined with Nigeria, (concentrate now), while the remaining southern part joined with east Cameroon in a confederation of two states. Then, after more than a decade of flirting, thinking about it and long, sigh-filled conversations, east and west Cameroon got together as a single state in 1972. (And as a result of all this, border disputes are on-going with Nigeria, particularly over the oil-rich Bakassi Peninsula.)

But almost immediately, there were marital problems. Because half of the Anglophone part of Cameroon had been given away to the Nigerians, what was left was considerably smaller than Francophone Cameroon. The Fish-and-Chip-eaters were vastly outnumbered. Since 1960, politics in Francophone Cameroon had been dominated by Ahmadou Ahidjo and his Cameroon National Union, so when east and west re-unified, Ahidjo continued to dominate, much to the annoyance of the west Cameroonians.

Not that they could do much about it. They didn't have enough votes to put Ahidjo out of office, and even if they had, they didn't have a candidate. Cameroon was a one-party state, where dissent was dealt with quickly and brutally. (The best you could hope for was a beating. Political opponents regularly 'disappeared'.) Ahmadou went on to be re-elected president four times. But given that his was the only name on the ballot sheet, this is hardly surprising.

As President, he had almost total power. He appointed the cabinet, the prime minister, the judiciary and reserved the right to rule by decree if anyone got lippy.

In 1975, Paul Biya, a well-educated Christian, (this becomes relevant later on), was appointed Prime Minister. Biya had been taught by nuns (which may explain the ruthless streak), then studied at the Sorbonne in Paris. When he returned home he held various civil service posts, and obviously caught the eye of Ahmadou.

Of course being Prime Minister didn't entail having any real power – that all lay with the President. But in 1982, when Ahmadou stepped down of his own volition, Biya was named as his successor.

What followed is still the subject of heated debate in Cameroon (though not too loud; you never know who's listening) and comes down to whom you believe and how generous you are. Was Paul Biya a good man frightened into becoming a despot? Or was he just a git prepared to use any excuse to win power?

What is certain is that shortly after his mentor's departure (Ahmadou went to live on the French Riviera), Biya started talking about introducing a liberal democracy.

And then changed his mind. Suddenly, he fired his prime minister, and several other members of the cabinet and accused them of plotting to overthrow him. He replaced them with members of his own ethnic group, the Beti. There may have been a genuine plot, or Biya may have simply been using a trick he learned from the Old Man. No one knows.

What we do know is that the Old Man was furious.

From his retirement home in France, Ahmadou – without any sense of irony – accused Biya of trying to create a police state. In return, Biya sentenced Ahmadou to death *in absentia*.

So then there was a real coup attempt. The Cameroonian 'government' pardoned Ahmadou. Elements of the palace guard still loyal to the old president revolted.

But hang on: why would anyone in Cameroon want to bring back Ahmadou, a ruthless dictator who rigged every election he ran in? Don't underestimate the power of tribalism. As far as many Cameroonians were concerned, Biya's mob, the Beti, had now seized power – which in effect they had. This was compounded by the fact that not only is Cameroon divided 200 ways along tribal lines and twice along Anglo/French lines, but also twice along religious lines: Ahmadou was a Muslim from the north, where it is predominantly Muslim, while Biya is a Christian from the south. There were plenty of people ready to fight, and for a dazzling variety of reasons.

It only lasted three days, but there were hundreds of deaths. Biya remained in power. Ahmadou stayed in France.

So Paul Biya continued on in pretty much the same vein as his predecessor: controlling all the media, brutally repressing any opposition, most of which had now fled to France anyway. Killing. Torture. Corruption. Again, displaying no sense of irony, he changed the name of the Cameroon National Union to the Cameroon People's Democratic Rally.

Did he do it because he felt he had no option or because of the threat from other tribes, from Ahmadou, from

Muslims? Or was it what he had always planned? In Cameroon, you will find people to argue passionately for both versions of their president, and some of this has to do with the fact that they know so little about him. Despite his total control of the country, he remains a remote, mysterious figure. And into this void, Cameroonians have packed their own speculation: some of it sensible, and as we'll see later, some of it almost demonically sinister.

What was clear was that he had no intention of loosening his hold on power. He staged an election in 1984 and won an astonishing 99.98% of the vote: cheeky, even for Cameroon. Perhaps the forest pygmies came down specially to exercise their ballot.

Biya was helped by the fact that Cameroon had become quite a prosperous country. Like other parts of the world, (see *Brunei*), people don't mind being oppressed so much if there's a few bob in it. The country had modest amounts of oil and had also spent a good deal on developing the infrastructure and agriculture. It has the highest literacy rate in Africa, and is also the most plane-friendly country in the continent: because building roads into the dense mountain forests would cost too much, they built lots of small airports instead. The sight of people hopping on and off commuter planes in Cameroon is quite common.

But the price of oil fell and the economy went into sharp recession, so in 1990 the ungrateful Cameroonians staged a prolonged nationwide strike. To defuse this, Biya ended one-party rule and initiated a multi-party system.

Cameroon's first multi-party election was held in 1992, by which time the Social Democratic Front's John Fru Ndi (from the Anglophone section) was presenting a major challenge.

But for reasons which Biya chose not to reveal, a state of emergency was suddenly declared. Fru Ndi was put under house arrest and Biya 'won' the election. There were widespread allegations of bribery and intimidation; yet still Paul only scraped home.

Nonetheless, the President was now an enthusiastic convert to multi-party politics – and bribery and intimidation. In 1997, there was another election, and this time Paul romped home with 92.57% of the vote. Indeed, this time the vote-rigging was so bad the other parties didn't even bother taking part. The official figure for the turnout was 80.5 per cent; the opposition groups claimed it was more like ten per cent.

More recently, Biya has refined his electoral fraud techniques to make it seem a little more believable. In the National Assembly elections of 2002, the opposition was allowed to win 22 out of the 180 seats. Just to keep 'em interested.

Though God help you if you don't do what you're told. In those 2002 elections, one local official in the south of the country, Mbachu George Ngah, ignored a written instruction 'to do everything possible and to use all means available to ensure a landslide victory for CPDR candidates'. Roughly translated, this meant he refused to remove the names of opposition candidates from the ballot sheet.

By May of the following year he had survived several attempts on his life. However, on May 11th 2003, during a highly convenient power failure in his home town of Kumba, a group of unidentified men broke into his house, robbed him and shot him in the head.

Miraculously, Mbachu George Ngah survived this attack, (the bullet didn't penetrate his brain), but shortly afterwards his parents' home burned down. He is now in hiding.

Even still, Paul Biya – the man who may have once been honest – makes noises about bringing in more democracy and decentralisation. Yet no one believes him: to survive, he has had to make too many deals with vested interests (most significantly, politicians from his own Beti tribe) who would not want to relinquish power. Even if he really wanted to change things, he probably couldn't.

Right across the country, President Paul has a series of cosy arrangements with local tribal leaders. They defend and enforce government policy, and in return he lets them rule their areas like mini-despots. And occasionally, he throws some development money their way.

As a result, Cameroon probably has one of the most cynical electorates (if you can call them that) in the world. Not surprisingly, there is now a large independence movement in the Anglophone province, which is far less developed. In 1999, secessionists announced a breakaway republic, and the following year named Judge Frederick Ebong Alobwede as its president. For their trouble, many of them were jailed or killed.

Elsewhere, corruption is endemic.

No: not endemic, much worse than that. Put it this way: Cameroon holds a world record. It is the only country *ever* to be named by the anti-corruption organisation, Transparency International, as the most corrupt nation on earth *two years running* (1998-99). It currently lies at 13th position.

Cameroon stinks from corruption. The country is covered with police 'checkpoints', the purpose of which is to extort money from motorists. Failure to pay up means jail.

It was widely assumed that at least half the money allocated for public works projects – such as road building – finds its way into officials' personal bank accounts, and from there into the conspicuous building of luxurious new private houses. Many civil servants do virtually no work.

Parents have to bribe the headmasters of government schools to get their children admitted. Getting a driving licence entails little more than paying cash to an official. Even the Catholic Church in Cameroon (which regularly denounces this corruption) admits it has had bishops and priest on the take.

Every now and again, Biya announces the start of a drive to get rid of it, (usually if the World Bank or the International Monetary Fund is giving him hassle), yet little happens. A few policemen get caught, but never *le grand poisson* – unless Biya wanted to get rid of them anyway. A couple of years ago the home of a sacked Finance Minister was raided. He had 7.7 *billion* Cameroon francs (€117 million) *in cash* in his house. He was awaiting delivery of the world's largest brown envelope.

Yes, there's money to be made in Cameroon. Both the black and white economies are still doing reasonably well. Apart from the oil, (a major pipeline between Cameroon and Chad was opened in July 2003), Cameroon is now one of the largest exporters of timber, though conservationists estimate that already half its rainforests have been lost through intensive harvesting. There are government restrictions, but these are ignored: concessions are won by bribing officials. It has been predicted that Cameroon could run out of commercial timber within 15 years. And, as the forests have come down, there has been a boom in poaching antelope, chimpanzees and gorillas.

And, of course, Cameroon's human-rights record remains poor. Opposition politicians and human-rights activists are harassed or jailed. A recent UN report concluded that torture is widespread in Cameroon's prisons and police cells. The security forces are notorious for extra-judicial killings and summary executions. Journalists are regularly beaten up and intimidated. In 2002 a journalist was jailed for suggesting that Biya had had a heart attack.

Naturally, no one really knows if he had or not. A fanatical golfer, the President spends much of his time at a vast estate – complete with an eighteen-hole course – that he built with state funds near his native village. (He no longer lives in Yaounde, the capital. According to popular legend this is because the ghost of Ahmadou Ahidjo – who died in 1989 – haunts the State House there.) He also has mansions in France and Germany.

It sounds a bit lonely. But at least he has the compensation of being the richest man in Cameroon. A French weekly magazine, *L'Evenement du Jeudi*, put Biya's fortune at 45 billion Cameroon francs (€68 million). Article 66 of the Cameroonian constitution states that the president should publicly declare his goods and assets. He has never done this. Much of this appears to be oil revenues or tax money which has simply disappeared, though thanks to another nifty clause in the constitution, the President is entitled to funnel money to an account solely controlled by him, 'in case of need.' Whose need, it doesn't say.

Certainly, money has been spirited out of Cameroon at an astonishing rate. Some estimates have it that between 1988 to 1993, 230 billion Cameroon francs (€350 million) in oil revenues disappeared, while in the same period 2 000 billion Cameroon francs (€3 billion) evaporated due to tax evasion. There are also allegations that Biya and his cronies effectively sucked dry the Cameroon Bank, which eventually went into liquidation.

But this is the problem when you continually get what you want: some observers believe that Biya has been losing interest in his job. There have been long and frequent holidays abroad. Not only he is rarely seen in public, there are rumours that he has only attended two cabinet meetings in the last five years. There are ministers who apparently have never met him, while the ordinary Cameroonians know virtually nothing. Except to keep their mouths shut.

Yet ironically, he has never been in such a strong position. There are 168 legal political parties in Cameroon, yet they seem unable to agree on any sort of strategy to dislodge Biya or what shape Cameroon should take afterwards. The only individual who might stand a chance is Cardinal Christian Tumi, who has both a pulpit and a newspaper to criticise the President. But the Cardinal already has a job, and ain't interested.

And there seems little international pressure on him. US state department reports have noted the lack of human rights and the extra-judicial killings. However, in 2003, when the US was trying to win Cameroon's vote on the UN security council, Colin Powell described Cameroon as "an island of stability in that area of Africa. The United States government will make all possible efforts to strengthen M. Biya's government," he added, promising to help Cameroon's economy as well as "their efforts to fight terror". In March 2003, Paul's wife, Chantal Biya (who likes startling hairdos, designer clothes and to do charity work: she has several hospitals named after her and heads up the Chantal Biya Foundation) had a cup of coffee in the White House with Laura Bush.

Not very good news for those Cameroonians who were hoping they might get to actually vote for their leaders.

But now that we've mentioned the Cameroonian First Lady, let's talk a bit about Paul Biya's marital status. Chantal was not his first wife. When he returned from Paris in the early 1960s, he brought with him Jeanne-Irene, a midwife whom he had just married.

Ironically, given her profession, they never had any children together. No one knows why, but rumours abound. She was sterile. He was sterile. He was gay.

Certainly, when she died in August 1992, the news came as a total shock to Cameroonians. There had been no prior indication of illness, and afterwards, very little information on the circumstances of her death. Only two days before she had appeared on television, looking perfectly healthy, yet for her funeral the casket was closed because – so went the official line – she looked too terrible to be displayed in public.

Many have claimed that she looked 'terrible' because she had a large bullet-hole in her forehead. The story goes that two bodyguards were assigned the task of killing her, and then, to keep the story quiet, a government official killed the bodyguards. However, Jeanne-Irene had already confided her fears of a plot to kill to her to two French nuns. The nuns were also subsequently found dead.

Of course, this is speculation, but the story won't go away and many Cameroonians believe it as fact. Certainly there was a mysterious spate of killings at the time: the bodyguards, the nuns, a cook plus three closer advisors to Paul Biya who may also have been a bit too close to Jeanne-Irene.

As to why she was killed – if she was killed – is again down to speculation. This was just before Cameroon's first multi-party elections, and one theory runs that Jeanne-Irene was just about to publicly disown her husband. Another was that, tired of her husband's homosexuality, she had begun an affair with an Army officer.

Whatever the truth, Paul didn't spend too much time grieving. He married Chantal, (a major hate figure for Biya's opponents), who promptly produced three children. In 2002, a journalist enquired whether the president would be holding any commemoration to mark the tenth anniversary of his first wife's death. The journalist received no reply, and shortly afterwards had to go into hiding.

Another presidential election is due in 2004. (Thanks to a change in the constitution in 1996, Biya can go for a fourth consecutive seven-year-term.) It is widely believed that Biya will once again romp home with 104% of the vote.

Basically, the only hope for Cameroon is Biya's boredom or death. He was seventy in 2002, so the effort of oppressing his country may have become a little tiring. However, when Paul Biya pops his clogs, the prospect is not a rosy one: Cameroon is now so tribalised that there is a good chance the country will fracture internally and massive bloodshed will ensue.

And then there will be a fourth reason to have heard of Cameroon.

PRESIDENT HU JINTAO

of the People's Republic of China

Obviously, the first thing about China is that it's big; mind-bogglingly big: twenty-two provinces, four special municipalities, five autonomous regions. A workforce of 711.5 million people; a population of 1.3 billion. A country so populous that in the 1980s the government attempted to limit families to just one child each.

It's also old. Very old: a continuous culture which stretches back 4 000 years and gave the world inventions such as paper, gunpowder, credit banking, the compass, paper money and Soy sauce.

Yet for such a huge, colourful, wonderful land, modern China is a drab place, and in recent times it has seen little joy. Here are the highlights:

1949: the People's Republic of China is established, headed by Mao Zedong. (You know: the chubby, bald-headed guy who wrote *The Little Red Book*.)

The ousted Chinese government move to Formosa – now Taiwan. Taiwan and China have been bitching at each other ever since. China claims Taiwan as part of its territory but doesn't want to antagonise the US by invading.

1950: China invades Tibet instead, eventually making it an 'autonomous' region.

1958-60: the little bald-headed guy announces the Great Leap Forward to collectivise agriculture and create a socialist paradise. 40 million people don't have enough to eat and end up going to the other paradise.

1966: to create a genuinely proletarian state, Mao announces the Cultural Revolution. 800 000 proletarians die.

1986: there is some liberalisation, particularly in the arts and culture.

1987: the Communist party decides the liberalisation was a mistake and a massive clampdown ensues.

1989: students protest in Tiananmen Square in Beijing and other cities. The government declares martial law and runs them all over with tanks. Thousands die.

2000: China signs international deals as preparation for joining the World Trade Organisation.

China is changing. It has to: if it doesn't start doing business with the outside world, a large proportion of those 1.3 billion people won't have enough to eat, especially in rural China where there is a much lower standard of living. (In a most un-communist manner, social welfare payments, such as pensions, tend to be lower outside the cities.)

But the metropolitan areas are feeling the pinch too. Increasing numbers have no jobs: in the summer of 2003 alone, two million university graduates came onto the employment market.

But while it may want to bring in a more liberal economic system (and already in China there are people doing well; young cocky guys whizzing around Beijing in their Ferraris are not that uncommon), the Communist Party (with a membership of forty million people) still wants to control just about every other aspect of Chinese life. Chinese jails are jammed with millions of dissenters; thousands are tortured; hundreds are executed. Ratting on your friends, neighbours, even members of your family is openly encouraged.

Every aspect of culture – the arts, the media – has to be approved or directly controlled by the propaganda department of the Communist Party. In 2003, most Chinese people didn't even know that their country was about to put a man into space – until he arrived back safely.

In recent times, hundreds of Chinese people have been jailed for the heinous crime of 'expressing opinions on the internet'.

China is such a closed society that it prefers to keep things quiet even when it is clearly in its interest *not* to. When the SARS virus was first discovered in the southern Guangdong province of China in November 2002, local officials decided not to inform the Chinese Health Ministry, fearing that they might somehow be blamed for it. But when millions of people criss-crossed China the following February for the

New Year celebrations, it triggered an epidemic which spread into Hong Kong and other Asian cities.

Yet still the Chinese government denied there was a problem: in April of 2003, officials from the World Health Organisation arrived in Beijing to inspect the thirty-seven 'official' cases of SARS. In reality, there were hundreds. But in an attempt to keep this quiet, the patients were put into ambulances and driven around the city until the WHO officials had left town. Only when the epidemic began to threaten the economy did China admit there was a big problem. It promptly announced that it would jail for life or even execute anyone caught intentionally spreading the virus.

However, in early 2004, China reacted in exactly the same manner to a bird flu epidemic which swept Asia and claimed hundreds of human lives. It failed to inform the WHO that it had any outbreaks at all, and fired Chinese journalists who attempted to report on the disease.

Yet despite the tightness of this control – or perhaps because of it – the Chinese Communist party is riddled with corruption: it is common practice to buy high-ranking civil service jobs. You can become head of a transport bureau for €24,000 or head up a tobacco bureau for just €19,000. Think of all those free cigarettes.

As a result of an anti-corruption drive launched in early 2003, 1 252 Communist Party officials committed suicide, another 8 371 fled overseas while 6 528 simply disappeared. It is not known how many were imprisoned or executed, but it's likely to be many times greater than these numbers. But don't get the impression that Chinese fellas are mad into killing themselves; invariably, these people were 'encouraged' to commit suicide by other corrupt officials keen not to get caught.

The official estimate is that €5.5 billion has been siphoned out the Chinese economy as a result of corruption.

China is a huge, messy country, yet for decades the Communist Party (CCP) has put enormous effort into attempting to regiment every aspect of Chinese life, mainly through the deployment of a juggernaut of bureaucracy: even the most unimportant jobs have long-winded titles or confusing acronyms; for every aspect of public life, there are committees upon committees upon committees. It's not just the Thought Police who have stifled Chinese life; it's all the form-filling.

And as you might expect, the leaders of China pride themselves as being exemplars of this drab and humourless way of life. Communism was never viewed as a fun way of organising society, but even by its dreary standards, Chinese communists are particularly colourless. And none more so than their current big chief, Hu Jintao

Hu Jintao was appointed President of the Republic of China in March of 2003, and absolutely no one was surprised.

He was already vice-president, while the year before, in a carefully choreographed meeting, four of the five members of the CCP's Central Committee had resigned, allowing younger men to take their place. Hu was the only one who remained, making him the Senior Guy on campus, and thus General Secretary of the Communist Party of China.

That he would be president had long been speculated about. Now it was a foregone conclusion: once you've become General Secretary, you get the presidency within the year.

In Chinese politics, little is spoken about openly, but everything is planned ahead in the tiniest detail. Spontaneity is a hanging offence; sometimes literally. Hu Jintao became ruler of China not just through careful shepherding of his career, but because he best fitted the profile of what a president was expected to be. In China, it is not an individual who is the despot, but the Chinese Communist Party (CCP) and the system it has created. If you want to get on in Chinese politics, you become what is required. As one commentator put it, Hu Jintao 'has played the role of heir apparent brilliantly. He hasn't mistimed a single move – largely because he hasn't made one'.

Since his elevation to the big job, the official profiles of Hu have stretched so much to make him sound heroic and interesting, it borders on the comic. In New York, we are told, he 'braved the rain'; he visited Mongolia despite the fact that it was 'freezing'. Weather holds no fear for this leader.

The truth is that Chinese rulers are invariably a mixture of cunning, cruelty and utter dullness. One early official biography mentioned that Hu had a fondness for table tennis and ballroom dancing. But after he began his climb up the Communist Party hierarchy, this detail was deleted: you wouldn't want people thinking he was some sort of Wild Man.

So let's see how he did it. He was born in Taizhou City in the eastern Jiangsu Province in 1942, just seven years before the Republic was established. Years later, this helped make him a suitable candidate for leadership, as he was, just about, a 'child of the revolution'. (It's referred to as the *Fourth Generation* in China.) He was a smart kid too – he is said to have a photographic memory – and after school enrolled in the prestigious Qinghua University in Beijing where he chose to study hydroelectric engineering.

Please: don't nod off. It was a grindingly tedious subject to choose, but in Chinese politics, it is the practical disciplines, such as engineering or agriculture which have the most cachet: it implies a desire to build things, a willingness to get one's hands dirty like all the proletarian heroes of the revolution . . . OK, it is dull, but that's the way it is in China. If you choose to study poetry or even economics, you're never going to be leader. You'll probably end up in prison.

Anyway, for the young Hu it wasn't just the choice of subject, it was the university that was important. Qinghua is the Oxbridge of China, reserved for the very smartest cookies in the communist box. It was, and still is, one of the few institutions in the country where they get to study groovy subjects like European social-democratic political parties, free-market economics and Western management methods: all the stuff that evil capitalists go in for.

Not that any of its graduates are expected to become raging Richard Bransons afterwards. The reverse is more the case: by being entrusted with this knowledge, they are expected to do all in their power to prevent China ever embracing such wicked notions.

And Hu didn't disappoint. He graduated from Qinghua in 1965, having completed a study of the thrilling world of Hub Hydropower Stations. During his time there he also met his future wife, Liu Yongqing, with whom he now has a son and daughter. (Both of whom also studied at Qinghua.) More importantly though, Hu had joined the Communist Party the year before and had a volunteer job as a 'political instructor', i.e. junior brainwasher.

He stayed on at Qinghua until 1968 to teach. This, however, was during the Cultural Revolution, when members of the elite had to demonstrate their solidarity with proletarian heroes etc etc, or get thrown in prison. So he took a year out to work as a manual labourer in Gansu province, which, both politically and geographically, was in the middle of nowhere. (Today, there are still parts of China where they have never seen a television or white people.)

It was something of a flamboyant gesture: Hu had so much solidarity that he was prepared to live and work with his comrades in a part of China so mountainous and remote you're considered posh if you own shoes. Indeed, the party were so pleased with this commitment that in 1968, they sent him out there again.

For the next twelve years he held various posts, all to do with water and engineering; all of them dull. Except that he wasn't *just* working as a water engineer: in China, especially if you are a party member, everything is about politics. When he became Secretary of the Gansu Provincial Construction Committee (GPCC), it was as much as a result of his lobbying in the local party as it was of his engineering expertise; particularly the close ties he established with Song Ping, an elder of the Party who still had connections back in Beijing

And it was Ping who got Hu his first big break: in 1982, Hu was appointed Secretary of the Gansu Provincial Committee of the Communist Youth League. Wow. The Big Time. In 1982, Hu was forty years of age. In China, they have a rather elastic definition of 'Youth'.

Still, the new job meant a transfer back to Beijing to where the real action was. Not that Hu was an action sort of a guy. The Communist Youth League is generally considered the reformist wing of the Party, yet Hu came over as a bit of a soppy-pants. One report of the time describes him as 'rather soft and unforceful, without sufficient trailblazing spirit'.

But that was the point: Hu wasn't trying to present himself as a passionate politician, but rather as a Safe Pair of Hands: just the sort of guy the conservative leadership would like to promote. Hu didn't propose any radical change, and as much as possible avoided criticising anyone. One of his few recorded statements of the time includes the sentence: 'success requires resolve, attention to concrete matters and courage in making decisions'. Makes you think, doesn't it?

At all costs, the future leader of China avoided saying or doing anything. Instead, he networked like a madman.

Even folks in China who hate Hu's guts admit his networking abilities are extraordinary. Perhaps it comes with being a bit dull – people neither liked nor disliked him – but Hu got to know just about everyone, and today is recognised as having the best network of political contacts in China.

Within two years he had networked his way to the top job: Secretary of the Central Committee of the Communist Youth League. In 1985, he was made a full member of the Central Committee of the Communist Party proper and appointed Party Secretary of the Guizhou province – effectively, Governor of a region. This entailed another move out to the middle of nowhere, yet still it was an impressive achievement: he had been given an entire province to run and at the unusually young age of 42. Hu was well on his way.

However, it was his next appointment which may have raised a few eyebrows in Beijing. In 1988, the Party Secretary of Tibet, Wu Jinghua, suffered a heart attack. This may not have been entirely surprising, as Tibet wasn't exactly regarded as a plum job. China had occupied Tibet since 1950, yet the unappreciative natives had still to thank Beijing for bringing them the great gift of communism. They had demonstrations, strikes and riots. The Dalai Lama, their spiritual leader, kept travelling around the world giving out about it: so much so that he eventually won the Nobel Peace Prize.

China addressed this problem by appointing a series of Party Secretaries with military backgrounds, each of them more kick-ass and oppressive than the last. But it hadn't worked, so with Wu Jinghua a more conciliatory line had been adopted: Tibetans were promoted within the local government, to at least give a semblance of autonomy.

But this didn't work either. If anything, it made the situation worse.

Thus the choice of Hu as Wu Jinghua's replacement was indeed an odd one. Hu would be the first Party boss in Tibet without a military background. And for a man already identified as being in favour with the Communist Party, to send him even further away from Beijing seemed a little strange.

Yet according to one account, Hu was mad keen to go: 'like a soldier, asking for a battle assignment'. But perhaps this was the point: before he could finally join China's ruling elite, Hu had to pick up some experience of dealing with the military – and most importantly, demonstrate just how far he was prepared to go to maintain the system.

Suddenly, things weren't so dull. Hu's appointment was announced on December 9, 1988. The next day the Tibetan capital, Lhasa, played host to a massive demonstration. The police opened fire, killing several people.

Hu arrived the following month and at first tried the Nice Guy approach. He convened a meeting with the most senior Buddhist leader, the Panchen Lama, (he's number two to the Dalai Lama), during which Hu declared that he considered himself a member of the Tibetan people and promised to 'work wholeheartedly for their benefit'.

But the Panchen Lama – displaying a rather unhealthy degree of courage – effectively told Hu to shag off. He delivered a scathing critique of Chinese rule and said the Chinese occupation had resulted in far more harm than good to Tibetans.

Unhealthy courage indeed: a few days after the meeting, the

Panchen Lama suddenly died, creating a vacuum in the Tibetan local leadership which has still to be filled. There's no proof, of course, but most Tibetans are convinced that Hu had him taken out.

So convinced were they that the demonstrations started almost immediately, eventually building to a three-day riot in March of 1989 which came dangerously close to an uprising. Around 130 Tibetans were shot by police. On March 7th, after consultations with Beijing, Hu announced martial law, effectively rolling back all the reforms introduced by his predecessor. Thousands of troops poured into Tibet. Hundreds of Tibetans were arrested.

Hu had shown he could be tough. But, of course – if he wanted to have a future career – this was exactly what he had to do. Even the smallest sign of weakness would have meant him being passed over for promotion. But just to be sure Beijing got the message, he sent a telegram of *congratulations* to the leadership later that summer: for taking the decision to drive tanks over the demonstrating students in Tiananmen Square.

The Party had paid for the Dull Man's soul, and they were delighted with the purchase. In the summer of 1990 even CCP General Secretary Jiang Zemin paid a visit: the ultimate gesture of confidence in Hu Jintao's good work.

Hu was no doubt pleased, but even more so when in October of that year, he moved back to Beijing and ruled Tibet from there. The official reason was that Tibet's mountainous terrain gave him constant altitude sickness; his official biography claims that Hu suffered from 'highland anoxia' yet still 'braved the region's hostile natural conditions, including a shortage of atmospheric oxygen'.

The truth was that he hated the place. *The Guardian* journalist Jonathan Mirsky later wrote: "I once had a chance encounter with Hu. Not knowing that I was a journalist, he told me how he disliked Tibet's altitude, climate and lack of culture. He was keeping his family in Beijing, he told me, and feared that if there were ever an uprising against the Chinese, no Tibetan would protect him."

True enough. Anyway, by crushing Tibet, he had done what was expected of him. Now it was time to slither up the well-greased pole of leadership. Eventually, he was replaced as Tibetan Party Chief by Chen Kuiyan, who took an even more hard-line approach.

Curiously though, in more recent years Hu seems to have moderated his position. During a press conference in Berlin in 2001, he said the Chinese government was willing to "negotiate with the Dalai Lama when he declares Tibet and Taiwan are inalienable parts of China". This doesn't sound like much – in fact it is the standard line on the issue – yet usually it is couched in far more vitriolic language. The fact that Hu didn't abuse the Dalai Lama for being an enemy of the proletarian heroes of China was construed by many China-watchers as something of a climb-down. Perhaps his 'good work' in Tibet did leave a bad taste.

But anyway: back to the pole-climbing. Hu expected rewards, and he got them. In October 1992 he was promoted to the sexily-titled Standing Committee of the CCP Central Committee, reportedly at the personal behest of President Deng Xiaoping. This made Hu the seventh most powerful man in China.

The following year Jiang Zemin – who already had a liking for Hu – was appointed President. It was looking good, so Hu did what he always did: he said and did nothing, and as usual, it worked a treat. By 1998 he was appointed Vice-President of the People's Republic, which, in the totally confusing way of these things, made him the fifth most powerful man in China. (The next year, to reinforce his hard-line credentials, he made one of his rare appearances on television. Following the 'accidental' bombing by the US of the Chinese embassy in Belgrade, Hu officially authorised (i.e. ordered) spontaneous demonstrations outside the US and British embassies in Beijing.)

Yet out of the five most powerful men in China, Hu was by far the youngest – 55 – so it was then that the speculation began to grow that he would be China's first 'Fourth Generation' leader.

There was, however, one small amount of grooming still to be performed on the future president: he may have known a lot about being bland, building hydroelectric schemes and killing Tibetans, but he knew damn all about foreign affairs. So in October of 2001 he was dispatched on a whirlwind tour of foreign capitals: a chance for various world leaders to have a look at the new Chinese guy, and for the new Chinese guy to demonstrate his charm and diplomacy.

In fairness, Hu Jintao can be diplomatic – his ability to say nothing while using words is close to superhuman – yet there are axe-murderers with more charm. He visited Moscow, Paris, Berlin, Tokyo, Amman, Minsk and Madrid, and while in every capital he was furnished with the full diplomatic whistles and bells, all were left slightly puzzled by his flat, expressionless face. He made warmish noises about the War on Terror, yet said little else, apart from the slightly-less-hostile-than-usual reference to the Dalai Lama.

When George W Bush visited China in February the following year, he didn't even meet Hu, who at that time had yet to be elevated to General Secretary. They finally got together late in 2002 when Hu made a trip to Washington, but according to one report, 'he left but a faint imprint'.

The dullness which had proved so effective in Chinese

politics ain't so lethal when you're trotting around the world.

Yet it's unlikely Hu will worry about this too much: he can leave it to others to concentrate on the foreign PR. His main problem is where China goes next. The economic reforms are continuing, yet still there are many forces within China who would wish to ensure that they don't go *too* far – that they don't start leading to – gasp – democracy.

Chief among those is Hu's mentor, Jiang Zemin. Despite the fact that he virtually gave Hu the job of president, he still retains some power as Secretary of the powerful Military Commission. In China, you don't trust your friends. It's expected.

But would Jiang have a reason not to? Based on how Hu has acted so far, certainly not. Yet still there are whispers: talk about Hu's days at Qinghua University and the effect it had upon him. There is speculation that Hu favours the introduction of a Western-style civil service system; that he secretly admires the organisational principles of Western social democratic parties.

But even if he does, Hu would be far too sly to do anything about it soon. He'll wait until he has a much firmer grip on power; in other words, when Jiang – who is in his late seventies – has gone to the great politburo in the sky. If Hu is going to bring in any reforms, it won't be until after he begins his second term as President in 2007.

The key word is *if*. In the meantime, 1.3 billion Chinese people will have to put up with keeping their thoughts to themselves, with following the Party line. With imprisonment, with torture. With dying of hunger . . . and boredom.

PRESIDENT FIDEL CASTRO
of the Republic of Cuba

Cuba: now this is a tricky one. To many people, especially those of a beardy, left-leaning nature, the very idea of including Fidel Castro in a list of despots can prompt screams of indignant horror: Fidel isn't a baddie, he's a *hero*. Fidel gave up a career as a lawyer and risked his own life to liberate his people; he has faced down the Yanks for more than forty years and survived numerous assassination attempts. Most importantly of all – despite the US embargo and the end of billion-dollar dig- outs from the Soviet Union – Fidel established a regime with the highest standards of health, education and housing of any Latin American country – with a literacy rate exceeding that of the United States.

And it's all true: Castro has brought about astonishing changes to his country since he seized power in 1959; he is arguably the only person in history who made a socialist system of government actually work. More or less.

Yet, yet, yet: Fidel may have improved the lot of millions of Cubans, but has done so without the impediment of democracy. When was the last time you heard the phrase 'Cuban elections'? You haven't.

In the land of quality tobacco, Fidel has come close but not quite earned that cigar. By sticking it to the Yanks he has become a poster-boy for the Left and one of the US' Top Five Hate Figures. And the Americans really, really hate him.

But we'll get to that. First, it's worth explaining that the average Cuban ain't too enamoured of the US either, and for very sound historical reasons.

Discovered by Columbus in 1492, Cuba was first settled by the Spanish back in the sixteenth century. At the time the island had an indigenous Indian population, but the wise Spanish, foreseeing all sorts of ethnic tensions later on, solved this problem by killing them all.

Thus it remained for the next four centuries. After the first three hundred years or so the Cubans started to get a bit uppity and looked for independence. The Spanish were having none of it, but changed their tune considerably when they came second in the Spanish-American war of 1898. At the insistence of the US, Cuba was granted its freedom.

Hang on: isn't this the US doing Cuba a favour? Well, not really. About two minutes after independence was granted, US troops arrived on Cuban soil and stayed there for the next four years, the logic being that since Cubans had never been allowed run their own affairs, they were bound to make a mess of it. Annoyingly, the Americans were proved right.

In 1902, the troops went home. Sort of. By this time Teddy Roosevelt was US president. Famously, Roosevelt outlined his foreign policy as consisting of speaking softly while carrying a big stick. Yet it was his fondness for big sticks that many Cubans will remember him for. To President Teddy, most Latin Americans were 'little brown brothers' who were a bit too, well, *brown* to be allowed total freedom to run their own affairs. So as a way of demonstrating just how much he cared for his little brown pals, Roosevelt gave Cuba the Platt Amendment.

Grafted into Cuba's new constitution, this gave the US the right to intervene in Cuban affairs whenever it felt like it. This America did regularly for the next three decades. In effect, the regime in Cuba was directly controlled by the US. Newspaper proprietor William Randolph Hearst was given the job. Here: have a country. Thanks. I can't wait to get home and play with it.

This was a trick that the Yanks had pulled off with several of their Latin American neighbours: America controlled them politically through a proxy – and usually poxy – government, while the country was solely dependent on the US to buy its exports. In Cuba's case, it was sugar. In the case of many South American countries, it was bananas.

Hence the term: banana republic.

But the Americans liked Cuba so much they couldn't bear to give it all back. In 1903 it 'leased' a naval base at the eastern end of the island and even now, more than one hundred years later, keep forgetting to return it. It's called Guantánamo Bay. Yes, you've heard of *this* place. Guantánamo Bay is the location for Camp X-Ray, that fun-filled holiday destination much-beloved by people from Afghanistan and Iraq. Oh, how they love to sit in those cells with black bags over their heads. It's a little piece of America, but without the Geneva Convention.

Anyway: things rattled along in this manner for the next five or six decades. One corrupt, self-serving 'President' was replaced, or overthrown by another. Political ferment and violence were almost constant: so much so that eventually even the US loosened its grip on the country. There were other places to get sugar.

Into this Fidel (Faithful) Castro was born on August 13, 1926. But unlike a lot of Cubans, the Castros were doing quite well: Fidel's daddy, originally from Spain, owned a 23 000-acre sugar plantation. Thus the young Fidel received a private education from Jesuits and during the summer built up his tan by working on the plantation. It was also during this time that he developed his love of cigars: Dad presented him with his first when he was just fifteen.

But it was the University of Havana that really moulded the future despot. While studying for his law degree he, like a lot of his peers, became intensely politicised, sickened by the widespread poverty and corruption most Cubans had to endure. Fidel wanted to see change, though at this stage it was unclear exactly *what sort* of change. The young Fidel may not have been entirely sure himself.

During this period Cuba had had various Presidents, yet the real power lay in the hands of General Fulgencio Batista, who, as the title implies, was the head of the army. General Batista would find some corrupt weasel, install them as president, then depose them a few months later on the grounds that they were a corrupt weasel. And he did it again in 1952, just prior to scheduled elections – elections in which Fidel had planned to offer himself as a parliamentary candidate.

Somewhat miffed, Fidel took Batista to court, respectfully suggesting that to seize power by force of arms just might be a wee bit unconstitutional. Unsurprisingly, he lost the case.

So with no legal recourse left, Fidel decided to stage his own revolution. Just like that.

Say what you like about Fidel Castro, but the man is stunningly optimistic. In July 1953, along with his brother

Raul and just 165 untrained men, he launched an attack on an army barracks in Santiago de Cuba.

It was a miserable failure. Half the men were killed before they even took a shot while the rest were easily captured. The 'coup' was so laughable that even the normally paranoid and vengeful Batista didn't bother having the insurgents executed or even tortured: he threw them in prison for a couple of years. And when he finally stopped laughing, he let them out.

Fidel and Raul promptly left the country, travelling first to the US and then to Mexico. The Castro brothers had caught the revolution bug, and were keen to meet others who wanted to give it another try. And they did: though not as many as the last time. Spurred on by Fidel's almost psychopathic optimism, a force of just 82 men returned to their homeland with the aim of overwhelming the Cuban army.

Well, eventually they returned. First they had to sit in their yacht for two days to let some bad weather pass by – thus allowing plenty of time for the Cuban army to find out about their plans. Then, to make things even more challenging, they accidentally landed the yacht in a swamp. A fire-fight with Batista's troops ensued, followed by a week-long chase into the mountains. Finally, the revolutionaries managed to shake off the army, but at this stage there were only twelve of them left. They had seven guns.

Apparently, this was when Fidel exclaimed: "The revolution has triumphed!" For the rest of them, it was probably a bit annoying at the time.

Yet he was right. Eventually. The twelve remained within the Sierra Maestra mountains and waged a guerrilla war against the Batista government. They blew up power stations, cut railway lines and burned sugar plantations – including Castro's own. Their force grew to an estimated 3 000, and more importantly, garnered widespread support through the Cuban population.

No slouch on the PR front either, Fidel even developed a nifty knack for propaganda. Despite having virtually no resources he managed to con a *New York Times* journalist into believing that his troops were numerous and well-armed: mostly by arranging to have 'runners' interrupt Fidel with 'news' from fronts that didn't exist.

Finally, General Batista skipped town on New Year's Day, 1959, and pretty much everyone was pleased. Except for Batista. Fidel was a hero. He was young – only 31 – good-looking and came from a wealthy family. He had given up a comfortable life to liberate his country and everyone expected him to deliver what he had been promising: a Cuba that was democratic, Catholic and stable. Even the Yanks seemed pleased, and recognised the new government within a week.

But whatever books Fidel had been reading in the mountains, *Capitalism For Beginners* wasn't one of them. The new government began seizing American-owned properties by way of compensation, and then set about nationalising farms and industries – including Fidel's own family's farm. It caused a rift with his sister Juanita which exists to this day. She now lives in Miami.

And as you might imagine, the Americans weren't too thrilled either, especially when, in February 1960, Cuba announced it had signed a deal to buy Russian oil. The US broke off diplomatic relations. Privately, President Eisenhower resolved to bring the Castro regime down. Even the Pope got annoyed. Fidel was excommunicated from the Catholic Church after declaring himself an atheist and ruling that Catholics couldn't be members of Cuba's new ruling Communist Party: a party which now controlled virtually all aspects of Cuban life.

Suddenly, the US had a commie country only 70 miles from its border – thus starting one of the most tragicomic sequences in US history.

In 1961, with John Kennedy now US president, a group of 1 300 Cuban exiles (armed by the CIA) landed in the Bay of Pigs in Cuba with the aim of seizing power. But someone in the US State Department had forgotten that it's best to keep these things secret: the Cuban Army was waiting for them. The promised US Air and Naval support never arrived – so the Kennedy administration could preserve 'plausible deniability'.

Fidel 1. Yanks: 0.

The fiasco made the US look like a bunch of dopes. So to test if they really were that stupid, the USSR decided to station a few nuclear ballistic missiles in Cuba. Up until now, Soviet ICBMs could only reach Western Europe. Now they were only 70 miles from Miami.

Obviously, President Kennedy wasn't too pleased, so we had the Cuban missile crisis. Kennedy immediately instigated a naval blockade of Cuba and got on the hot line to President Khrushchev of the USSR, warning him to move the nukes, or else.

For thirteen days, the entire world tottered on the brink of nuclear annihilation.

Luckily for us, Khrushchev blinked, and the nukes went back to Moscow. But as part of the deal, the US agreed to accept over a million Cuban refugees: all the people, it turned out, who Fidel wanted to get rid of anyway . . . opposition groups, criminals, the insane and homosexuals. (Cuba isn't a good place to be gay, but we'll get to that presently.) Most of these people and their families now live in Florida where the bulk of the anti-Fidel resistance is based. In the last thirty years, Fidel has repeated this process many times.

Fidel 2. Yanks: 0.

Oh, the Americans really hate Fidel Castro.

In the space of two years, Fidel had managed to make the world's most powerful nation look like Luxembourg – yet on the second occasion he had done so by risking the destruction of the entire planet. A bit irresponsible, you might think. Yet in fairness to him, he might not have had that much choice. Accepting the Russian rockets was probably part of the price he had to pay for all the lolly they handed over: money which he used to build enviable health and education systems. At its height, the USSR was doling out annual subsidies of $4-5 billion.

In turn, Cuba has also supported revolutionary movements in various Latin American and African countries, though it seems as if this support petered out in the 1990s. Members of some groups – such as the Basque group ETA – have taken refuge there.

But it was, and still is, a one-party state in the classic communist mould. The only media is state media, which a lot of the time features Fidel's long speeches. (Very long: it's not been uncommon for him to talk for seven hours.) Opposition figures were jailed, executed or deported. Religion was suppressed. You get three years in prison automatically for disagreeing with the state. And the more pressure the US put on Cuba – such as the 40-year-long trade embargo – the more oppressive Fidel seemed to get.

However, not all of it seemed to be about maintaining the purity of the revolution. Some of it was just plain old bigotry. During his guerrilla days, Fidel's struggle was supported by a popular left-wing journal, *Lunes de Revolución*. However, a couple of years after Fidel got his feet under the government desk, *Lunes de Revolución* was closed down – mainly because it employed gay writers.

Homosexuality was then declared illegal (even though

Fidel had earlier declared that "there are no homosexuals" in rural Cuba). There were mass round-ups without trial. Many ended up in forced labour camps along with all the other undesirables: criminals, political dissidents and Catholics.

The most famous example of this is the case of the writer Reinaldo Arenas. Having fought with Fidel's rebels, he published an internationally-acclaimed novel, *Singing from the Well*. However, his follow-up work *Hallucinations* was refused publication on the basis of its 'deviant' content. Arenas had the book published overseas, for which he was jailed for several years, then deported to the US. He committed suicide in 1990, aged 47.

A softening of the line on homosexuality didn't really take place until the early 1990s, when the world outbreak of AIDS – along with a lot of international pressure – forced the Cuban government to take a more tolerant approach. In 1992, Fidel declared that to be gay was a 'natural human tendency'. However, the Cuban Association of Gay and Lesbians, formed in 1994, was suppressed three years later, and its members arrested. You now can be gay in Cuba; just not very.

Yet despite all this, there is a thing about Fidel – a thing which really infuriates US governments. No matter what he has done, both he and Cuba have a sexy image. The beard, the cigar smoking, the rather louche atmosphere of Havana with its rum and sun and 1950s American cars sliding past crumbling bars leaking Latin jazz music. Even at the height of the Cold War, when Communism was officially the Most Evil Thing in the World, Fidel was still a bit cool. After all, one of the men who helped him liberate Cuba (the only non-Cuban of his troop) was the Argentinian Che Guevara: literally and metaphorically the poster boy for left-wing revolution.

No wonder the Americans really, really hated him.

So they decided to get the CIA to kill him. And the CIA tried. By some reports, the CIA tried around six hundred times. It was code-named Operation Mongoose. "If surviving assassination were an Olympic sport," Fidel once told an interviewer, "I would win the gold medal."

After the Watergate scandal in 1975, many sensitive US government papers were made public, including various proposals on how to take out the Cuban leader. They demonstrated imagination, determination and probably a certain amount of drug abuse. So we present to you, from the files of Operation Mongoose:

SEVEN WAYS TO KILL FIDEL CASTRO

1)   Inject his cigars with poison. Made sense really: like, the guy has one in his mouth constantly. And this plan almost worked. Except for the fact that, like all men who have smoked cigars since the age of fifteen, Fidel is rather fussy about his. He likes to smoke Cohibas and doesn't much care for anything else, so when the poisoned ones arrived – and when they weren't Cohibas – well, he didn't smoke them. In fact no one knows what eventually happened to the lethal stogies: the poison may have been discovered or, far worse, some poor minion may have decided to help themselves.

2)   Put explosives into his cigars. Quick and effective. But suffers from the same flaw as idea 1). This was abandoned.

3)   Put drugs in his cigars. Loath to completely give up the cigar-centred plots, but rather worried that the guy was impossible to kill, the CIA came up with the fantastic wheeze of putting an hallucinogen into one of the aforementioned

Cohibas, in the hope that he would appear in public obviously out of his trolley and lose credibility at home. This was abandoned.

4)   Thallium Salts. Having finally learned to let go of their cigar obsession, (Yes, Doctor Freud), the Company further pursued the idea of eroding Fidel's credibility with his people. Adhering to the strict logic that the source of Fidel's power, rather like Samson's, lay in his hair and beard, they planned to deposit Thallium Salts into his shoes. These salts would make all the hair on his body fall out, thus destroying his credibility. This plan was abandoned on the basis that it was stupid.

5)   Scuba diving 1. Upon learning that Castro had a hobby apart from smoking cigars, the CIA went into a frenzy of concocting diabolical scuba diving plots. The first consisted of presenting Fidel with a diving suit contaminated with tuberculosis and, as a spiteful extra, a foot fungus. A mix-up resulted in him being given the wrong suit, and once again, another minion developed a bad cough and smelly feet.

6) Scuba diving 2. Not only did they know he liked diving, but the CIA had also discovered the location of one of his favourite diving spots. So they hatched a plan to place an exploding conch shell there. Rather bizarrely, given plans 1-5, this was eventually scrapped as being too impractical.

7) Get God involved. Without doubt the most ambitious and astonishing idea came from General Edward Lansdale, the man in charge of the covert war on Castro during the Kennedy presidency. The general hoped to spark a counter-revolution by spreading the word to devout Cuban

Catholics that the Second Coming had happened. Jesus was on TV in the US (naturally) and naming Fidel as the anti-Christ. But to whip Cuban Catholics into a real frenzy, he further planned to have 'Jesus' surface off the shores of Cuba aboard an American submarine, with flares illuminating the sky around him. Once given the nod by God, it was hoped, Cubans would then overthrow their satanic leader. This was eventually considered slightly less impractical than the exploding conch plan

Despite such Austin Powers-like ingenuity, Fidel Castro is still alive and still in charge. Very annoying. Yet for such an iconic figure, not that much is known about his personal life. He was married in 1948 (in a Catholic church) and divorced in 1954. He has one son, born in 1949 (christened in a Catholic church) who has since served as head of Cuba's Atomic Energy Commission.

People who have met the Cuban despot usually comment that he does have genuine charisma and does come across as vigorous and committed.

But he's not getting any younger. Now in his late 70s, Fidel Castro is sick and grey, a visibly failing figure. Rumours of serious illness – heart trouble, brain tumour, Parkinson's, take your pick – have been gathering momentum. The Cuban authorities have always played them down, but it is an open secret that soon Fidel will die or retire. He's even given up the cigars, though he can still do the odd seven-hour speech.

Like Fidel, Cuba too has been in decline since the cash from the USSR dried up in 1991. The following year he announced the end of all funding to insurgent groups or friendly governments abroad, while the Cuban military, now facing massive cutbacks, began establishing farms, business and construction brigades to help pay for itself.

Many predicted the end of the regime then, yet it survived. Despite the economy shrinking by more than 60 per cent and the continuing US trade embargo, a modest recovery has been made with the help of Canadian, European and Latin American investments, especially in tourism. Some economic controls have been relaxed, with companies allowed to import and export without seeking permission and a number of free trade zones opening up.

But the introduction of a little bit of capitalism – and the legalisation of the US dollar – have brought with it the ugly face of western economics. There are grim divisions between those with US currency and those without. Native Cubans aren't even allowed into the tourist hotels. They are rationed eight eggs a month. There have been increases in prostitution, corruption, and black marketeering. And people continue to leave

Quietly, there is something of an opposition movement in Cuba. But they can't risk becoming too visible. It is estimated that there are as many as five hundred prison camps across the country. A recent wave of arrests attracted international condemnation.

Another open secret is that Fidel's younger brother Raul – vice-president and head of the Cuban Armed Forces (they are called 'Raul's Party' in Cuba) – will succeed Castro Senior when the time comes. Raul, of course, has been there since the very beginning, and it is believed that even as far back as 1959, Fidel was telling his followers that the younger brother would one day take over from him.

Certainly, all important government meetings have to take place with Raul present, while recently he has represented Cuba abroad several times: in China, Italy and even the Vatican.

Yet by choosing his brother, Fidel is doing more than just keeping the family business alive: as head of the Cuban

Army (who are very loyal to him), Raul wields enormous influence in Cuban society. If the boss dies suddenly, Raul can make sure that no cocky underling grabs power.

Of course, this arrangement won't last forever; Raul is no teenager either. He is viewed as more pragmatic than his brother: so his ascension could well spell a further softening of the communist regime, but probably not a total collapse. Out of principle, stubbornness and not a little nostalgia, Raul will try to keep Fidel's inheritance alive. For a few years more.

After he goes, who knows? Many of the top government and communist party posts are held by men in their thirties and forties: young enough to be ambitious, but not well known enough to command widespread support.

In the meantime, the US still views Cuba as the Home of Evil. Unsurprisingly, Tony Blair recently gave a speech in the House of Commons supporting this stance. However, there is also a widespread view, especially in Europe, that now might be the time to establish more contacts with Cuba and encourage them to democratise.

Or put less kindly: their time is almost over. Fidel will die, then Raul, and then the greedy young men will scrabble for power while the US navy steams towards Havana, determined never to let *that* happen again.

Even for a man as optimistic as Fidel Castro, this must be difficult to contemplate.

PRESIDENT TEODORO OBIANG
NGUEMA MBASOGO

of the Republic of Equatorial Guinea

It really is amazing what a small country can achieve. And Equatorial Guinea is a very small country, divided up between six even smaller countries, with a total population of less than 500 000. Yet year after year, it is named as one of the top despotic regimes in the world – consistently within the top fifteen.

Not bad, because if you knew anything previously about Equatorial Guinea – or EG – it was probably in the context of failure. Back in the 2000 Olympic Games, a swimmer from EG, Eric Moussambani, entered the record books as having won his 100m freestyle heat in the slowest time ever in the history of the Games.

In the one minute 52 seconds (over double the world record time) it took Eric to complete the hundred metre swim, he barely managed to keep his head above water. But something kept him going. Eric said it was the Olympic spirit, but it may also have been the fact that the other two swimmers in the race had already been disqualified for false starts. After the first few seconds, Eric knew he had it won.

Bit like elections in his home country. But we'll get to that.

Afterwards, Eric was a hero: he gave over 100 interviews to the world's press. He was the main item on NBC's nightly sports coverage. Fans queued to get his autograph. It wasn't just that someone who could barely swim had won an Olympic heat; it was the charm with which he admitted it. "I had never been in a pool that big before," said Eric. "I was very scared."

It turned out that Eric, who was unemployed, trained in a twenty-metre pool: because that is the biggest one they have in Equatorial Guinea. It made the victory of Eric the Eel (as he became known) all the more heroic. But poignant also: there should be a fifty-metre pool in Equatorial Guinea. There should be ten of them. In fact, if Eric the Eel and his family didn't have the misfortune to live under two crazy despots in a row, there's a good chance he would be quite well off. Really.

But first: where is Equatorial Guinea? What is Equatorial Guinea? In the post-colonial way of these things, EG is a bit of a hodge-podge. First thing you should know is that it's in West Africa: and as we've learned, no one cares about West Africa. Second is that there are six separate bits to it. The biggest is Rio Muni, a rectangular piece of land squeezed in between Cameroon and Gabon, while the rest of EG consists of five islands: all of them located much closer to Cameroon than Rio Muni. And despite the name, it's not on the equator. But it's close to it.

Given that Rio Muni is the biggest bit, most of the population live there: 75 per cent. But just to be contrary, the capital of Equatorial Guinea, Malabo, is located on the largest of the islands, Bioco, where pretty much everyone else lives. Confused? You should be. It's a confusing place. On the mainland bit, Rio Muni, ninety per cent of them belong to the Fang ethnic group, (who still maintain traditions such as black magic), while on Bioco, the population is pretty equally divided between Fangs, Bubis and Creoles. And if you parachuted into any part of Equatorial Guinea, you wouldn't have a clue where you were: apart from the usual mix of local languages, such as Bantu, everyone speaks Spanish. It's the only part of Africa to do so.

So let's have the bit of history. The Portuguese landed on the islands back in 1470, but weren't too interested in the place, so they did a deal with Spain to swap them for a few Brazilian territories. The Spaniards had plans: they wanted to establish Bioko as a major slave-trading port. But all the settlers they sent died of yellow fever, so they gave up.

The British moved in next, during which time freed slaves settled on Bioko. The Brits didn't die of yellow fever, so the Spanish wanted the place back. They re-occupied in 1884 and for good measure took over the mainland part, Rio Muni. In 1879, a Cuban penal settlement was established on Bioko, and descendants of those prisoners still live there.

In 1959 EG was divided into two overseas provinces of Spain, but by then there was already a fledgling independence movement, so in 1963 it was re-united, christened Spanish Guinea and given its own parliament and president, Ondo Edu. The vice-president was Francisco Macias Nguema, a supposed leftist and leading light of the independence movement. Macias was a member of the majority Fong tribe.

Full independence came in 1968. Spanish Guinea called itself Equatorial Guinea. After an election, Macias Nguema was named president. Then the fun really started.

The following year, the Foreign Minister, Atanasio Ndongo attempted a coup, and got a bullet in the head for his trouble. Why he attempted the revolution remains something of a mystery, though at the time, some British tabloids speculated that it had really all been engineered by the thriller writer, Frederick Forsyth. Forsyth was living in the capital, Malabo, at the time, and working on his novel *The Dogs of War*: a story of how twelve Western mercenaries and fifty soldiers from Biafra take over a small West African country. The papers claimed that Freddie had masterminded the coup attempt to see if his plot could actually work.

It didn't, but hey: you can't buy that kind of publicity. *The Dogs of War* was a huge bestseller – Richard Burton and Harris were in the film version – and everyone went back to forgetting where Equatorial Guinea was.

It was still in the same place, but very quickly going down the plug-hole. In the year of the attempted coup, 1979, there were violent anti-European demonstrations, which blossomed into inter-ethnic riots. Any Europeans living there scuttled home. (Freddie Forsyth had already gone.) For about a year afterwards Equatorial Guinea existed in a state of near-anarchy. The President had to take control.

So he did: and how. First, he merged all existing political parties into his own, the United National Party, whether they liked it or not. He dissolved parliament and the constitution and appointed himself president for life. In every key political and military post, he installed either members of his own family or members of his Fang tribe. With a militia of just 2 000 men and a small Youth Army, he grabbed total control of the country.

He then set about purging all foreign influences. He persecuted intellectuals and Catholics, eventually banning the Church altogether. Anyone who gave any lip at all was killed, thrown into the notorious Black Beach jail in Malabo or driven into exile. During Christmas celebrations in 1975, Macias ordered his militia to bring 150 of his political opponents into the Malabo stadium and shoot them while the loudspeakers blared music. Apparently, the song was *Those Were The Days, My Friend*. At least he had a sense of humour.

Of the parliament he dissolved in 1970, Macias had managed to kill two-thirds of them by 1976.

President Macias was in charge, but like all tragic heroes, he had a fatal flaw: he really wasn't that smart. Even the most ruthless of despots know that you have to keep some parts of the country ticking over: you have to have allies, both internally and externally, and you have to make it worth their while to stay on your side. Macias didn't seem aware of this, and so over the next decade destroyed his country. Here are some examples:

* Because of his anti-European purge, Spanish plantation owners shut down their cocoa operations (the backbone of the economy), fuelling massive unemployment. EG broke off diplomatic relations with Spain in 1977.

* When migrant Nigerian workers looked for higher wages, Macias brutally crushed their protests. Eventually, Nigeria paid to bring all the workers home. Diplomatic relations between the two countries disintegrated, while agricultural production in EG dropped by 90 per cent.

* Huge numbers of Guineans fled the country, straining relations with neighbouring Gabon and

Cameroon, who were forced to take them in. During Macias' reign, the population of Equatorial Guinea fell by one third: around 200,000 people, including all the teachers, doctors and engineers.

* He banned fishing and destroyed EG's fishing fleet – believing the boats were being used to spirit people out of the country. Which they were.

* Overseas aid dried up because pretty much all of it was being diverted into the regime.

* In 1973 he expelled the representative of the United Nations Development Program, one of the few agencies still providing aid.

By the time Macias had finished, the bush had reclaimed all the cocoa and coffee plantations. All the schools were closed – EG had previously had one of the best school systems in Africa – along with all the clinics. The water was turned on for one hour a day. Typhoid, cholera and cerebral malaria were rampant. The Post Office and National Bank were closed. The population were almost entirely barefoot. After Macias was deposed, the Chinese sent a boatload of shoes.

The *Unique Miracle*, as Macias came to call himself, really had to go. So how did it happen? Don't forget that Equatorial Guinea was a tiny, unimportant place – it didn't even export cocoa any more – and so was hardly going to grab the interest of any Western countries. Its African neighbours weren't going to do anything either. Cameroon and Gabon had their own problems.

But the Spanish retained a distant, if secretive, post-colonial interest. No one knows how much they were involved in the subsequent coup, but they certainly weren't against it. And it came from where dopey, paranoid Macias least expected: his own family.

One of the relations he gave a job to was his nephew, Obiang Nguema. Obiang, the third of ten brothers, was a military man. In the early sixties he had trained in Spain, and, naturally, when Uncle took over the shop, gained rapid promotion. He was military governor of Bioko and director of Black Beach Prison. In 1973, Obiang was given the job of expelling the UN Development Program representative. By 1979, he was vice-minister of the inappropriately-named Popular Armed Forces: a job which gave him enough clout and contacts to organise a move against Macias. Backed by the military, Obiang led an almost completely bloodless coup against his uncle.

Almost bloodless: after a quickie trial for crimes against humanity, Macias and five others were executed by a Moroccan firing squad. (Moroccan? This will be explained.) Now installed as head of the ruling Supreme Military Council, Obiang called his predecessor 'an envoy of the devil and president of sorcerers'. Indeed.

It was a new start, with all the usual promises: reform, democracy, a Fiat Punto parked outside every house. And for a while there it looked like Obiang might actually do it. He lifted all the restrictions on the Catholic church, re-established ties with Western governments and was suitably grateful when foreign aid poured in.

Naturally, Obiang invited all those Guineans in exile to return home. Yet curiously, most of them didn't take up his kind offer. Perhaps they knew something. *Of course,* they knew something: Obiang, after all, was no innocent; he had been deeply involved in the brutality of his uncle's regime. Yet at his trial Macias made no attempt to implicate his nephew. It is speculated that Obiang had promised his uncle immunity in return for his silence. And the uncle was dumb enough to believe it.

Economically, things got a little better, but that was about it. A small number of exiles returned. Many of them were slung into Black Beach Prison for their trouble. Oh-uh.

Yet still Obiang liked to talk the talk. In 1982 he and the Supreme Military Council approved a new constitution which called for a more democratic political structure. You'll notice the words: *called for*. While they continued calling, Obiang got himself re-elected president twice – in 1984 and 1989. He was the only candidate.

And in the meantime, he got up to a lot of Macias' old tricks. Political opponents were arrested, deported or 'disappeared'. Freedom of expression was *verboten*. The people remained dirt-poor.

In fact, he even managed to surpass his uncle's moral vacancy. In 1985, Obiang allowed the then apartheid South African regime to build an airstrip on Bioko – disguised as a cattle ranch – which the South African military used to launch attacks against Angola. In a subsequent interview with the *New York Times*, Obiang said that he was opposed to apartheid, but supported the free market. Yuk.

Meanwhile, the oppression continued. The security forces were untouchable. There were regular reports of torture and rape in Black Beach jail. The Malabo Chief of Police, sentenced to two years in jail for murdering a peasant, simply didn't bother to serve his sentence. He continued on as Chief of Police.

But then in 1992, an astonishing thing happened: Obiang ditched the old constitution and announced a new one: to usher in multi-party democracy. As constitutions go, it wasn't any great shakes: the prime minister would still be appointed by Obiang, while a clause was tucked in giving the president immunity from prosecution for life. Yet still it established an 80-seat legislative assembly. It was something. So why on earth did he do it? Two reasons:

1) They had just discovered oil off the coast of Equatorial Guinea. Obiang figured that international oil companies prefer to deal with democratic regimes. (A mistaken assumption; they don't care.)

2) He had no intention of allowing anyone to actually win the elections. Apart from himself.

Parliamentary elections were scheduled for the following year, 1993. But even before the voting started, everyone knew what the result would be: Pedro Motu, a prominent military figure who had joined the opposition, was suddenly arrested. The following day he was found dead, having 'committed suicide'. Opposition groups were not allowed to canvass or hold election rallies. Their leaders were arrested or had to flee the country. Eventually they had no option but to boycott the election

Yet even on polling day – just to be sure – armed soldiers stood outside polling booths asking each citizen who they intended to vote for. Anyone foolish enough to name a party other than the president's was invited to go for a little stroll with one of the soldiers.

Thus in Equatorial Guinea's first multi-party elections, Obiang's Democratic Party of Equatorial Guinea won a landslide victory. The system worked.

And it worked again in 1996 when Obiang himself garnered an enormous vote in the presidential elections.

Indeed, the vote-rigging was so blatant that even the usually shameless Americans closed their embassy there: though they never admitted this was the reason. Officially, it was due to 'budgetary constraints'.

So to make things a little more 'believable', Obiang allowed the opposition groups to win six out of the 80 seats on offer in the 1999 parliamentary elections. The government even trumpeted this fact to the world's press as evidence that EG was now a truly democratic country. The six lucky winners, however, refused to take up their seats: one reason being that Obiang's major opponent at the time, Eloy Elo Mve, had been shipped off to Black Beach Prison for some re-education. (Trussing up prisoners like chickens and smacking the soles of the feet is one of the favourite torture methods) Happily, Eloy managed to escape and *in absentia* was sentenced to 101 years in jail.

But you can't have too much of a good thing: following another huge clampdown on the opposition, Obiang romped home with 97.1 per cent of the vote in the 2002 presidential elections. Twenty opposition parties have now been forced to flee the country, taking up residence in either Spain or Cameroon. (Not a great place for democracy either.) As a result, Obiang demonises his neighbour whenever he can, blaming Cameroonian immigrants for an increase in crime. He has even encouraged his citizens to attack Cameroonians to make them go home. Thankfully, they haven't.

Of course, this is the old story with despots. After a while it's not about having a lot of hard neck; it's about actually believing your own press releases – and being surrounded by people who aren't going to tell you any different. Obiang was becoming more and more like his uncle. He even gave himself a nickname: *El Jefe*. It means: Boss.

In 1998, *El Jefe* gave an interview to an English journalist. The journalist was allowed to bring along a tape recorder, but had to use an official interpreter. Afterwards, the journalist quite shrewdly got everything interpreted again, and discovered that when he had asked Obiang about human rights abuses, the interpreter had asked the President: "What does Your Excellency think about the lies peddled about our country by your enemies?" You don't tell Your Excellency anything he doesn't want to hear.

The oil money probably has a lot to do with it. It's like God has rewarded him for all his oppressing. And it's such a terribly big reward.

The oil started pumping in 1996, and since then production has increased more than ten-fold. EG is now the third-largest oil producer in sub-Saharan Africa. The US imports 15 per cent of its oil from this region; a figure set to double over the next five years. Oil now accounts for 90 per cent of Equatorial Guinea's exports, giving the country a truly stratospheric annual growth rate of 65 per cent. However, few Guineans work for the oil industry or any of its ancillary services: apart from people related to Obiang. All foreign companies are obliged to take out a private security contract with Sonavi, a local company which just happens to be owned by Obiang's brother, Armengol Ondo Nguema, who also just happens to be a General in the Army and head of national security in EG. Naturally, the oil companies are all happy to comply, whilst also bringing in their own private security people, mostly former US military.

Yet in a recent BBC interview, EG's energy minister bragged about how the money was being put to good use. "You can see a lot of projects going on," he said. "Building roads, hospitals, schools, electricity generation."

And he's not lying: the joke in EG is that if you put your tongue out, someone will start construction on it. But where he may have departed slightly from the truth is in giving the impression that all this building will benefit the plain people of Equatorial Guinea. The ugly truth is that their lot has barely improved since Uncle was ousted in 1979.

There's building all right: offices, hotels, banks, a new phone system and swanky new restaurants; state of the art homes for the president and senior members of his government. In Bata, the main city of Rio Muni, they are building a hugely expensive road into neighbouring Gabon. The locals say they have little use for it. But the President travels on it for state visits.

Keep in mind that this is a country so small that the phone book only runs to four pages – and everyone is listed by their first name. To care for such a small population – in a country earning billions of dollars a year from oil revenues – would be relatively inexpensive.

Indeed, it's been estimated that if the economy of Equatorial Guinea had been organised differently, most of its tiny population could be very wealthy by now.

Yet Eric the Eel had to train in a twenty-metre pool. And he was one of the lucky ones. Although agriculture accounts for only five per cent of EG's Gross Domestic Product, it employs 70 per cent of the workforce According to a World Bank estimate in 2000, the average daily income was $2 a day. Although not banned any more, Obiang has done little to encourage the fishing industry; fearing, like his predecessor, that boats would allow people to flee the country. Which they would.

For the unemployed, there is $0 a day. There is effectively no social welfare system in EG. Drug trafficking is rife. Education levels are also poor: over 25 per cent of Guinean women are illiterate, while the government does not enforce a legal minimum age for child employment. Even the kids who get to go to school would rather work. Health care is atrocious: it has been reported that in Rio Muni – by far the poorest part of Equatorial Guinea – there are only five doctors. Only forty-three per cent of the population have access to fresh water. Power cuts are a daily occurrence. One in ten babies dies at birth. The average life expectancy is just fifty-one years of age. Fifty-one miserable years.

Although external aid accounted for twenty-five per cent of EG's income before the oil, Obiang now feels cocky enough to give the finger to the EU and the World Bank, both of which previously helped keep the country afloat. He has refused to cooperate with the International Monetary Fund, providing no external audits of its economy or details of government bank accounts abroad.

Of course, not. It's impossible to know how much money EG has made from oil, or where it has gone. There are estimates of $700 million a year; there are reports that Obiang personally stashes $50 million a month in a Washington bank. He says he has to do this to avoid corruption.

But we do know where some of it went: In 2000, Obiang bought himself a house in Washington D.C. for $2.6 million and another one in Rockville, Maryland for $1.15 million. His son, Teodoro – more of him later – owns several radio and TV stations in EG and recently bought a house in Bel Air, Los Angeles, for $5.8 million, just across the street from Farrah Fawcett. Oh look: it's the despot's son. He also loves Paris, where he has a flash pad, two Bentleys, a Rolls, a Ferrari, and a Lamborghini. And that's just in France.

As a hobby, Teodoro also runs and owns a Los Angeles-based record company called TNO entertainment, which specialises in rap artists. The company is said to be losing money hand over fist. Bet Teodoro doesn't care. It's not his money. (In keeping with *Bling* image, Teodoro has a couple of drug convictions.)

However, it would be wrong to say that Obiang hasn't spent any of his money on improving the country. He is rather keen on modernising the armed forces, which are in something of a tatty state: the army has around 1 300 members, the Navy 120 and the Air Force just 100. Seven of the Army's Generals are related to Obiang (including the aforementioned brother and 'security consultant', Armengo), while the remaining two come from Obiang's tribe. Discipline is poor and training virtually non-existent. There is one reasonably well-disciplined troop of 350 soldiers who make-up the Presidential Guard – but they are from Morocco. Obiang brought them into EG when he staged the coup against his uncle (it was the Moroccans who carried out the executions), and he has hung on to them ever since. That Obiang would depend upon a bunch of mercenaries to provide his personal security demonstrates just how little he trusts his own army. It's like a Freddie Forsyth book.

So in 1998 EG approached Military Professional Resources Incorporated, a private American military company which has trained troops in the Balkans, Latin America and Africa. According to some reports these included such charming regimes as Charles Taylor's Liberia, now deposed, and Nigeria, where the government accused them of spying. Obiang told MPRI that he wished to have a more professional army so he could introduce democracy. Well, of course.

Unfortunately, the US State Department was a bit more cynical about Obiang's motives, and denied MPRI a licence to operate in Equatorial Guinea. MPRI appealed, and was eventually – in 2002 – granted a licence to train only the Guinean Coast Guard: which probably wasn't what Obiang had in mind. According to the MPRI website, MPRI did prepare a report detailing how to revamp all aspects of the

EG's armed forces, and implementation of this report 'is projected to begin shortly'.

And well it might: because after a principled withdrawal of their embassy from a despotic regime in 1995, the Yanks suddenly decided to set up shop there again. A new embassy swung open its doors in October of 2003, to wails of protest from various human rights groups. Unfortunately, none of those wails were heard due to the thunderous sound of oil coming out of the ground. The official reason given was that, with 3 000 US citizens now working in EG, they needed an embassy to look after them. The real reason is that West African oil is easier to refine – and compared to the way things are in the Middle East (see *Saudi Arabia*), even Obiang's regime is relatively stable.

But is it? For all its superpower might, the US does have a habit of getting these things wrong. (See *Iran*). There are many rumblings of discontent. Everyone resents the Fang tribe for being in control. Within the Fangs, they resent the Mongomo Clan (of which Obiang and his uncle were both members), for the same reason. In Rio Muni, they resent Bioko for being better off, and talk about breaking away. Opposition groups in Spain and Cameroon campaign against the regime. In 2002, following another wave of arrests, there were reports of an attempted coup. Obiang can't trust the army, and most annoying of all, even his son is starting to cause trouble.

Teodoro, record producer and neighbour of Farrah Fawcett, has for some years been considered his father's heir apparent. Apart from his more showbiz activities, he is also Minister for Water, Forests and the Environment. Which may explain why the water, forests and environment in Equatorial Guinea are in such a poor state. Yet in the last couple of years Teodoro has been using his TV and radio stations to direct criticism at Daddy's government. (And they are not used to this sort of thing in EG: in July 2003, state-operated radio declared that the president is a god who is "in permanent contact with the Almighty."). In 2001, one of Teodoro's radio stations was actually closed down.

Why he is doing this is something a mystery. Despite his government job, Teodoro doesn't spend that much time in EG, preferring shopping in Paris or hanging with his homies in LA. It could be simple boredom.

Whatever the reason, it does expose a weakness in Daddy's regime which some, – especially all those seven General uncles – might think about exploiting. If Teodoro doesn't take over the family business, then it's going to be one of them. And if it's going to be one of them, they'll be thinking of getting rid of the opposition. Sooner rather than later. No wonder Obiang doesn't trust the army. One slip and Equatorial Guinea will descend into chaos once again, and Eric the Eel will wish he could swim a damn sight farther than 50 metres.

In March of 2004, it nearly happened. Simon Mann, a former Etonian and SAS officer, was arrested in Harare airport in Zimbabwe, along with 64 other alleged mercenaries. They were bound for EG and were apparently just about to pick up a shipment of guns. Mann has quite a long history as a mercenary in Africa, though more recently he has diversified into acting: he appeared as a British Army colonel in the 2002 film *Bloody Sunday*. The claim is that Mann had been planning the coup attempt since before Christmas 2003, when he recruited some former South African soldiers. It is believed South African intelligence got wind of this and tipped off the Zimbabwean and EG governments.

So when Mann's Boeing 727 with the blacked-out

windows touched down at Harare, the Zimbabwean security forces were waiting for him. At the same time, Equatorial Guinea arrested 15 members of what it said was an advance party led by another South African, Nick du Toit. In no time Nick was being wheeled out in front of television cameras to confess: he claimed the plan was to spirit Obiang out of the country and install Severo Moto, an opposition leader living in Spain. The EG authorities claimed the operation was funded by Ely Calil, a London-based Lebanese businessman with substantial oil interests. Naturally, Moto and Calil have denied any involvement, as do all the mercenaries: they claimed they are legitimate private security guards, on their way to Equatorial Guinea to guard a mine. True or not, the EG government has used the alleged coup attempt as an excuse to deport hundreds of foreigners, mostly Ghanaians and Cameroonians

That an oil company might wish to topple Obiang does make sense: to bring in a more stable regime would protect the oil supply and probably reduce the number of kickbacks that have to be aimed towards Obiang and his cronies. However, Nick du Toit does have a share in an EG-based security company named Triple Options 610. Another major shareholder is Armengol Ondo Nguema: the 'security consultant', General and Obiang's brother. Oh-uh. He might have some explaining to do.

At the moment, Mann, du Toit and the other mercenaries are rotting in prison cells awaiting trial. They could receive the death penalty. As Freddie Forsyth would tell you, the mercenary business is a tough game. It's not a bit like *The Dogs of War*.

SUPREME RULER AYATOLLAH ALI KHAMENE'I

of the Islamic Republic of Iran

Curiously, the story of Iran could turn out to be a happy one. Not that it's going to be easy: Iran, after all, is a part of George W. Bush's 'Axis of Evil', accused of secretly developing all sorts of dread weapons and of hosting coffee mornings for Osama's mob, Al-Qaeda.

Worse still, the country is ruled by a bunch of autocratic Imams who are – to put it very mildly – somewhat inflexible.

Despots are usually a bit crazy. Usually, the greed and power and self-glorification has perverted them to such a degree that they cannot see how monstrous they have become, how hypocritical they are.

However, the Imams who rule Iran, and particularly Ayatollah Ali Khamene'I, aren't like that. If there's one thing you could never accuse them of, it's hypocrisy. These boys are living the Islamic dream. The harsh rules they inflict on everyone else they are more than happy to live by themselves. In practice, this makes the Ayatollah the worst sort of despot: the one with God on his side.

But we're getting ahead of ourselves: first let's see what's been happening in Iran since the fifth century. Not that it's Iran at all: it's really Persia, and has been for a long, long time. (The name change occurred only in 1935.) And Iranians are not Arab. Although Iran is usually lumped in with the *Arab World* (or the even more confusing *Arab Street*), they have their own distinct culture and language. And when we say the fifth century, we mean the fifth century *BC*: that was when the modestly-titled Cyrus the Great established the Persian Empire.

About a thousand years later, Islam arrived, and after that, there was all the usual stuff. War with Genghis Khan. With Afghanistan. With Georgia. With Armenia. With Russia. With Britain. There was a lot of war. Even before anyone knew about oil, Iran had value to the colonial powers, being strategically located on the Persian Gulf. In 1907 Iran established its own parliament, but Britain and Russia continued to meddle. They occupied the country in 1941 and 'persuaded' the (pro-German) Shah (Persian for Emperor) to abdicate in favour of his (pro-Allies) son; after the Iranian Prime Minister had the gall to nationalise the Anglo-Iranian oil company in 1953, the Brits helped the Shah stage a coup to get rid of the PM.

In retrospect, that may have been a mistake. Once he had power back, the Shah decided not to share it, with anyone. Iran's constitutional monarchy effectively became a dictatorship with the government appointed by the Shah; elections were rigged to favour candidates the Shah liked. In 1957, with some help from the CIA and Mossad (the Israeli Secret Service), the Shah established his own Secret Police, the Savak, who quickly became notorious for the range and imagination of their torture techniques. The government, such as it was, was riddled with corruption.

The Shah was not a very nice man.

Everyone – the Iranian people, the Americans, the British – they all agreed on this. Except the Americans and the British didn't really care. Britain had an exclusive oil contract while the US regarded Iran as a valuable ally; again, due its strategic location: in the Middle East and bordering the then-USSR. Perfect for spying on the commies.

As long as the West was getting what it wanted out of Iran, the Shah could torture whoever he liked.

Understandably, having their country regarded as little more than a glorified listening post/petrol station somewhat irked the Iranian people. They showed their irritation in small ways: chanting slogans like *Marg Bar America* (Death to America) for hours on end and by listening to cassettes. During the late 1970s, recordings of sermons delivered by Ayatollah Khomeini were smuggled into Iran and duplicated on a massive scale.

Khomeini was also very big on the whole *Marg Bar America* thing, for which he had been forced to live in exile in Paris for fourteen years. A cleric of the highest rank, (Source of Emulation is the technical title), Khomeini came from a wealthy family who claimed to be direct descendants of the Prophet himself. It is said that he had memorised the Koran by the age of seven. This guy really liked his job.

And his tapes – largely on religious subjects and Islamic theories of governance – seemed to do the trick. By 1978, Iran was on the brink of disintegrating into civil war.

So the Shah took decisive action. He ran away.

Within a matter of months, Iran completely transformed itself. Ayatollah Khomeini returned, promising that no Iranian would ever have to pay for oil, gas, electricity or water. (It never happened.) A referendum voted in favour of establishing an Islamic Republic – with the Ayatollah K as its Supreme Leader.

A revolutionary court, presided over by Ayatollah Khalkhali, sentenced thousands of the Shah's supporters to death. The story goes that after the Shah's prime minister, Hoveida, received his one-way ticket to meet Allah, Khalkhali was pestered with phone calls from across the globe to not execute the poor PM. When the umpteenth call had come though, Khalkhali asked the caller to hold on for a moment, walked out the room, shot the Prime Minister in the head, then returned to the phone and announced: "I'm sorry, but the sentence has already been carried out."

And when they heard the Shah was now living in the US, a mob of students stormed the American embassy in Teheran and took everyone hostage. They were released a year later in exchange for military equipment.

The Yanks were not pleased. Apart from the hostage embarrassment, the US had lost a perfect puppet regime in a very sensitive part of the world. And in its place were a load of blokes in funny hats chanting *Marg Bar America*, whatever that means. No. Not at all pleased. Apparently, their intelligence analysts didn't see the revolution coming. Twenty years later, the same guys told us there were Weapons of Mass Destruction in Iraq.

So: Islamic Iran. This is how it works. There is an elected president, plus an elected parliament. However, everything they do must be approved by the twelve-member Guardian Council, who are not elected and who are all Imams. In turn, they defer to the most senior cleric, the Supreme Ruler. The Supreme Ruler appoints the head of the judiciary, the head of radio and television, the commanders of the armed forces, the members of the Guardian Council and confirms the election of the President.

Being a strict Muslim country, pubs and lap-dancing

spots are a bit thin on the ground. (Going on picnics is a popular pastime.) Women have to keep themselves covered up, but unlike a lot of Middle Eastern countries, they are allowed to drive and work. Until recently, it was commonplace for women to be arrested for wearing make-up. If seen in public with an unrelated male, they could be dragged off for a virginity test.

The legal system is based on Sharia Law, with public flogging one of the most popular punishments, though what the Iranian Courts really like is a good execution. After China, Iran executes more people than any other country in the world. It's usually by hanging, and often in public. The other favoured method for doling out justice was to bury the convicted felons up to their waist and then stone them to death, though this practice was halted in 2002. Probably ran out of stones.

As with many other Muslim countries, Iran operates a 'blood-money' system where a murderer can avoid execution by paying a fixed fee to the victim's family, usually 150,000,000 Rials (€14,100). However, this was the fee if the victim was a man. For a female victim, the murderer only had to pay 75,000,000 Rials: legally, the life of a woman was only worth half that of a man. The murder price structure was also changed in 2002.

The Shah's secret police, the Savak, are gone, but in their place are the Basijis: young, ruthless, well-paid men who keep a constant watch on the population.

No, Iran doesn't sound like a jolly place, though by all accounts Iranians are a jolly people: friendly and open, and back in 1978, genuinely pleased with the new regime. But alas for them, the smiles didn't last for too long. In 1980, following a dispute over territory, Iraq launched an attack against Iran and captured large sections of the country.

Now as we all know, when Iraq invaded Kuwait in 1990

for similar reasons, the United States jumped up and down with outrage and wasted no time in assembling a military coalition. But back in 1980, not a peep out of them. You see, things were different then. Obviously, the US and the West didn't much like Iran, and they actually quite liked Iraq, to whom they sold weapons with which to bomb the crap out of the Iranians.

And then – in secret – the US supplied arms to Iran as well. In an attempt to release hostages held in Beirut – supposedly by groups backed by Iran – the Yanks thought shipping a few guns to Teheran might get their people home. It didn't work, but eventually caused a huge stink in Washington, successfully distracting the world's attention from the fact that millions of Iraqis and Iranians were dying in a vicious, pointless war.

The war ended in 1988, but it wasn't long before Iran was back in the headlines again. In 1989, Ayatollah Khomeini issued a *fatwa*, or religious decree, denouncing *The Satanic Verses*, the latest work from the novelist Salman Rushdie. Rushdie had to go into hiding for some years. To much of the Western world, Khomeini looked seriously bonkers.

But then he died following surgery. Khomeini, that is. But hang on: isn't Ayatollah Khomeini our despot here? No actually. Look at the title again. Check the spelling. Perhaps they did it to confuse us infidels, or perhaps they did it because they were too lazy to have to remember a new name, but the new Ayatollah, (elected by the Assembly of Experts, a council of 96 Islamic clerics), was called Khamene'I.

Similar name, similar guy. The Ayatollah Version 2 was born in 1939 to a dirt-poor family. (Locals in his home town of Mashhad still refer to him as *Ali Geddaa* – Ali The Beggar.) He studied under Khomeini, and from there became involved in radical Islamic politics: in 1977 he was one of the founder members of Combatant Clerics

Association. (No, really.) For his troubles, he was detained by the Shah's secret police for a year and upon his release, banned from holding public meetings.

After the revolution though, there was no stopping him: he held various government positions, ending up in the (highly influential) position of Leader of the Friday prayers in Tehran. No stopping him – yet there were those who tried. In 1981, while preaching in a mosque, a booby-trapped tape-recorder exploded and left him without the use of his right hand. It is generally thought that the attack was carried out by Mojahedin-e Khalq, a tiny Marxist opposition movement.

Didn't stop our boy though: he declared his survival 'a gift from Allah' and went on to serve two terms as President. His ascension to Supreme Leader, though, wasn't entirely popular. Although as hard-line as they come, he lacks charisma and Khomeini's religious credentials: the Iranian constitution had to be amended to allow Khamene'I, a cleric of lesser rank, to take over the Big Job. Some even publicly questioned his suitability for the position. Shortly before they were arrested.

Alas for him, it was also proving to be a more difficult job. Following the imposition of trade sanctions by the US in 1995, (for 'sponsoring terrorism'), the Iranian people have started to get a wee bit fed up with their Islamic paradise. What with the international isolation, the wars and the poverty, the discontent has grown so much that some even harbour nostalgia for the Shah. (He died in 1980, but his son, Crown Prince Reza Pahlavi, is available for work.)

Not that this has affected the Ayatollah one jot. As far as he's concerned, the Western world is a sewer he wants nothing to do with. Not that he knows that much about it: in one recent rant on Radio Tehran, he blamed the Beatles for undermining Western civilisation. "Nihilism and Beatleism and all kinds of misfortunes have affected the Western world since thirty or forty years ago," he fumed.

But apart from his obvious shortcomings as a music critic, the Ayatollah doesn't seem much of a diplomat either. He has slammed as 'suicide' any attempts to repair relations with the US. "There are individuals who want to prove, with their rotten pens, that the US is not our enemy and interestingly, they do all this in the name of reform," he said, adding that "any newspaper or writer wanting to renounce the fundamental principles of Islam . . . is an apostate and liable to the death penalty." Ouch.

So where are these reform noises coming from? Curiously, from the government itself. Iran is probably the only country in the world where the democratically elected parliament and president now form the opposition.

This needs explaining. In 1997, Mohammad Khatami was elected president with a huge majority.

Although also involved in the anti-Shah movement when a young man, Mohammed has always been a bit better disposed towards the outside world, possibly because he spent some years as head of the Hamburg Islamic Centre in Germany. His platform of reform and modernisation has become enormously popular, especially with younger voters. In 2000, Khatami-supporting reformists took 170 of the 290 seats in the Majlis, the Iranian parliament.

All of which adds up to exactly nothing. The politicians and the people might want change, but they have virtually no power to make it come about. As far as the Ayatollah and the Imams are concerned, they know best: they are, after all, on the Hot Line from Allah. The actual democratic wishes of the people are irrelevant.

They *really* believe this.

Many reforms proposed and approved by the President

and Mejlis have been simply thrown out by the Guardian Council on the basis that they were 'incompatible with Islam'.

However, it would be unfair to say that Khatami has made no difference. Although the state may control TV and radio, a vibrant opposition print media has sprung up, (the individuals with the rotten pens referred to earlier). Of course many of them have been just as quickly closed down and many journalists have been jailed. But Khatami has been able to provide them with a measure of protection – especially to his brother Reza, managing director of one of Iran's most successful reformist dailies.

The public have played their part too. The closure of a pro-reformist newspaper in 1999 set off six days of rioting which left three people dead. (Naturally, the US was blamed for inciting the riot.) Even the Imams have had to tread a bit carefully. A bill aimed at strengthening press freedom led to violent scuffles within the parliament itself, but was never passed.

There is, in effect, a power struggle going on between President Khatami and Ayatollah Khamene'I. But this being Iran, neither can admit to it. The Ayatollah has to maintain his image of being spiritual and otherworldly and not involved in the grubby business of day-to-day politics, while Khatami can't utter a word of criticism of the Ayatollah.

Yet inch-by-inch, the situation is taking on all the trappings of a good old-fashioned political slanging match. In 2001, when Khatami was re-elected by a landslide, (despite attempts by the state-run media to down-play the whole event), the Ayatollah tried to postpone his swearing in – prompting a small constitutional crisis. More than 100 members of the Mejlis wrote an open letter to Khamene'I warning that Iran faced a choice between democracy and dictatorship. Khamene'I backed down.

Since then, relations have hardly improved. It is widely believed that certain Imams now 'shadow' members of Khatami's government in the same way that opposition parties in democracies 'shadow' government ministers. Except that here it's the other way around, sort of. Even after the 2003 earthquake in the Iranian city of Bam, Khamene'I made sure to make an 'unannounced' visit several hours before the President turned up.

And no matter when he speaks, the Ayatollah never misses the chance to mouth off about his three great hates: the US, Israel and the Iranian reformist press, or 'mercenaries of the enemy' as he calls them. But everyone knows who he's *really* talking about.

More sinister though was a partially successful attempt by the Ayatollah in 2004 to stage a bloodless coup. In advance of parliamentary elections, all candidates must be approved by the Guardian Council. So in mid January, 2004, a little over a month before the elections were to take place, the Council announced that around 3 600 of those candidates – nearly half of the total – would not be allowed to run on the basis that they were 'incompatible with Islam'. By an astonishing coincidence, virtually all of them were reformists. The list even included 83 members of parliament hoping to run for a second term – and Khatami's aforementioned brother, Reza.

The Ayatollah's stroke caused such ructions that the MPs staged a sit-in at the parliament, all 27 provincial governors threatened to resign and even the normally woossy European Union complained. A group of Iranian MPs wrote another open letter to the Ayatollah, this time posting it on the internet. It was removed within twenty-four hours.

The Ayatollah himself had to go on radio and appeal for calm. Naturally, the whole thing was the decision of the

Guardian Council and had nothing to do with him. But as the sit-in dragged on and the threat of riots grew, Khamene'I eventually 'intervened', ordering that the 83 members of parliament be allowed to run and that others be 're-evaluated'.

Then it was announced that 100 candidates – out of 3 600 disqualified – would be allowed run. Then another 200, though in both cases, no names were revealed. More were promised, but not until February 10 – just ten days before the election: leaving them virtually no time to campaign. Repeated attempts to have the election postponed were rejected by the Guardian Council.

After a 26-day protest in the Iranian parliament, just one third of 3 600 disqualified were allowed back in the race. Still too few, and too late: the reformists couldn't possibly win, and almost immediately a row started over what to do next: boycott the poll altogether and hope for an embarrassingly low turnout or continue to run on the principle that a reformist presence should be maintained in parliament.

So naturally, they did both: 550 candidates withdrew from the election, including many sitting MPs. They criticised Khatami and his supporters for giving this 'parliamentary coup d'état' legitimacy by continuing to participate.

So the hardliners romped home. The reformists ended up with around 65 seats in the 290-member house – compared to the 170 they won in 2000. In southern Iran, an argument over alleged vote-rigging developed into a riot. Eight people were killed.

The turnout was the lowest for a national election since the 1979 revolution – 50.6 per cent – yet not quite low enough to embarrass Khamene'I and his chums

It was a thoroughly cunning piece of political engineering, aimed at robbing Khatami of the only real power he had: the support of the population. Despite being elected twice in the hope of reforming the oppressive system, the Imams knew damn well that a lot of the electorate were fast becoming disillusioned with his inability to bring about any change; especially the younger voters: two thirds of the population are under thirty. Khatami's now emasculated presidential term will come to an end in 2005, and already the Guardian Council are plotting who his successor will be. Most of the smart money is on Hassan Rohani, naturally a hard-liner, but apparently something of a pragmatist.

Yet in the villages and towns of Iran, increasing numbers of people don't care about any of this. Instead of trying to change the system, many young Iranians now simply ignore it, operating within their own sub-cultures. They secretly listen to western music and have 'unapproved' relationships. They buy under-the-counter alcohol and go to 'X' parties: illegal raves. Friday mosque attendance among young people has plummeted. And as long as they keep it discreet, the Imams seem happy not to notice.

Young people don't bother to vote either, believing it won't make any difference. In local elections in 2003, only fifteen per cent of the electorate in the cities bothered – compared to eighty-three per cent in the presidential elections only two years before. That's a fairly spectacular loss of faith.

Within Khamenei's hard-line followers, there seem to be two schools of thought: (1) the ideological hard-liners, who promote US-hating and Zionist-condemning as a lifestyle choice; (2) the pragmatic hard-liners, who argue that it might be better long-term to liberalise the economy and restore relations with the US, while still maintaining total control domestically – exactly what China is currently attempting to do.

Recently, as a sop to the pragmatists and reformists, a law was passed which legalised holding hands in public, but such a wildly liberal move seems unlikely to win young people back to the Islamic state. Another form of escape – drug use – is now a growing problem in Iran. One estimate has it that there are over one million addicts. And they can't blame the Beatles for that.

Anyway, pushing Khatami out of the political picture hardly solves the Ayatollah's problem: the fact is that the majority of Iranians still don't like the system, especially those not old enough to remember how bad the Shah was. February 2004 saw the twenty-fifth anniversary of the revolution, but the celebrations were dull and unenthusiastic. No one cares any more. It is speculated that even many low and middle-ranking clerics are unhappy. Sooner or later, that overwhelming lack of support may come back to bite the Ayatollah in a part of his anatomy he would consider it a sin to mention.

Meanwhile, Iran continues to be squeezed from the outside. With George's W Bush's policy of pre-emptive action a constant threat, Khamene'I must be all too aware of the fact that he now has US troops on two of his borders – in Iraq and Afghanistan. If the US did decide to attack, we'd only hear about it the following day. And despite the embarrassing lack of weapons of mass destruction in Iraq, George W continues to bleat on about Iran having the bomb.

In October of 2003, Britain, France and Germany brokered a deal whereby Iran agreed to halt its uranium enrichment programme (which both Khatami and Khamene'I claim is for entirely peaceful means), and to allow spot-checks from UN inspectors. Yet suspicions that the Iranians may have been – and still are – lying through their pearly whites have been re-activated by revelations that they were given nuclear secrets by Abdul Qadeer Khan, Pakistan's top nuclear weapons scientists. (Well, not any more he's not.)

Some US officials believe that Iran is operating a second, totally secret, uranium enrichment programme with the sole aim of producing a nuke.

Even if true, it's unlikely Iran would ever own up. After agreeing to allow in UN inspectors, the Ayatollah still raved against the American Devils: "anyone who ever tries to challenge Iran's peaceful nuclear programme will be slapped in the face".

A slap would be the best we could hope for. Given Persia's blood-splattered past, it seems almost inevitable that someone – the US, the Ayatollah, the reformists – will pick up a gun. And begin the story all over again. And this time it might be a happy one. But don't hold your breath.

PRESIDENT NURSULTAN ABISH-ULY
NAZARBAYEV
of the Republic of Kazakhstan

It's a terrible thing to say, but Kazakhstan isn't really a place where anyone would want to live. Well, anyone with an option; which most Kazakhs don't have. Apart from the lack of democracy, the corruption and the oppression, it's also one of the most polluted countries in the world, thanks to years of Soviet nuclear testing. Thanks to nature, large sections of it are uninhabitable. Thanks to years of Soviet rule, it is still a grey, dull country. Thanks.

Not a great location either. It's at the bottom of the old Soviet Union, on the Caspian Sea. It borders jolly places like Turkmenistan and Uzbekistan (dealt with elsewhere in this book), and is directly across from Iran. It's in the cockpit of the War on Terror. Great.

And it's a huge country: the size of western Europe. It has mountains, where not many people live, energy-rich, heavily mined lowlands, where not many people want to live, a Siberian climate in the north and arid, empty steppes in the centre. But for such a big place, the population is tiny: just 16 million, and going down. *Quelle surprise.*

Yet it must have something: Kazakh nomads have lived here for centuries. Being nomads, they didn't go in much for systems of government or defence forces, so it was pretty easy for foreign armies to swoop in. The Arabs came in the eighth century and introduced Islam, while in 1854 the Russians invaded and established the garrison town of Almaty, which eventually became the capital of Kazakhstan. (Until the president changed his mind. But we'll get to that.)

After the Russian revolution, Kazakhstan proclaimed independence, but the whole not-having-an-army thing proved a fatal flaw in their aspiration: 150,000 of them were killed while another 300,000 fled the country. Kazakhstan joined the Soviet Union in 1924 as an 'independent' Republic.

It seemed as if these Kazakhs didn't really know what was good for them. But luckily, Josef Stalin did. He collectivised agriculture, in the process causing one million of them to starve to death.

The Ruskies had another go at the whole farming concept in 1954 with the so-called 'Virgin Lands' scheme, whereby large tracts of useless land were reclaimed. Not trusting the Kazakhs to do it properly themselves, the USSR exported a massive number of Russian settlers: effectively making the Kazakhs a minority in their own country. The Russians then proceeded to run pretty much everything else: a sort of central Asian Northern Ireland.

But change came, as it inevitably does. The Soviet Union fell apart in 1991, and suddenly Kazakhstan had to make its own way in the world. Not that it wanted to: the then head of the Kazakh Communist Party, Nursultan Nazarbayev (he had been appointed in 1989, the first Kazakh to hold the position), had been a die-hard Gorbachev supporter and opponent of going it alone. Kazakhstan was the last Soviet republic to declare independence.

But when a super-power disintegrates, what are you going to do? Nazarbayev shrugged his shoulders and got on with it, deciding that if he had been head of the old oppressive regime, then it only made sense he should be head of the new one. And just so he wouldn't be lonely, he brought in all his old Communist Party cronies with him.

Yet still it seemed all new and shiny. With inflation running at 2 000 per cent, Nazarbayev made all the right noises about being liberal and free-market etc: the things western governments love to hear – especially from a country that has oil – lots and lots of untapped oil. Because of corruption, bureaucracy and sheer laziness, Kazakhstan's vast underground lakes of black stuff had been barely explored during the Soviet era. Even today, with oil companies drooling all over the place, they still don't know exactly how much is down there: it could have the largest reserves of oil *in the world*. Oh yes: and there's loads of natural gas too.

(Plus, if you like mining, Kazakhstan is the place to be: it produces 40 per cent of the world's chrome ore. There are also deposits of iron ore, nickel, cobalt, vanadium, titanium, copper, lead, wolfram, zinc, gold, silver, tin, tungsten, molybdenum, uranium, cadmium, bismuth, pyrophyllite, barite, phosphorites, magnesium, phosphorous, asbestos, manganese and bauxite. No wonder it's polluted.)

Nazarbayev made all the right political noises too. There were even free parliamentary elections in 1994 which returned a predominantly pro-Nazarbayev assembly.

But it wasn't all holding hands and singing songs in those early days: there was discontent, much of it ethnic-based. Even though a lot of the Russians cleared out after independence – leaving Kazakhs back in the majority again

– the country is still a hodgepodge of Ukrainians, Germans, Chechens, Kurds, Koreans and Central Asian ethnic groups. The remaining Russians particularly resented the lack of dual citizenship and having to pass a rather tricky Kazakh language test in order to work for government or state bodies. (Kazakh is spoken only by about 40 per cent of the population, and was only recognised as an official language in 1989. Most everyday business communication takes place in Russian.) And understandably, the Kazakhs weren't too crazy about the Russians either.

It wasn't a major problem – more grumblings rather than naked ethnic strife – though there had been a few riots in the communist days. The danger was there that it could escalate. And given that Kazakhstan still depended economically on trade with Russia, the President couldn't afford to be too mean to the remaining Russians.

Nazarbayev thought about it for a little while and finally decided that there was only one responsible thing to do: make himself dictator. In 1995, he selflessly dissolved the Kazakh parliament, the Kenges, and drafted a new constitution. The constitution gave the president the power to rule by decree and appoint government and regional heads. He made himself a life-long member of the State Security Council – thus giving him permanent influence over future foreign and domestic policy. Oh, and immunity from prosecution for life. Just in case.

Naturally, everyone was thrilled with this decisive action. No, really. Well, maybe not thrilled, but there was a general acceptance that something had to be done. In the short life of the Kenges, an inordinate amount of time had been taken up with a debate on wages and benefits for the elected members.

Of course, there were a few nay-sayers (aren't there always?), who claimed that Nazarbayev had effectively staged a bloodless coup and turned himself into a despot. But he proved them wrong: in 1999 he held a presidential election and romped home with over 85% of the ballot. Of course, he was the only candidate, but that wasn't his fault: through a truly freaky series of accidents, all the opposition leaders were either dead, in jail or had fled the country.

A parliamentary election was held at the same time, but subject to a few minor changes to the electoral laws: religious parties were banned (you wouldn't want to encourage any sort of Islamic vote), while all candidates had to undergo a compulsory Kazakh language test – effectively barring sixty per cent of the population. And if you still wanted to run for office, you also needed to cough up a non-refundable deposit of $130,000.

But at least he now had a mandate, and could get on with running his country.

So what kind of a job has he done? What word would best sum up Kazakhstan?

Horrible.

It has a dilapidated infrastructure, high unemployment, inflation, poverty, prostitution, drug addiction and Aids. The Red Cross estimates that more than 70 per cent of the population lives at minimal subsistence levels. During the 1990s, the country's Gross Domestic Product – a key indicator of wealth creation – dropped from $39 million to just $15.9 million.

Then there's pollution: because Kazakhstan is big and flat with not a very large population – and because there was nothing the natives could do about it anyway – the Soviet Union used it as a dump, space-port and rocket testing ground. In Semipalatinsk there is huge contamination caused by repeated nuclear detonations; there is a massive problem with abandoned toxic waste; in Baykonur, the land is polluted from Russian space vehicles dumping their fuel.

Things are so bad that the national atomic company, Kazatomprom, proposed that Kazakhstan import *more* toxic waste as a way of making money to pay for the clean-up. A bill to reverse the country's ban on importing toxic waste even went before the Kenges. But eventually, it was dropped.

And thanks to overuse of the two rivers feeding into it, the Aral Sea is drying up: fishing ports once located on the sea are now 60 miles from its coast.

Drilling for oil certainly isn't going to help. Already there are reports of the waters around Kazakhstan being covered with an oily film.

There's a lot of stuff to give out about in Kazakhstan. Except you're not allowed to. They don't seem to like journalists there. Here's an example:

In 2002, Journalist Sergei Duvanov was jailed, accused of having raped a 14 year old girl. Curiously, a press release announcing the arrest – which originated from the President's Office – was put in circulation *before* Duvanov was taken into custody. In reality, Mr Duvanov was just about to travel to the US to talk about repression in Kazakhstan. Despite widespread international objections, he's still in jail.

Then again, it's not like he didn't see it coming: a few months before this, Duvanov had been due to travel to Warsaw for similar reasons. But he was attacked by three men outside his apartment. They beat him unconscious and carved a cross into his chest.

Other journalists have been hit by cars or had their children killed in mysterious circumstances. Television stations, magazines and newspapers have been shut down for minor media licence infractions: one favourite wheeze was a regulation that fifty per cent of programmes must be in the Kazakh language, despite the fact that it is spoken by only forty per cent of the population. Workers for human rights organisations have also died mysteriously. Opposition newspapers are unable to publish because of government control over printing presses.

In 2000, Nazarbayev gave the National Kazakh Security Committee (the former KGB) the right to monitor e-mail traffic, access to the internet, faxes and phone calls by any 'organisation, company or person it deemed suspicious': in other words, everyone.

Conditions in jail are thought to be horrible, with torture commonplace. There are repeated reports of beatings, choking, rape, partial suffocation and sleep deprivation.

However, one area in which Kazakhstan is up there among the best is the (literally) cut-throat world of human trafficking – which is not specifically illegal under Kazakh law. This relates particularly to women, who are used for prostitution. In the last decade it has been estimated than anything between 5 000 and 70 000 women have been sold and exported. They are usually recruited with the promise of a good job overseas: to places like Saudi Arabia, Israel, and Greece.

To cap it all, Kazakhstan also appears to be one of the most boring countries on the planet. In 2001, to celebrate ten years of independence, what did President Nazarbayev lay on? A chess tournament featuring Gary Kasparov.

Indeed, probably the most exciting thing to happen in Kazakh history took place in 1997 when Nazarbayev decided to move the capital of Kazakhstan from Almaty – one of the most scenic cities in central Asia, within view of snow-capped peaks and with access to great skiing – to the town of Astana, an ugly, mosquito-ridden dump on the steppes where electricity and airline flights are erratic. They had to quickly re-tarmac the runway so Nazarbayev could land his Lear jet there. It was originally called Akmola, meaning White Grave, but was re-named Astana because that means, er, Capital.

Reasons given for the move were that Almaty was in an earthquake zone and it was a bit too close (200 km) to the Chinese border. However, the real reason was probably that Nazarbayev wanted to locate the capital in an area which once had a Russian majority: a symbolic poke in the eye to the Ruskies which most Kazakhs failed to pick up on. Many foreign embassies have refused to move there, and most of the political action still takes place in Almaty.

But things might get better, at least economically: the opening of an oil pipeline in March 2001 could potentially transform the economy. Nazarbayev has bragged that Kazakhstan will turn into another Saudi Arabia. Of course, they don't have elections there either.

In the meantime, the American money rolls in: thanks to their proximity to Afghanistan and Iran, annual US aid to the five Central Asian states of Kazakhstan, Uzbekistan, Kyrgyzstan, Tajikistan and Turkmenistan is nearly US$600 million, twice its pre-September 11 level. Arms and training have also been supplied, while there is also a deal for the US Air Force to use Almaty Airport. Many speculate that it is only a matter of time before the US sets up a permanent presence: a move which certainly wouldn't thrill the neighbouring Chinese, (Kazakhs have ethnic links with China), but probably wouldn't bother the Kazakhs too much: although Kazakhstan is an Islamic country, there is little radicalism there: Nazarbayev has made sure of that. It would threaten him as much as George Bush.

As for the man himself, he's as dull as his country, though he's no dope when it comes to making a few bob.

He was born in 1940 and is a metallurgical engineer by trade. He has written dozens of pamphlets, with exciting titles like *The Steel Profile of Kazakhstan* (1984). He is married to an economist and has three grown-up daughters. Apparently, he enjoys reading books on history, philosophy, and economics. He also enjoys tennis, volleyball, and hunting.

How he finds the time to do all this remains a mystery. Not only does Nazarbayev have a country to run and enemies to jail and murder but he is also reputed to be the eighth richest man in the world. Bet you didn't know that.

A lot of his citizens don't know it either because *by law* it is an act of treason to even talk about Nazarbayev's business affairs (or that of his family) or to take photos of any of his palaces.

So where did all his money come from? Well one clue might be that since 1996, U.S. authorities have been investigating allegations that around $78 million from various oil companies has been funnelled into Swiss bank accounts controlled by President Nazarbayev and some of his friends: as part of the deal to pump oil out of Kazakhstan. In 2003, Swiss investigators also got involved.

President Nazarbayev has admitted that these Swiss accounts exist – but claims that they are 'rainy day' stashes for the country. In the US, the case has already been dubbed Kazakhgate and is involving some big names: such as Condoleezza Rice, who was a consultant to Chevron's oil dealings in Kazakhstan.

Naturally, he denies all charges of corruption, claiming they have been cooked up by exiled political rivals; the few who are still alive. Transparency International, the corruption-busting organisation, doesn't entirely agree. It rates Kazakhstan as the 15th most corrupt country in the world.

As we've said, journalists who have attempted to report on any of this have been jailed, exiled, beaten, fire-bombed or simply found dead. TV and radio stations have been closed down. However, there are independent TV stations which have thrived in Kazakhstan: five of them, in fact, along with four independent radio stations and two newspapers – all of them previously state-run. And by a freak coincidence, they all happen to belong to President Nazarbayev's daughter, Dariga.

Nazarbayev has three daughters. And what a bunch of overachievers they are. Dariga, the eldest is the media mogul. She's married to Rakhat Aliyev, who is chairman of the scary-sounding Committee on Tax Police: they investigate corruption allegations and can freeze the bank account of anyone they don't like the look of. And they frequently do.

Meanwhile, the middle daughter, Dinara, is married to Timur Kulibayev. He's vice-president of the national oil and gas company, Kazakh Oil, and as such has control of the billions of dollars of oil revenue which pour into Kazakhstan every year. Lucky devil.

The youngest daughter, Aliya, seemed to have done even better when she hooked up with Aidar Akayey, son of the President Akayey of Kyrgyzstan. But they separated a few years ago so we'll say no more about it.

But let's not forget Mammy: Sara Nazarbayeva runs a number of charitable organisations. She has the power to hand out tax-exempt certificates to other charity outfits.

My word, but owning your own country sounds like tiring work. And it's a long way from being over yet. Nazarbayev is only in his sixties, has no health problems anyone knows about, and says he is ready to contest the presidential elections in 2006.

Nonetheless, there has been mucho speculation as to who might take over from the big man. And mucho of that mucho speculation has rested upon his eldest daughter, Dariga.

Of course, even Nazarbayev can't just hand her the job: especially now when he's trying to re-package himself into the President of Reform. Things have started to change in Kazakhstan; ever so slightly. Although he merrily harasses and kills journalists whenever he can, even Nazarbayev hasn't been able to keep them all quiet: and some of the print media is now owned by *nouveau-riche* capitalists who aren't quite as scared as the President would like them to be. And anyway, Nazarbayev's strategy from way back was that the people wouldn't mind him having absolute power as long he improved their standard of living. Which didn't happen.

As a result, even some members of his own government have got a bit uppity: in 2001, several members of his cabinet resigned, publicly declaring that not enough was being done to tackle corruption. The following year, the Prime Minister Kasymzhomart Tokayev also asked for his pension. He was replaced by Imangali Tasmagambetov, a much more reliable old commie, yet still the jig was up: to defuse the mounting opposition, Nazarbayev had to give himself a democratic makeover.

The following year, and without a hint of irony, the President engineered a national conference for Kazkh journalists, the first of its type in the country's history. And you can imagine the hacks' joy when the Big Man himself turned up to address them. He said this:

"Under conditions of the initial accumulation of capital and of a wild market, journalism has appeared under pressure from sacks of money that are trying to buy and corrupt it. Today people know about the media not only by the names of their editors or observers, but by their owners who are businessmen and oligarchs, or by the companies that established them. The media are being used as an information weapon for settling scores between state officials, politicians and financial and industrial groups."

Politicians manipulating the media? Pressurising it for their own ends? My Lord.

Still maintaining a completely straight face, Nazarbayev went on to propose the creation of a media council to deal with any disputes between politicians and journalists – the idea being to create a buffer between the media and undue political pressure. Naturally, it would enjoy the protection of the Office of the President.

For the journalists present – many of whom had been beaten, threatened and jailed by this man – it must have been a supremely surreal moment. Yet the Kazakh hacks went on to vote in favour of his proposal. He's obviously crazy. Don't anger him.

It was clearly a political stroke, yet it worked. For the next few days the media – both inside and outside Kazakhstan – reported that Nazarbayev was now taking a more conciliatory stance towards reform. On top of that, the Congress of Journalists elected themselves a Chair: the President's daughter, Dariga.

Phase two of the makeover was a new electoral code, to come into force before parliamentary elections in the autumn of 2004. The provisions – heartily backed by the President – included a supervisory role for all political parties, transparent ballot boxes and measures designed to improve the accuracy of voter lists. Even the Office for Security and Co-operation in Europe (OSCE), which hadn't been behind the door in branding previous Kazakh elections as unfair, gave the measures a guarded welcome. The Kenges passed the bill with the near unanimous vote.

Effectively, the President had now stolen the reformist clothes of the opposition parties. During 2003, he could hardly open his gob without words like transparency, development, free and fair tumbling out.

The opposition reformist parties had been outmanoeuvred. Most of them, anyway. In January 2004 a new political party was launched, called Asar, (All Together). It too wants change: modernise the economy, address social hardship, especially for pensioners and take on the huge ecological problems. Asar confidently claimed that it expected to win half the seats in parliament in the autumn elections: and already ten sitting MPs have pledged their allegiance to the new party.

In keeping with this bold, modern image, Asar is led by a woman. She has a doctorate in political science, speaks four languages and as a child learned to sing opera in secret because her father disapproved.

Indeed, Asar made such a huge impression that the President couldn't resist throwing his full support behind it. It is, he proclaimed 'a party of specific deeds,' which would 'put into practice progressive ideas of economic development'.

And who is the head of this new party? Of course you know already. It's Dariga Nazarbayeva.

Naturally, Dariga says she's not seeking high office for herself. At least not yet. But in a surprisingly honest, but also rather chilling admission, she said she would have no qualms about exploiting her family and media connections to the full to push her party's agenda. Sound like a threat to you?

In a part of the world where despotic leaders regularly pass on power to family members, Nazarbayev is attempting to do the same, while also appearing reform-minded. Whether the poverty-stricken, polluted, oppressed and depressed citizens of Kazakhstan buy it or not remains to be seen. Yet even Nazarbayev's harshest critics admit that it was one piece of very smooth operating.

And while he changes his image at home, Dariga's TV stations can broadcast pictures of Daddy travelling around the world and being feted by world leaders. Look: everyone loves him.

In 2001, he visited Washington, where he and George W Bush signed a joint statement pledging Kazakhstan to international standards of governance, including freedom of religion, human rights, an independent media and free and fair elections. You've got to hand it to the boy: he has some neck. (A few months later, to demonstrate his solidarity, he ordered all Kazakh men pursuing Islamic studies abroad to return home immediately. George W must have been thrilled.)

In 2002. President Nazarbayev made a state visit to London, where he received the Order of the Knight of the Grand Cross of St Michael and St George at Buckingham Palace.

The day after he had tea at Downing Street with Tony Blair and various ministers: after a lunch in his honour at the Café Royal.

However, one of his most interesting trips was made in January of 2003 to Switzerland – home of his $78 million bank account. The President wasn't dipping into it, you understand: he's not allowed to. Pending the result of the on-going investigation by Swiss and US officials, that account has been frozen. What's caused a lot of speculation is that it was unclear *why* he travelled to Switzerland at all: did he go to speak to the investigators? Was he making a deal to get himself off the hook in return for grassing up some of his old colleagues?

Probably doesn't matter anyway. With oil and the right location, you can get away with anything.

PRESIDENT GENERAL KHAMTAI SIPHANDON

of the Laos People's Democratic Republic

Laos? Laos? Where the hell is Laos? Wasn't it big in the sixties? It was, and we'll get to that. But since then it has kept itself to itself and hoped the rest of the world wouldn't notice. The rest of the world has been more than happy to accommodate.

There are two reasons why Laos wants you to ignore it:

1) It doesn't want decadent westerners coming in and contaminating the place. Laos is one of the few hard-line communist states remaining on the planet. As such, the real despot isn't Siphandon so much as the creaking, septuagenarian politburo of the Lao People's Revolutionary Party. (LPRP). In turn, the LPRP does pretty much everything Vietnam tells it to. Which brings us neatly to:

2) Deep down, Laotians have a wee bit of an inferiority complex.

Laos is land-locked, surrounded by states that have always been more dynamic and high-profile: Vietnam, Burma, Cambodia, China and Thailand. Flashy, look-at-me places that think they are great. Laos has had rows with all of them: Thailand especially, with whom there are continuing border disputes. Over the last thousand years or so, Thailand has controlled Laos or vice versa.

Yet despite the chip on its national shoulder, Laos has done little to compete with the neighbours. It is a sleepy place. The population is around five million, though no one is too sure; they've never done a census. In some of the jungles and around the huge Mekong river, they are not even too sure where the border lies. The old joke is that the Vietnamese plant rice, and the Laotians listen to it grow.

Appropriately, the national currency is called the Kip.

Laos doesn't have oil wells or a strategic location. It hasn't produced any famous people. The main crop is rice, grown on the fertile floodplain of the Mekong River, along with vegetables, fruit, spices and cotton. In keeping with the soporific mood, Laos is the world's third largest opium producer. (Vang Vieng, just north of the capital, Vientiane, is reputedly full of opium dens.) *Third* largest, you'll notice: we could have made more, but, ah, you know.

It's not a rich country. Life expectancy is about 55.

Not to sound too cruel, but it's amazing anyone could be bothered with the place. Apart from Laotians, obviously, who would probably have been too lazy to move. Yet a long list of powers have been keen to use and abuse Laos. At least it was wanted: the Chinese, the Burmese, the Siamese (Thais), the Vietnamese, the French and the Japanese have all occupied for a while. Laos has been split in two, then put back together again, then split in three. And put back together again.

Laos has been a kingdom since the 13th century. Back

then it was called the Kingdom of Lane Xang, meaning Kingdom of a Million Elephants. The descendants of King Fa Ngum ruled Million Elephants Land in an unbroken line from the 13th century until 1975. (Interesting aside: most Laotians do not regard themselves as belonging to the same ethnic group. There are three main tribes: the Lao Lum, who live at low altitudes; the Lao Theung who live on mid-mountain slopes and the Lao Soung who live at even higher altitudes. The Hmong, whom we'll meet in a moment, are Lao Soung. Most Laotians are Buddhist, though with colourful local variations: some worship the spirits of various animals, some worship their ancestors, while one group – a so-called 'Cargo Cult' – believe Jesus will one day arrive in a Jeep, wearing combat fatigues. Really.)

But back to the elephants: it did boost the self-confidence. In the 1600s, Laos was quite developed and go-ahead, establishing contacts with European traders, probably attracted by the idea of picking up a few cheap nellies. First it was the Dutch, then the Italians. True to form, the Europeans didn't quite see the difference between 'trading with' and 'colonising' so Laos became a French protectorate in 1893.

Curiously, it was probably the period after this which did the most to erode Laotian self-esteem. Not because of the colonising itself, you understand, but because the French seemed to regret the decision. Laos doesn't have that many natural resources to exploit, so the Frogs simply lost interest. In fact its' only use seemed to be that it contained the Mekong trade route to China. Humiliatingly, officials from neighbouring Vietnam were drafted in to run the country.

Thus things remained until World War II. With France already occupied by Germany, the Japanese captured Laos without too much bloodshed. When it was over – and following a short guerrilla campaign – Laos declared its independence. France pretended to be hurt for a few minutes, then recognised Laos in 1949.

It was a constitutional monarchy, the emphasis being on monarchy. King Sisavang Vatthana's main pastimes seemed to be building palaces and statues of himself. For a country that still secretly idolises its royalty, Sisavang managed to make himself astonishingly unpopular.

Most countries have a civil war after independence, but the Laotians really couldn't be bothered. It was more like a period of great political tension interspersed with the odd bit of violence. From 1949 to 1975, there were three factions struggling for power:

1) Conservatives, commanding, among other forces, a 30 000-men army of the Hmong hill tribe.

2) Neutralists, organised by a feudal Prince, Souvanna Phouma. They supported the Laotian monarchy.

3) Communists, or Pathet Lao, led by Souvanna Phouma's half-brother, Prince Souphanouvang

It was your classic cold war division. The conservatives got a few bob from the US and the communists were being funded by Moscow. There were spurts of violence, followed by coalition governments consisting of two or three of the above, usually led by the Neutralists.

And it might well have remained that way, except that the US then decided to invade Vietnam.

Laos promptly declared its neutrality, but no one was going to pay much attention to that. There was an area in Northern Laos (then controlled by Laotian communists), called the Ho Chi Minh trail – used by the neighbouring commies, the Viet Cong, as a supply line. So the US bombed that part of Laos rather enthusiastically. Very, very enthusiastically. The US spent $2 192 125 *a day* dropping bombs on Laos. They dropped more bombs on Laos than they did world-wide during World War II *in total*.

On a per capita basis, Laos is the most heavily bombed nation in history. 200 000 Laotians died. They are still clearing the ordinance today. Live phosphor bombs are still maiming children, while the resulting defoliation made agriculture impossible for decades.

And while this was going on, the CIA was training, arming and funding the conservative Hmong tribesmen, particularly with a mind to launching attacks against the Viet Cong passing through the Ho Chi Minh trial. It was *Colonel Kurtz/Apocalypse Now/Heart of Darkness* stuff: an ex-marine named Tony Poe, tasked by the CIA to train the Hmong, did go bonkers and establish his own little kingdom deep in northern Laos. He paid the Hmong for each communist they killed, asking for ears as proof. Occasionally, he would send a few ears to the American ambassador in Vientiane. Tony sent ears. How thoughtful.

There are still a number of US ex-military involved in that operation who never went home. Most of them live in Thailand, and regard Poe as a hero. Poe now resides in San Francisco. He is an alcoholic, and maintains his mission failed simply because he didn't kill enough people.

Naturally, at the time, none of this was happening, as it flagrantly violated the Geneva Accord. (To get around the rule, pilots wore civilian clothes and flew unmarked planes.) The US flatly denied having any involvement in Laos until years later.

Eventually, the Yanks pulled out of Vietnam and the Viet Cong took over, essentially paving the way for a communist victory in Laos. Aided by better-trained and battle-hardened

Vietnamese units, the Pathet Lao marched into Vientiane with virtually no bloodshed. Prince Souvanna Phouma, head of the neutralists, resigned as Prime Minister, though he was kept on as an advisor to the government. Pays to have your half-brother as head of the opposition.

King Sisavang Vatthana abdicated about ten seconds before the monarchy was abolished. The King, along with his wife, Queen Khamphoui, and son, Crown Prince Vong Savang, were shipped off to a labour camp. They were all dead within three years.

Another son, Sauryavong Savang, escaped Laos by swimming across the Mekong. He now lives in France, where for a while he worked for car manufacturers Renault. His nephew, Prince Soulivong Savang, also lives in France. As the eldest son of Crown Prince Vong Savang, Prince Soulivong is heir to the Laotian throne. We'll come back to them.

The Lao People's Revolutionary Party was named as the sole legal political group.

Prince Souphanouvang became President. Kaysone Phomvihane was named Prime Minister, while future president General Khamtai Siphandon became Deputy Prime Minister, Minister of Defence and Commander of the Armed Forces: Khamtai had been Military Commander of the Pathet Lao.

The communists were in control and set about transforming society into a workers' paradise.

Yet curiously, the workers didn't seem aware of this. Many of them are still not. Although the Communists did have a large measure of public support, virtually none of this had anything to do with ideology: most of it was down to a personality cult around Souphanouvang. He was thought to have magical powers and is regarded as a sort of Buddhist saint. As far as many Laotians were concerned, they had swapped one monarch for another they liked better.

Were they in for a surprise. What followed was a harsh, neo-Stalinist regime. In 1985, to celebrate the tenth anniversary of the revolution, the population was instructed to be on the streets at 4am to listen to a few hours of speeches and marches. Then they went off to work.

Just like in neighbouring Cambodia, the Laotian Communists established 'Re-education Centres' where something like 30 000 people were sent away to be taught how fabulous communism is. However, being Laos, they didn't execute this scheme with quite the same degree of savagery as the Cambodians. Thousand died, rather than millions. So everyone ignored Laos.

Which was not great news for all those Hmong tribesman, secretly backed by the US. Suddenly without support from their friends in the CIA, many of the Hmong fled to Thailand, where there are still refugee camps. But many more, having no choice, remained where they were. A guerrilla war between the Laotian government and the Hmong is still raging today, with sons and even grandsons of the original rebels now involved.

Ex-pat Hmong groups in the US claim that something up to 70 000 Vietnamese troops are helping in this war, and that chemical and biological weapons have been used. They claim that since 1975, the communists in Laos have killed 300 000 of their own citizens, including 46 000 civil servants from the former regime. The problem has been worsened by the fact that Thailand isn't too keen on having all these refugees, and since 1985 has been forcibly repatriating people back into Laos. Many of these people are going back to certain death.

But hey: it's only Laos. The expatriate Hmong in the US

have virtually no political clout, while the government at home have been very effective in controlling information. Being a former head of propaganda, Khamtai is particularly keen, and particularly good, at maintaining the veil of mystery around his country. In 2001, his government passed a regulation which requires Laotian journalists to cover news 'in a manner favourable to the government'. Western journalists are allowed in occasionally, but none are based there. Some have been jailed for trying to meet with the Hmong guerrillas. (Laotian prisons, usually labour camps, are particularly brutal, torture being the main pastime.) Politburo members, Khamtai included, are rarely seen in public and virtually never give interviews, that job usually being reserved for a designated government minister. These days it's the Foreign Affairs man, Somsavat Lengsavad. When asked recently about the lack of human rights in Laos, he replied: "Some people are not friendly to Laos and envy us."

Oh, yes, there's so much to be jealous of. Laos does have ministers, a government and an elected assembly, but in reality all the decisions are made by a nine-man politburo, all of whom have been there since the revolution. Seven of them, including Khamtai, are Generals. Not one of them is younger then seventy. Khamtai is in his eighties. The *de facto* government of Laos is a festival of hearing aids and colostomy bags: men who stubbornly resist change, despite the chronic suffering of their people, yet who are quite happy to follow orders from Vietnam. Ever since Vietnamese troops marched into Vientiane with the Pathet Lao, Laos has basically been a client state to its neighbour. Back to that inferiority complex. Partially because Hanoi still sends cheques, partially because it is land-locked and depends on Vietnam for access to the sea, and partially because they still think they are a bit crap, the Laotian government clears all its major policy decisions with Vietnam first.

They don't want change, but they are not averse to a bit of window dressing. In 1989, Laos had the first elections to its new national assembly, the Sapha Heng Xat. Only snag was that candidates had to be approved by the LPRP: out of the dozens of independent candidates who applied to run, only four were approved – against the 155 party members. Voting was compulsory and monitored: no secret ballot in Laos.

So the communists won 108 seats out 109. Presumably, the 109th went to the Monster Raving Loony Party of Laos. Elections in 2002 came out with exactly the same result. In 1991, the parliament approved a new constitution which declared that the LPRP should be the only legal party. You'd wonder why they bothered.

And what a fantastic job the LPRP have done: despite money coming in from the USSR and Vietnam, the Laotian economy never prospered, mainly due to bureaucracy and corruption. By 1980, the country was plagued by widespread food shortages, while a tenth of the population had fled overseas. Encouraged by Mikhail Gorbachev, it had no option but to introduce some modest market liberalisation in the mid-80s

Didn't work though: the fall of the USSR meant no more cheques from Moscow, while the Asian economic slump in the 90s hit Laos particularly hard. The value of the Laotian currency, the Kip, plummeted. Self-confident as ever, the Politburo asked Vietnam what to do. Vietnam told them to go back to communism.

So docily, the Laotians obeyed. Market reforms were rolled back, scaring off the little foreign investment there was. If they were running a bit short of cash, the Politburo simply printed more of it, creating massive inflation. Today, with an inflation rate at over 100 per cent, the Laotian Kip is almost worthless. One euro will buy you 12 889 of them.

Laos is one of the poorest countries in the world. Around 85 per cent live on subsistence agriculture, while one third of Laotians live entirely outside the money economy, depending on barter to survive. Illiteracy rates run at 66 per cent for women. There is no rail network, only a few pot-holed roads and not much of a telephone service

Another quote from spokesman Somsavat Lengsavad: 'Talk that the government is not managing the economy well is groundless'. He accused 'anti-government subversives' of attempting to sabotage the Lao economy. In Laos, these subversives are always to blame.

More recently, Laos has again been making noises about economic liberalisation: probably at the behest of Vietnam, which is doing the same thing. It joined the Association of South-East Asian Nations (ASEAN) in 1997 and says it wants to join ASEAN's free-trade area by 2008. It sort-of admitted to a problem with poverty and even sucked up to the US a bit, finally coaxing it to drop a 20-year aid embargo in 1995. This was probably helped by the fact that, since the early nineties, the Laotians have been cooperating with US attempts to find the bodies of US service personnel who took part in the secret war against Laos. At the last count, they found 174; 391 still remain unaccounted-for.

There is a modest backpacker tourist trade, but little economic progress other than that. Vietnam still throws Laos a few bob, though no one knows how much. Money has a habit of disappearing. A few years back the Asian Development Bank lent millions to Laos to build colleges, yet no colleges appeared. Similarly, funds for a scheme to build a hydro-electric station also evaporated. As a result,

Germany and the World Bank have both cut back on aid schemes. The IMF refuses to have anything to do with Laos. Singapore and Malaysian Airlines have both stopped their services to Vientiane, while Lao Aviation is internationally blacklisted due to a failure to meet maintenance standards.

Almost certainly, some of the money is ending up in the bank accounts of politburo members. Laos is riddled with corruption, – and there are claims that the LPRP is involved in drug trafficking in order to gain hard currency. On top of that, the Laotian military has also gone into business for itself. Logging is its main source of income, though not too long ago it opened a casino just north of Vientiane.

Recently, opposition groups in the US have named six members of the Laotian politburo who between them have allegedly deposited $788 million in foreign bank accounts. They include the president, Khamtai Siphandon

Yet Laos could be rich. If the doting politburo were ever awake for long enough. Laos has largely unexplored reserves of gold, along with modest deposits of oil and coal.

However, they do have a national lottery now, which, understandably, is very popular.

Everything else is tightly controlled. There is a midnight curfew in Vientiane. Sex between foreigners and Laos is illegal. It is virtually impossible for a foreigner to marry a Lao: unless you are prepared to wait years and do a lot of bribing.

So what do we know about Khamtai Siphandon? Look, let's not skirt around the point here: the answer is, virtually nothing. Because of the communist system in Laos, Khamtai barely exists as an individual at all. Indeed, he might not exist *in actuality*: to put it mildly, he's no spring chicken. When he buys the (collective) farm, the news could be held back for years, in order to avoid a power vacuum. He could be dead now. In some cases, when Politburo members died, the great Laotian public were not officially told at all: the news was announced through the Laotian embassy in Vietnam.

So here are the dry facts: he was born in the southern province of Champassak in 1924, and became involved with the Communists in the 1950s. He is married with five children. He was chief of staff of the Pathet Lao during the revolution and afterwards became deputy prime minister and defence minister, during which time he had a central role in propaganda. In 1991, after the new constitution, Kaysone Phomvilhane became president and Khamtai moved up to the Prime Minister's job.

The following year Phomvilhane died. Khamtai became president of the LPRP while Nouhak Phoumsavanh took over as president of the country. When Phoumsavanh resigned in 1998, Khamtai succeeded him, but retained his presidency of the party, thus making him the most powerful man in Laos.

He still has very little contact with the West, and is rarely seen in public. It is believed that some of the younger members of the party would like to open things up a bit and would rather have closer links with China than with Vietnam, but that's going to happen over Khamtai's dead body. Which shouldn't be too far off

This is all we know about him. And that's the way he wants it, though this also leads to a constant state of confusion in the country: rumours constantly circulate of his death, of power struggles. People keep their head down, just in case. Paranoia becomes a weapon of oppression.

Yet the state can't control everything. One of the few remarkable aspects of Communist Laos is the position of religion. Laos is a (mostly) Theravada Buddhist country, and this is so engrained in the people that even the communists realised they couldn't get rid of it. (Most Lao men become a monk for a short period, usually after school.) So it is tolerated, even somewhat appropriated by the state. And being a stoical religion, it probably helps them endure the miseries of living under King Khamtai, as some there secretly call him.

However, Christianity is a total no-no. It's been called the 'number one enemy of the state'. Christian missionaries are regularly arrested and tortured until they renounce their faith – which involves signing a form which asks that they be punished if they are caught practising Christianity again. One recent report claimed that some Christian missionaries were forced to drink blood.

Opposition groups operate outside the country, mostly in the US, while in Laos there have been occasional protests. Five students tried to unfurl a banner in 1999, but were arrested before they even got it open. They haven't been heard from since. It's not even known what the banner said. There was another attempt, again by students and teachers, a couple of years later, after which 100 people were arrested. And the day after a protest meeting at Vientiane's Dongkok University meeting, the chief organiser was killed in a 'traffic accident'.

No one knows what happened to those who were arrested. Sentences for such activity usually range between ten to twenty years in a labour camp. There is, at best, a 50-50 chance of coming back alive.

In 2000, – the year Laos celebrated twenty-five years of communism – there were reports of a dozen bomb blasts around Vientiane, all of which went off without warning and in crowded parts of the city. There were reports of up to ten dead, though, of course, no one can be sure. Officially they never happened.

It could have been the Hmong: some claimed

responsibility, but others denied it. However, shortly after the blasts, a group of armed insurgents attacked a Lao customs post at the southern border town of Vang Tao. For no obvious reason, they hoisted the old Royalist Loatian flag over the customs post.

Within hours, Laotian soldiers had retaken the post, leaving six of the rebels dead and dozens unaccounted for. It was a bizarre, reckless gesture. Rather suspiciously, the whole incident was broadcast live on Thai television.

Even more suspiciously, Prince Sauryavong Savang, the only surviving son of the dead king, just happened to be on a month-long fund-raising and lobbying tour of the US at the time. Looking suitably regal, he informed reporters that "the fact that the anti-communist fighters called for the return of the constitutional monarchy makes an excellent path for the restoration of liberty, peace and democracy in the country." He then rather pointedly avoided questions about the bomb blasts in Vientiane.

However, it was later claimed that the men who attacked the customs outpost were little more than mercenaries. They were paid $10 – ten times the average Lao wage – and told that they were part of a force of 30 000 men. If true, it means that the Laotian Royal Family were prepared to lure men to their deaths just for a bit of cheap publicity. As the cure for communism, the Laotian royal family might be worse than the disease.

Yet despite this – despite all the propaganda and re-education, the communists have never been able to completely eradicate the Laotian nostalgia for the royals. Many people keep pictures of them in their homes or the old bank notes with the king's picture. Some even keep the pictures thinking it will bring them luck in the national lottery.

And don't forget that the commies came to power in the first place because they were led by a Prince.

So in an attempt to cheer everyone up, Khamtai was in 2002 photographed at a statue of King Fa Ngum, who founded the kingdom of Laos – or a million elephants – back in the 13th century. Quite ironic given that it was Khamtai and his chums who sent King Fa Ngum's ancestors to their deaths hundreds of years later. No doubt, many Laotians saw this irony too, and were probably tempted to laugh. And they planned to: but, ah, you know.

LEADER OF FIRST OF SEPTEMBER REVOLUTION
COLONEL MU`AMMAR AL-QADHAFI

of the Great Socialist People's Libyan Arab Jamahiriya

If you were really, really bored one day, you could try this. Go on the internet and look up his name. To start you off, here's a few variants: Muammar al Qathafi, Muammar el-Qaddafi, Muammar Qadhafi, Muhammar Qaddaffi, Moammar Qaddafi, Muammar Gadafy, Moamar Gadhafi, Moammar Gadhafi, Muammar Gaddafi, Moamer Kadhafi, Muammar Al-Qaddafi . . . you get the idea.

There are, apparently, thirty-two ways to spell Mu`ammar al-Qadhafi. (This spelling is closest to the Arab pronunciation). It's partly to do with the difficulties of translating from Arabic into western languages, but it also says something about the man himself. Among despots – among *anyone* – al-Qadhafi is unique. And almost impossible to pin down.

Look at his life story and in equal measures you'll see great intelligence and sheer stupidity. You'll also see idealism, cynicism, bluster, pragmatism, eccentricity, cruelty, kindness, showmanship, charisma, confusion and creativity. Forget Saddam: in the late twentieth century, Mu'ammar al-

135

Qadhafi was the brand leader for despots whom western governments loved to hate.

And now, in the twenty-first century, they are starting to like him again. That's just how amazing this guy is: a mixture of Chairman Mao, Lawrence of Arabia and Austin Powers.

Here's an example: in July 2002, Mu'ammar attended the launch of the African Union in South Africa. He turned up with something of an entourage: two Boeing 707s, his own personal jet, two transport aircraft – including a giant Antonov transport plane – and a ship full of goat carcasses.

In typical style, he arrived late at the inaugural session. The speeches had already started when he swept in, dressed in swirling robes and a felt hat. He was surrounded by his all-female troop of bodyguards, dressed in red berets and green camouflage uniforms. No, really: they have guarded him for over ten years. (This is the Austin Powers bit.) Many of them have black-belts in karate, and some have lost their lives in assassination attempts. They carry AK-47s slung over their shoulders, and despite the uniforms, Mu'ammar encourages them to be as feminine as possible: to wear nail varnish, lipstick and perfume.

Naturally, everyone turned to watch.

The speeches resumed, during which Mu'ammar appeared to take detailed notes. Several of the leaders appealed for a more open and honest approach to the scourge of AIDS.

Then it was Mu'ammar's turn to speak. Ignoring the fact that a high-ranking EU delegation was present, he launched into a rant about how Europe was attempting to divide Africa, then shared his thoughts on the AIDs problem: "If you are straight, if you are clean, AIDS will not aggress you.

"And the mosquito and tsetse fly are God's armies to protect Africa from its enemies," he added, glaring at the Europeans.

Some of the delegates shuffled uncomfortably for a few minutes, yet no one was too outraged. This was just Mu'ammar; this is what he does. He's indulged, like an eccentric uncle. An eccentric uncle with the third largest supply of oil in the world.

When the summit was over, Mu'ammar didn't fly home. So taken was he with the notion of African unity that he decided to drive instead; to get some sense of what life is like for ordinary Africans. So off he went: accompanied by 70 armoured vehicles. This included two 46-seat buses, trucks containing sub-machine guns, AK47 assault rifles and rocket-launchers, a mobile hospital, several armour-plated limos and 600 security personnel. When he entered Swaziland, bystanders ran for cover, assuming the country was being invaded; in Malawi, his radio-jamming signals knocked out the country's phone system.

He also swept through Mozambique and Malawi, stopping occasionally at villages to chat with locals. When he didn't stop, he simply threw money out the window. A lot of money: most reports have it that during this mini-tour of Africa, he literally threw away $6 million in cash.

At the time, a Jordanian psychologist remarked: "I meet people like him every day in my hospital." Yet experienced Mu'ammar-watchers say that giving away all this dosh wasn't just a crazy attempt to buy popularity in Africa: it was also a sly commentary on how most aid money never reaches the people who need it. Mu'ammar is a kind of a madman, and a kind of a genius.

But what was he doing at a meeting of the African Union anyway? Isn't Libya an Arab country? It is, and has been for a very, very long time. The first recorded settlements there date back three thousand years. Various ancient civilisations came and went, including the Greeks who gave it the name of Libya in the fourth century BC.

The Arabs – and Islam – arrived in 643 AD, followed by the usual stuff: the Ottoman Empire, then the Italians, then the British and the French during World War Two. Independence finally came in 1951, though not democracy: the country was ruled by King Idris Al-Sanusi, who spent most of his time being sucked up to by western powers keen to tap into Libya's newly-discovered oil supply. Idris allowed in British and American military bases, granted oil concessions to two US oil companies and built an 104-mile pipeline.

Which is where Mu'ammar enters our story. No official date is given for his birth, though it's thought to be 1942: apparently in a tent, apparently the youngest son of a poor nomadic cattle-herder. They were a revolutionary family: Mu'ammar's father and uncles had fought against Italian colonial rule and served prison sentences.

Yet Daddy was obviously a cattle-herder with contacts: Mu'ammar studied history at the University of Libya, then entered the Royal Libyan Military Academy in 1963. Part of his training took place in the UK.

At the time, pan-Arab nationalism was sweeping the Middle East and influencing many young officers in the Libyan army: especially Mu'ammar, who idolised the great Egyptian leader, Gamal Abd al-Nasser and his ideas of a United States of Arabia. (Even though Egyptians are not ethnically Arab – they are Eastern Hamitic). Seeing himself as perhaps a Nasser Version 2, he set up the Free Officers Movement in 1964. Just five years later, the FMO had successfully infiltrated every echelon of the Libyan military. The coup (or Great Al-Fateh Revolution as it is officially known) took less than two hours to complete. Hardly a shot was fired.

The Revolution Command Council took control of the Libyan Arab Republic, with Mu'ammar as its chairman. So he promoted himself to Colonel.

Initially, the West wasn't too bothered by any of this. The UK and US recognised the new government, and sought assurances that all existing trade agreements (i.e. sales of oil) would be honoured. And Mu'ammar was more than happy to comply: he needed to sell the oil too. Transforming Libyan society wasn't going to be cheap. He set about instituting his own version of Islamic socialism: both anti-capitalist and anti-communist, with a strict moral code, nationalised industries and a generous social welfare system. The Libyan people loved it. To this day, Libya maintains enviably high standards of healthcare and education.

But while he respected the business deals, he didn't think twice about closing down those US and British military bases, and kicking out any foreigners he didn't like the look of. He especially didn't like the look of Jews, expelling tens of thousands of them.

Of course the expulsion was informed by Mu'ammar's pan-Arab philosophy. (He'd already proclaimed himself a 'defender of Islam and the Arab nation'.) Mu'ammar wanted to establish an Arab super-state, and he wanted to do it quickly. So quickly that he turned into something of a political slut, offering his country in union with anyone who took even the vaguest interest.

In 1971, a national referendum approved the proposed Federation of Arab Republics, consisting of Libya, Egypt and Syria. But it never happened, so the following year Libya and Egypt agreed on a merger. But this too failed to materialise. In 1974, it was Tunisia's turn to merge with Libya, but a few months later, nothing. On the rebound, Libya had another go with Syria in 1980, but this was also unconsummated. In 1989, Libya, Algeria, Morocco, Mauritania and Tunisia did form the Arab Maghreb Union, but not much has been heard about it since.

So why did things keep going wrong? Arab union has

long been a cherished goal in that part of the world. It could have been that, when it came to the crunch, national leaders didn't want to give up the power they had. It could have been that they suspected Mu'ammar of having ambitions to lead these new states. And it could also have been because they thought he was, well, a little weird.

Certainly, Libya wasn't developing the way any other Arab nations were. The quasi-religious personality cult growing around Mu'ammar wasn't that unusual, but the political ideas certainly were.

In 1973, Mu'ammar announced a 'cultural revolution' to eradicate all traces of imported ideology. This mainly involved the establishment of 'People's Committees' in schools, hospitals, universities and workplaces: a move which had the smack of democracy to it, of allowing people a say in how things should be run. Except that it was the direct opposite. This was his first step towards banning democracy altogether. Mu'ammar didn't believe in it.

All was explained three years later when he published the first of his Green Books, which espoused his Third Universal Theory of governance. Voting for leaders, it seemed, was far too sloppy, hypocritical and western a system for Libya. The committees would voice their opinions and Brother Leader would listen. Simple as that.

In 1977, there was a 'People's Revolution'. The name of the state was changed to The Great Socialist People's Libyan Arab Jamahiriya: Jamahiriya being a new makey-uppy word coined by Mu'ammar himself to mean 'A state of the masses'.

And in a state it was, the main problem being that no one really understood what the Third Universal Theory meant. Two more Green Books were published by 1980, but this didn't leave anyone any wiser. Under the new arrangements, Libya had no written constitution, no political parties and a murky system of committees and congresses which sometimes can and sometimes can't make laws. Officially, the country doesn't even have a head of state – Mu'ammar resigned from all official posts in 1979, retaining only the titles Colonel and 'Leader of the First of September Revolution'.

Yet he was still in charge of the country: now even more so as congresses and committees had to look to Mu'ammar to 'interpret' the Third Universal Theory.

So things started to get strange. He ruled that television commentary of football matches should refer to players only by their numbers, not their names: lest any person become more important than the People's Revolution. (This from the guy whose picture was plastered on every street-corner.) For a while, he even considered banning football altogether, comparing spectator sports to going to a restaurant to watch people eat. (Though he changed his mind later.)

In 1977, in an effort to achieve self-sufficiency, Mu'ammar decreed that every family had to raise chickens at home. Not long later, live chickens were delivered to every front door (and tent) in the nation – even to those who lived in inner city apartments. The smell of freshly-cooked chicken wafted over Tripoli for some days after.

Being a Muslim state, he switched from the western Gregorian calendar to an Islamic one – except that his differed from every other Muslim country – complete with new month-names thought up by Mu'ammar. He began conducting all his business from a tent in the desert. On a state visit to Egypt, he set up the tent in the back garden of the Presidential compound in Cairo.

Indeed, his interpretation of Arab and Muslim culture was so unique that he even breathlessly announced that a certain well-known Elizabethan playwright was not English at all, but Arab. Shakespeare was in fact Sheikh Speare or Sheikh Zubeir. Oh, no.

Meanwhile, all aspects of foreign and international policy were decided on by him, usually without any explanation and often on a whimsical basis. He intervened militarily in the civil war in neighbouring Chad and remained there until 1994, but, being Mu'ammar, completely denied it. He showed support to Idi Amin's Uganda, one of the most barbarous regimes in history. Most dangerously though – at least from the West's point of view – he began supporting 'revolutionary causes'; the kind of people the US would call terrorists.

Naturally, like virtually all Arab nations, Libya supported the Palestinians and Mu'ammar put his money where his mouth was by handing over cash, training and arms.

(Interesting aside: even though Arab countries support the Palestinian cause, they are not necessarily crazy about Palestinians. Apart from it being a great stick with which to beat Israel, most Arab nations would like to see a Palestinian state so they can get rid of their refugees. In places like Saudi Arabia, Palestinians have virtually no rights.)

However, what really got the West narky was when Mu'ammar began aiding 'revolutionary causes' in Europe. Relations with the US were already pretty poor: Washington had broken off diplomatic ties over the incursions into Chad, while an aerial fire fight in 1981 over the Gulf of Sirte (Libya claimed the US planes were in its territory) during which two Libyan planes were shot down, hardly helped matters.

But it was in 1984 that Mu'ammar really dirtied his diplomatic bib. During an anti-al-Qadhafi protest outside the Libyan embassy in London, someone in the building shot at the crowd, killing a British policewoman, Yvonne

Fletcher. And because of diplomatic immunity, no one was ever charged. Britain broke off relations.

In 1986, the Yanks got involved again. Following the bombing of Vienna and Rome airports, plus a Berlin disco frequented by American military personnel, the US attacked several sites in Libya, including Mu'ammar's palace. Around 100 Libyans were killed, including Mu'ammar's adopted daughter. Soon after this, a ship named the Eksund was intercepted by French police. It was carrying arms from Libya to the IRA.

But it got even worse. In 1988, a bomb hidden inside a radio-cassette player blew Pan Am Flight 103 to smithereens over the town of Lockerbie in Scotland. All 259 on board were killed, along with eleven people in Lockerbie. Mu'ammar refused to hand over two Libyans suspected of being involved. The UN imposed trade sanctions, including a ban on flights to and from the country, forbade the sale of spare parts for oil refineries and froze all Libyan funds abroad.

And while Mu'ammar was busily trying to annoy every other country in the world, things weren't too sunny at home either. Even with all that oil, Libya's increasing isolation was damaging the economy. And that 1986 American attack inadvertently advertised to the Libyan people that Mu'ammar's simple-man-living-in-a-tent routine was bullshit: he lived in a huge palace, just like all the other dictators do. (It's also said that beneath his colourful African robes, he wears regular, western-style underpants. But that's just a rumour.) There were rumblings of discontent: in keeping with the Third Universal Theory, all private bank accounts had been nationalised. So just to show the complaining students and intellectuals who was boss, Mu'ammar staged a series of public hangings in all the universities. Bet that was educational. Other political opponents who had fled the country were tracked down and assassinated.

But at least there was the occasional crazed outburst to pass the time. Following Princess Diana's death in a car crash, Mu'ammar proclaimed that "the whole world knows it was premeditated murder", later on adding that it was "not a suicide but a murder": demonstrating both his paranoia and inability to grasp key details. He also encouraged his people to live more frugally by buying smaller drinking glasses, and toyed with the notion of abolishing universities altogether. Each year there was a new set of directions, telling Libyans what to wear, what to eat, what to read. Seemingly on a whim, he would announce new national holidays such as 'Libyan Pride Day', where he cut all phone lines to the outside world.

For the Libyan people, these were difficult times: though not for Mu'ammar himself, you understand. The Libyan state investment arm, Lafico – solely controlled by the al-Qadhafi family – was busy making shrewd investments all over the globe. For a guy who believes that 'Wealth, weapons and power lie with the people,' Mu'ammar was pretty good as a capitalist.

Despite all the guff about Arab, and more lately, African unity, Lafico has invested relatively little in those two parts of the world: about $800 million. The vast majority of its interests – $6 billion – lie in the evil, decadent West. For a while, it owned a slice of the Italian football club, Juventus, (Mu'ammar's son, Saidi, was on the board), along with several other business ventures in Italy like Fiat. On top of that was $1billion invested in British property, including the Carlton Towers and Corinthia Hotel Groups.

So with financial security not much of a worry, Mu'ammar turned his attention to the future direction of Libya, especially in relation to the future of the Arab world.

After thirty years of offering himself as the new Nasser, Mu'ammar finally began to realise that his neighbours weren't that interested.

His solution was a classic Mu'ammar make-over: Libya wasn't an Arab country at all. It was African. In 1994, he gave back the chunk of neighbouring Chad his troops had been occupying, and began making noises about African unity being the way of the future. He declared that Africa "is closer to me in every way than Iraq or Syria." And to demonstrate his disdain for his Arab neighbours, he decried the ill-fated 1995 peace accord between Israel and the PLO as a sell-out. He then deported 30 000 Palestinians from Libya, who no doubt really appreciated this sign of solidarity in their hour of need.

Libya's external radio service, the Voice of the Greater Arab Homeland, was re-named the Voice of Africa, while Mu'ammar – now wearing all those glittery African robes – went about making lots of new friends on the continent, mostly by throwing money at them and encouraging various despotic regimes not to give into decadent western notions like democracy. He even befriended Zimbabwe's Robert Mugabe (see *Zimbabwe*). Mu'ammar gives cash-strapped Mugabe oil under a barter deal, while it's also been reported that Libya actually pays for Zimbabwe's embassy in Tripoli. (However, the Africanisation of Libya wasn't so popular with Libyans, who are apparently annoyed by the large numbers of African workers coming into the state. In 2000, there was a pogrom in which dozens of Africans were killed.)

Yet none of this was bringing Libya back into the greater international community. There were more internal rumbles. Islamic militants were crushed, (Libya is a Muslim country, but has never tolerated the nuttier extremes of fundamentalism), while it's been reported that there were two assassination attempts on Mu'ammar, in 1993 and 1995. And the man still couldn't keep his mouth shut. Following European elections in 1992 when the Green Party made sweeping gains, Mu'ammar claimed that this was because they had all read his Green Book.

It was time to make peace with the West.

Enter none other than Nelson Mandela, who after several years of cajoling Mu'ammar, finally talked him into handing over the two Lockerbie suspects, both of whom were said to be members of Libyan intelligence (naturally, this is denied by Tripoli). In their trial in 2001, one was found guilty, the other acquitted. In the same year, four Libyans were found guilty of the Berlin disco bombing of 1996.

No one was going to be inviting him out for a night with the lads yet, but it was a small step towards Mu'ammar's rehabilitation. UN and EU sanctions were dropped. The UK re-established diplomatic ties. The US, however, wasn't so easy to charm.

As is often the way in the cynical, self-serving world of international politics, Libya's chance came through the death of thousands of Americans. Libya was the first country *in the world* to condemn the September 11th attack. Mu'ammar ruined it a little by suggesting that the US should bomb Britain as well as Afghanistan because it too harboured Muslim militants, yet it was enough for the Americans to take notice. Especially when Libya offered to help out on the War on Terror; especially when it secretly offered the services of Al Mathaba: Libyan intelligence.

This was a suggestion the Yanks couldn't afford to ignore. They had the guns, the bombs, the planes and lots of square-jawed soldiers, yet it was all useless unless the US knew where the enemy was at: and Libya could tell them. Weeks after September 11, Musa Kousa, head of Al Mathaba arrived into London for secret talks with British intelligence. He even brought a pile of documents, detailing the names of Islamic militants and cells operating in Africa, Europe and the Middle East.

How did he know all this? Because Libya had paid for most of it: even though Brother Leader was no fan of militant Islam, he'd no problem funding it to attack the West. By stitching up his former revolutionary chums, Mu'ammar was buying back international respectability.

No one knows exactly what happened at that meeting, but it wouldn't take any great genius to figure the sort of deal that was agreed. Indeed, since then the world has seen the terms of that deal being played out:

* In 2002, Libya and the US hold official talks. At the same time, the Libyan Dinar is devalued by 51 per cent against the dollar: the first step in setting up a market-driven exchange rate between the two currencies.

* Later that year, Libya agrees to pay $170 million compensation to the victims of the Lockerbie bomb

* In 2003, Libya announces that it will stop developing weapons of mass destruction. In an obviously choreographed move, Tony Blair describes the announcement as 'historic and courageous' while the White House says Libya may now 'rejoin the international community'. International observers are invited to oversee the process, while the *de facto* Libyan prime Minister, Shokri Ghanim, comes to visit Tony at Number Ten. Libya subsequently revealed that it had tonnes of mustard gas and had

bought designs for a nuclear weapon from a Pakistani scientist *(See Iran)*

* In 2004, Libya opened talks with Israel. Mu'ammar had already invited the thousands of Jews he expelled in 1971 to return. "If they come as warriors, we will fight them," he said. "If they come trading cheese, we will buy cheese." Er, OK.

And things were changing at home too. In 2001, Mu'ammar persuaded the Libyan-born, American-educated Shokri Ghanim to become secretary of the General People's Council: effectively Prime Minister. Slowly – very slowly – Ghanim has been loosening the grip of the state on the Libyan economy, especially in the area of imports, which were once a state monopoly. And so far, Mu'ammar has backed him to the hilt.

The thing is that Libya has to change, and Mu'ammar knows it: he knows what the Libyan people are thinking. Although Libya doesn't have democracy or opinion polls, it is estimated that around forty per cent of the population have some sort of relationship with the Mukhabarat, Libya's internal secret police: it is common practice to receive perks, such as electrical equipment or scholarships abroad, in return for feedback on what the plain folks are talking about on the streets. Part tool of oppression, part market-research company.

And what the Mukhabarat have been telling Brother Leader is that sixty per cent of the Libyan population (5 million) are under twenty, most of whom are rather indifferent to the Third Universal Theory. The Green Square in Tripoli, once considered so sacred that citizens were forbidden from walking on it, now buzzes with young people. On the side-streets, small private businesses are starting up, selling western music and clothes. And the square isn't painted green any more.

There is now widespread access to the internet and satellite TV in Libya. And although the standard of living is still high, young Libyans want a piece of the outside world. And they may get it yet: part of Mu'ammar's strategy to become the Great African Leader might be to bring the world to Libya.

Although he thought about banning it for a while, Brother Leader seems to have changed his mind about football. Libya hosted the African Nations Cup in 1982, (during which Mu'ammar got to make a two-hour speech), and ordinary Libyans are still talking about it. They are besotted with football. David Beckham is a god; games can sometimes attract crowds of 100 000 people.

This passion has even infiltrated the al-Qadhafi family: Mu'ammar's second eldest (and apparently favourite) son Saidi was for a while on the board of Juventus, as we've already mentioned. But before that he was also chairman of the Libyan FA, where he worked tirelessly to raise the profile of Libyan football. He made a bid to host the African Competition again in 2004, (he failed), and now talks about a bid for the World Cup in 2010.

Until he decided that rather than organise the Libyan team, he'd rather play for it. As he didn't play for a club, he hired a personal trainer from Holland while also taking advice from close personal friend Diego Maradona (he was at Saidi's wedding to the daughter of the head of Libyan intelligence) and the national team's athletics coach, Ben Johnson. What a pair.

Oh no: you can see it, can't you? Embarrassment of sphincter-tightening proportions. At training sessions, the other Libyan players ran backwards rather than tackle him. At international matches, he was allowed to take all the corners and penalties. His style of play was described as a 'classic school-ground goal-hanger'.

Eventually, Libya's Italian coach, Franco Scoglio, dropped Saidi, pointing out that 'as a footballer he's worthless'. So Saidi – still chairman of the Libyan FA – dropped Scoglio. Saidi is now captain of the team. Later that year, 2002, Saidi resigned from the Libyan FA, and then things got even weirder: at 30 years of age, he was signed by Italian Serie A side, Perugia.

In interviews at the time, Perugia's manager admitted to having seen Saidi play only once, virtually admitting that the deal might have more to do with the publicity value and the fact that Saidi was a billionaire. Sadly, Saidi is yet to play for his new club. He tested positive for the banned steroid, nandrolone. Well: if you're going to hang out with Maradona and Ben Johnson, drugs are bound to get involved.

Yet still the whole episode had a curious al-Qadhafi logic: football could be a way of marketing Libya overseas – of even spawning a tourist industry – while it also seemed to provide a release valve for the masses. Libyan fans are notoriously stroppy, with riots commonplace.

However, it would be incorrect to assume that Saidi has a part in this wider strategy. If the family business is to be passed on, it won't be to him. Mu'ammar has six children, five of them with his wife, Safiya. (There was a previous wife about whom almost nothing is known.) Apart from the footballing Saidi, there's Mohammed, son of the first wife, who seems to be estranged from Daddy; Mualassim, also estranged and living in Egypt; Moutassim, the playboy with the nickname Hannibal. He was recently involved in a brawl in Italy which left six photographers in hospital; Aisha, the only girl, said to be the Claudia Schiffer of North Africa, and finally Saif: the sensible one.

If anyone takes over from the old man, it's going to be him. An architect by trade, he began studying Global Governance in the London School of Economics in 2002, but even before that was entrusted with many high-level diplomatic tasks, including re-opening talks with the Israelis. Since the move to London, he has given several interviews and demonstrated a politician's flair for not answering questions. In a *Guardian* interview, he said Libyan society was similar to Switzerland.

Then again, there's no immediate sign of the Old Man stepping down. He could get to be president of Africa yet, while there are all his new friends in Europe and the US to meet

Or perhaps not. Just as relations with the West were starting to get a bit rosy, Shokri Ghanim suddenly claimed that Libya was not responsible for Lockerbie or the death of PC Yvonne Fletcher: that it paid compensation only to buy peace. This was in direct contradiction to earlier written statements in which Libya took the blame.

Naturally, the UK and US were not too thrilled with this turn of events. The White House demanded a retraction and put on hold plans to rescind a travel ban to Libya. The Brits looked for 'clarification' and started muttering about problems with Tony Blair's planned trip to Tripoli.

Why Ghanem took it into his head to make this statement remains unclear. Some are putting the outburst down to a simple lack of experience. Although he previously worked for OPEC, this is Ghanem's first political job, while there are other reports that Ghanem really believes it: he is reported to have said privately that if his government had been responsible for blowing up Flight 103, he could not serve it. However, the following day the Libyan news service, Jana, said "recent statements contradicting or casting doubt on these positions are inaccurate and regrettable." The

SEAN MONCRIEFF

Americans lifted the travel ban. Ghanem has remained conspicuously silent.

As for Mu'ammar, he's in his sixties and dyes his hair these days, but he's still the big cheese: despite the lack of democracy, the odd bit of oppression and the indifference of young Libyans, there is no significant opposition to his regime. Under Colonel al-Qadhafi, life has been pretty good.

Not to mention entertaining: Brother Leader's mind is as sharp as a revolutionary razor. In 1999, to coincide with his thirtieth anniversary as boss, it was announced that Mu'ammar had invented the world's safest car. The Saroukh el-Jamahiriya (Libyan Rocket) is a five-passenger saloon with a pointy end and front that does indeed make it look like a rocket. Naturally, the prototype was green, and featured all sorts of safety gizmos. Apparently, the idea came to him during the era of sanctions, when he had spent much time 'thinking of ways to preserve human life all over the world'.

Production was supposed to be immediate, with a factory churning out 50 000 a year. But sadly, the Libyan Rocket has assumed a cloak of invisibility.

Still: we have Brother Leader's words to sustain us. In 2003, a Canadian company published an English translation of Mu'ammar's first work since the epic Green Books. It was penned, apparently, during one of Brother Leader's long sojourns in the desert. Consisting of eleven stories/meditations/polemics, Mu'ammar decries the destruction of the environment, wonders if communism is really dead, tells a story about an astronaut who commits suicide, recommends a herb which he claims is a cure for the 'mentally disturbed', relates information about the relative size of planets and gives an Arab perspective on the (first) Gulf War.

Escape to Hell is classic Mu'ammar: rambling, spacey, sometimes incoherent. Yet the reviews have been surprisingly kind. Just like the man himself, no reviewer was quite sure what he was going on about. But many felt there was definitely something in there. Part loony, part genius.

PRESIDENT COLONEL MAAOUYA
OULD SID'AHMED TAYA

of The Islamic Republic of Mauritania

Let's start with a true story. Cheikhna Ould Beilil is a 44-year-old animal-feed seller. In the market town of Guerrou, slap-bang in the middle of the desert and some 300 miles east of the Mauritanian capital, Nouakchott, he met Mint Bota. They married, had some kids and settled just outside the compound of the Arab family who Mint worked for.

Some time later, Ould Beilil squabbled with Mint's boss, so badly that he decided to move his family away from the compound. But the Arab family wouldn't let him. They informed Beilil that as a slave, his wife was their property; that according to centuries-old tradition, his children also belonged to them. Beilil could leave, but the rest of them couldn't.

So Beilil went to a local Sharia Court. The court said the family should remain together, but curiously ignored the allegation that Mint was a slave. Yet still the Arab family would not let Mint and her family go.

Beilil tried the police next. They advised him to forget about his family.

Having no option, Beilil made the 300-mile journey to Nouakchott, where he took the highly risky strategy of talking to foreign reporters. He told them that his wife and daughters were used for housework, while his son looked after the herds, and claimed that the head of the Arab family regularly beat them: both the mother and children.

And this isn't some Somerset Maugham reminiscence. Beilil spoke to reporters from the Associated Press: they filed their copy in February, 2004.

Estimates have it that across twenty-first century Mauritania, Niger and Sudan, there are around 200 000 people – all of them black Africans – who live, work and die as the possessions of other people. Mauritania, a country with a population of just 2.5 million, is the worst offender with an estimated 100 000 slaves.

Yet Beilil's story was unusual, and for two reasons:
1) Free men like him are not usually allowed to marry slave girls.

2) In all practical senses, speaking about slavery in Mauritania is strictly forbidden. Anti-slavery campaigners are regularly jailed, so it is rare when eye-witnesses are brave or desperate enough to come forward. Often, they disappear shortly afterwards.

Officially, of course, slavery is banned in Mauritania – since 1981, don't you know. In practice, it continues on pretty much as it did before. The government does virtually nothing to stop it: a government which is racist, corrupt, brutal and barbaric.

On the buffer between black Africa and the Arab world, Mauritania is a poverty-stricken mess, a post-colonial made-up country which has remained intact only because various political boot-boys have managed to keep the ethnic groups in their place. It is one of the few states on the planet which might actually benefit from being broken up, or merged with one of its neighbours. There are quite a few Mauritanians who would rather be somewhere else.

To understand how it arrived at this sorry position, we have to go back to the beginning.

And the beginning is a terribly long time ago. Atlas, the mythical character said to have balanced the world on his shoulders, was supposedly King of Mauritania.

Some years later, when planet-hoisting had fallen out of fashion, Mauritania was inhabited by the Soninke tribe, and later by their descendants, the Bafours.

After this, it gets complicated, so pay attention and no slouching. Between the third and seventh centuries, the Bafours were gradually driven out of Mauritania by migrating Berber tribes. The Berbers are also north African, though no one is sure exactly where they originate from. They migrated so much through the region that today their descendants live in Libya, Algeria, Egypt, Tunisia, Morocco and throughout southern Europe. However, because they moved about so much, their indigenous culture has been mostly lost: they intermarried with other races, especially Arabs. Over time, most Berbers came to regard themselves as Arab, thus greatly helping the spread of Islam and Arab culture through north Africa.

Today, Marrakech is the only place on earth with an indigenous Berber population.

So: you had Mauritania full of Berbers. The original African inhabitants were either driven south or enslaved. Eventually, Mauritania became part of the Ghana Empire.

Then the Arabs started coming. From the seventh century on, some came to spread Islam. But in the tenth century, others came to spread Islam and kick ass: Islamic warrior monks called Al Murabitun took over southern Mauritania, in the process defeating the Ghana Empire. But the darker-skinned Berbers weren't giving up easily. Off and on, they fought the Arabs for the next 500 years, culminating in the Thirty Years War (1644-74), a final effort to repel the Arab invaders.

Remember though, this process took five centuries: in between the various wars, the Berbers couldn't help but get married to some of those attractive foreigners. Islam became the predominant religion, while even the differences between Arab and Berber became muddied: over time, the population of Mauritania became known as Moors: a catch-all term for north African Muslims.

Not that they all lived as one big happy family. The Arabs were led by the Beni Hassan tribe, whose descendants became the upper stratum of Mauritanian Moorish society – and this is still the case today. They have a lighter skin colour and are known as Bidan Moors – or White Moors.

The descendants of the Berbers, who along the way had converted to Islam and intermarried with some Arabs and Africans, were the darker-skinned Black Moors. The Black Moors produced the majority of the region's Marabouts: holy men who taught Islam. But for the most part, the Black Moors were slaves.

By the seventeenth century, things had pretty much settled down into this pattern. Mauritania wasn't really thought of as a country at this point: there was no capital or even a large town. The Moors pursued a nomadic lifestyle, wandering around the Sahara desert. The White Moors rode on the camels, while the Black Moors carried the bags.

Then the Europeans started coming. There had been some

trade with Europe as far back as the fifteenth century, but in 1814, Mauritania came under the direct rule of France.

During the colonial period, the population remained nomadic, while some black Africans, whose ancestors had been chucked out by the Moors centuries before, began to trickle back into southern Mauritania. And the place still wasn't regarded as a country: Mauritania and what became Senegal to the south were both administered from the coastal town of St. Louis.

By the twentieth century, the French had banned slavery: 'banned' meaning they signed a piece of paper saying they didn't approve of it. But they did exactly nothing to curtail the practice.

After the Second World War, there was the usual clamour for independence. Limited self-rule for the region came in 1957, following by full independence in 1960.

The French, however, weren't about to completely relinquish their grip on the area. Fearing that a large west African state would be too powerful, they carved it up into a number of smaller countries: Mauritania, Mali, Senegal, which would all be still somewhat dependent on their old colonial master. France also knew that Morocco claimed Mauritania as part of its territory. Senegal's capital was transferred from St. Louis to Dakar. Mauritania's capital was transferred from St. Louis to the middle of nowhere.

Nouakchott had the Atlantic Ocean on one side and the desert on the other. There was no infrastructure, not many buildings, no electricity. Not even a water supply. The Mauritanian government had to build their capital from scratch. The French waved goodbye, happy in the knowledge that they had bequeathed the Mauritanians not only a possible war with Morocco, but an ethnic time-bomb within Mauritania itself. Gee, thanks.

The new rulers were the Mauritanian People's Party.

Mokhtar Ould Daddah, a French educated lawyer, became President. Obviously, there was a lot to do: 90 per cent of the population was still nomadic. There were no roads, not much of a health service or electricity and there was a capital city to be built. However, most pressing was the need to turn Mauritania into a one-party state. Given that most of the population was wandering the desert and didn't even know it had happened, this was pretty easy to accomplish.

Then Daddah had a good hard look at his people. And it seemed like he had inherited something of a mess. The traditional Moor slave system was still in place and, having operated for hundreds of years, was deeply engrained in the culture. There were Black Moors whose ancestors had been slaves for generations and knew no other way of life. Under Islamic law, slaveholders are required to free their slaves by the fifth generation, (isn't that nice of them), yet many of those who had been freed – known as Harratin – remained with their masters. They had no place else to go.

However, this wasn't what bothered Daddah. He was far more exercised by the numbers of black Africans, mostly from the Haalpulaar, Soninke, and Wolof tribes, who had drifted back into southern Mauritania, where they operated small farms. The population of the country was now pretty much equally divided in three between White Moors, Black Moors and Black Africans. And most Moors shared this concern. The Black Moors might be treated as subhuman by their White Moor masters, but the Black Moors despised the Africans.

Daddah's response was a vigorous programme of Arabisation. He pulled out of the African Union and joined the Arab League. In schools, all children were required to learn Arabic and French; towns and regions were given Arab names. The Mauritanian People's Party published a paper declaring that 'Arabisation of Mauritania is a long-term objective that will lead to the full rehabilitation of our Arabic language and our culture'.

Naturally, the African population weren't too thrilled about this. There were protests and riots, so Daddah sent the army to have a chat with them. To this day, sections of the Mauritanian army, mostly made up of Black Moors – essentially slave soldiers – patrol large parts of southern Mauritania. There is an on-going policy of evicting African farmers and expelling them from the country. In reward for this work, Black Moors are often given the land of the Africans they evict. Arab immigrants are welcomed with open arms.

As for the slavery, Daddah had no problem with it: he kept several dozen of them in his Presidential Palace.

And things weren't too fantastic on the foreign policy front either. Senegal was kicking up over the way black Africans were being treated, while – just as France had planned – Morocco was also getting shirty, claiming Mauritania as its own

Luckily, neither country was too keen to fight a war over the issue, so in 1975 Daddah, who was a wily old dog, finally managed to broker a deal with the Moroccans. Not only did he talk them into recognising the independence of his country, but they also agreed to share between them a slice of the Sahara just about to be relinquished by Spain.

Clever, but also quite dumb: neither country seemed to consider that the inhabitants of this part of Africa – now known as Western Sahara – might have their own ideas. Which indeed they did. Polisario Front rebels, armed by neighbouring Algeria, launched a bitter guerrilla war against Mauritania, during which they even managed to attack Nouakchott a couple of times.

Suddenly, Daddah didn't seem so clever any more. Much of the Moor population weren't particularly keen to fight the West Saharan rebels, with whom they held a common ancestry, while the African population – drafted in large numbers to fight this war – felt it had nothing to do with them. On top of that, the country was nearly bankrupt, mostly due to spending on the army which had increased from 2 000 to 18 000 men in just two years, while foreign debt had almost quadrupled: in June 1978 it had to borrow money from a local bank to pay civil servants.

The unrest grew so bad that 9 000 Moroccan troops entered the country to prop up Daddah's regime – a move which many Mauritanians saw as little more than an occupation.

So in July 1978 – backed by the then Army Chief of Staff Ould Taya – Daddah was overthrown. Colonel Mustapha Ould Salack was installed as president of the Committee for National Recovery. (Because of close family and tribal ties, most Moors have the word 'Ould' in their names.)

Daddah was held for a year by the military, then eventually allowed to travel to France for medical treatment. In his absence he was sentenced to hard labour for life, for treason, violation of the constitution and undermining national economic interests. He spent the next 22 years in Paris, living in a flat bought for him by the French president, Giscard d'Estaing. Poor old Daddah was penniless. However, he was allowed to return home in 2001. He died two years later.

Not long after the coup, Mauritania withdrew from Western Sahara. The Moroccans were not too thrilled, as this meant they now had to fight rebels – and control all of Western Sahara – by themselves. To this day, the legal status of the territory has still not been agreed.

So what did the new president do? Well, not very much. It's confused and confusing.

So here we go:

Salack attempted to set up a 70-member national council to prepare the country for a return to civilian rule, but, as usual, it contained just ten seats for Black Moors and Africans, who refused to cooperate.

So Salack was overthrown by Mohamed Mahmoud Ould Louly. The Committee for National Recovery became the Military Committee for National Salvation.

Lieutenant-Colonel Ahmed Ould Bouceif was Vice-President and Prime Minister, but two months later, Bouceif was killed in a plane crash. He was then replaced by Colonel Khouna Ould Haidallah.

In 1980, Haidallah ousted Louly as President of the Committee.

That year, Haidallah cobbled together a civilian government with limited powers. However, just a few months later there was an attempted coup by an opposition group, the Alliance for a Democratic Mauritania They had been supported by Morocco. Diplomatic relations with Morocco were broken off.

So the following month – April 1981 – they went back to Plan B with military rule. However, less than a year had gone by when another coup attempt was discovered: this time involving ex-President Saleck; the one we started with.

And this is a simplified version of events: reshuffles, palace coups and attempted coups became so routine that some overseas Mauritanian diplomats stopped writing the names of presidents or ministers in their reports home – that person would most likely have lost their job by the time the report reached them.

Part of the reason for the coups against Haidallah – apart from simple greed for power – was that he was relatively liberal: in fact, he was a bit of an Arab-lefty in the mould of Mu`ammar al-Qadhafi. (See *Libya*.) He introduced educational reforms which allowed African languages to be taught in schools, and set up the grand-sounding Structure for the Education of the Masses or SEMs: basically a series of local committees (based on the Libyan Popular Committees) which would be used to carry out local improvement projects, fight illiteracy and to discuss grievances.

Most significantly, he banned slavery in 1981. The term for slave, *Abd*, was replaced with *hartani,* meaning freed man. Black Moors now refer to themselves as Harratin.

Of course, saying it and doing it are quite different. There were now distinct murmurs of discontent from the Black Moors, but to really end slavery would involve forcibly parting the White Moors from their 'possessions'; it would involve education and training: giving the Harratin somewhere to go and something to do. (And this is still the situation today. Out of the 100 000 figure quoted earlier, the majority are 'part-slaves': technically free, yet still in servitude to White Moor masters.)

If that was Haidallah's plan, he didn't have much of a chance to carry it out. In 1984, he was overthrown by Colonel Maaouya Ould Sid'Ahmed Taya, our current despot.

Yes, it took a while to get to him, but it is this background of racism and oppression which informs all politics in Mauritania. Taya seized power ostensibly to end corruption and pave the way for democracy, but in reality it was to re-launch the Arabisation of the country. Many speculate that he was gently encouraged by the French, who didn't like the look of Haidallah. (Taya had met François Mitterand only months before.) And given that all the other colonials had had a go at running the place, it was probably his turn.

A quiet-spoken man who did his military training in France, Taya had no intention of forging better links with his African neighbours. He already had a new friend: Saddam Hussein. While waiting to take over power, Taya and several of his cronies had formed strong links with Saddam's Ba'ath Party, who happily supplied Mauritania with military aid. In retrospect, it was a bit of a dumb move.

At the time, Taya was probably too busy oppressing Mauritania's African population to give it much thought. In 1985, he jailed over 100 black intellectuals who had prepared a manifesto calling for civil rights. In 1987, he carried out a purge of the Army, removing most of the African army officers and executing three of them.

However, it was in 1989 that things got really exciting. Widespread demonstrations by black Africans turned into riots, followed by a pogrom against the Africans. They were organised through the local committees established by Taya's predecessor, Haidallah. (The SEMs were now little more than a tool for spying on the population.) When it was over, at least 1 000 Africans had been killed, while tens of thousands were expelled from the country, mostly into Senegal, where there are now over 200 refugee camps. Senegal and Mauritania broke diplomatic relations.

The following year 4 000 Africans were detained without trial. Just under 500 of them died in custody. Shortly afterwards, Taya declared: "Mauritania cannot be in the process of Arabisation as it is already an Arab country."

As far as the regime was officially concerned, there was no ethnic problem, apart from a few African 'criminals'. There was no slavery either. It had been banned, and that was that. Yet in 1989, a visiting Kuwaiti journalist reported in *al Wattan*: "At the end of my last visit to Mauritania, among the gifts given to me by my Arab friends – which I strongly refused – was a black slave". The following year the human rights group Africa Watch reported: "Our criticism is not that the Mauritanian government has tried to eradicate slavery and failed, but that it has not tried at all."

But the world was a bit distracted around then. Taya's best bud Saddam Hussein thought it would be a really spiffing idea to invade Kuwait. Again, Mauritania voiced its support, much to the displeasure of many other Arab and Western powers. When Saddam came second in that little dispute, it may have occurred to Taya that he had backed the wrong political horse.

Meanwhile, he attempted to woo the folks at home. He decided to have a go at this democracy lark. In 1991, he introduced a new constitution. There would be a president, a prime minister and an elected assembly. The president would run for a six-year term and have the power to appoint the PM and dissolve the parliament.

The constitution stated that Mauritania is an Islamic, Arab and African Republic whose national languages were Arabic, Fulani, Soninke and Wolof: parity of esteem for the country's three main groups. It also guaranteed freedom of the press. However, a separate Press Law passed that year gave Taya the power to seize any publications which negatively reported on the government: a power he uses on a regular basis. In Mauritania, there is no freedom of the press.

Taya also declined the offer of consulting with any opposition groups before preparing the constitution, claiming that 'these are merely brawlers, exiled and jobless, who publish and distribute leaflets'.

Nonetheless, he did legalise opposition parties. Well, sort of. They were forbidden to be organised on racial or regional lines, or to be 'opposed to Islam'. As it turned out, whenever a party looks like presenting a significant threat to Taya, he bans it: usually due to involvement in 'terrorist activities'.

The following year, 1992, Mauritania saw its first presidential elections. Not to be seen to be too greedy, Taya helped himself to just 65 per cent of the vote. In the parliamentary elections, non-white Moors won just 11 of the 79 seats on offer, despite the fact that they made up around 70 per cent of the population.

German observers said the whole thing was rigged.

Almost as if to confirm this, Taya, handed out 17 of the 20 cabinet seats to White Moors. The Blacks got Sport, Transport and Public Works. All the important posts

But what you gonna do? For a lot of people in Mauritania, even this sham-democracy was probably better than what went on before. And Taya made some improvements. He built a few roads (mostly through White Moor areas), he tried to do something about the teeming slums around the capital. But not too much: as the country's economy stabilised, it was the White 'Bidan' Moors who benefited: through state jobs and lucrative contracts. For everyone else, things remained pretty much as they had before. Violent protests over a rise in the price of bread in 1995 were met with arrests. (To date, Taya has managed to arrest more opposition figures than all the other Mauritanian leaders put together.)

Not that there was much foreign capital pouring into Mauritania anyway: thanks to his support for Saddam, most western countries didn't want to know, while thanks to his racist policies, most African nations ignored him: out of the 47 black African nations, only three have embassies in Nouakchott.

And the slavery continued. Members of a newly formed anti-slavery group, SOS-Slavery were occasionally jailed for speaking out. The US – not too keen on Taya anyway – finally placed a ban on all military and economic aid to Mauritania until something was done. Internationally, Taya was isolated. Apart from the good old French, of course. In September 1997, President Jacques Chirac visited Nouakchott and is reported to have described Mauritania as a 'good example of democracy working in Africa'. The same year, Taya publicly denounced the work of anti-slavery activists.

Certain that the vast majority of Mauritanians agreed with these sentiments, he held another presidential election in late 1997. There were four other candidates, yet despite this Taya romped home with 90 per cent of the vote – proof indeed that slaves like being slaves. Naturally, the opposition groups claimed the whole thing was fixed, but you can't please everyone.

Anyway, Taya had more important concerns. He sorely needed to win some friends and influence some people overseas. So he changed his mind. In a policy reversal of truly acrobatic proportions, he broke off relations with Iraq and established full diplomatic ties with the great Zionist enemy: Israel. Mauritania is only the third Arab League country to do this.

As a piece of international sucking up, it was both obvious and effective. Gradually a thaw has come about: in 2001, Taya signed a €70 million a year deal to allow European Union fishing boats into Mauritanian waters. It has devastated the local fishing industry – which makes up about ten per cent of the Mauritanian economy – but at least it got some lolly into the national coffers, most of which was used to service crippling foreign debts. After September 11th, Taya made all the right noises, and is now enjoying the benefits of a $100m US plan to bolster his border controls; all part of the 'War on Terror'. The previous ban, aimed at ending slavery, is now forgotten.

So too is the abysmal condition of the vast majority of Mauritanians. Mauritania is one of the world's thirty poorest nations. Half the population live below the poverty line, with an average yearly income of around $300. Life expectancy is just 52 years. Only thirty-three per cent have access to sanitation and clean water. Literacy among women is thirty-two per cent. The ratio of doctors to the population is seven to *ten thousand*. In 2002, a drought brought the threat of famine. The World Food Programme has launched a massive aid scheme.

Meanwhile, in Nouakchott, the Bidan Moors cruise in their four-wheel drives and shake their jewellery at each other. Soldiers loyal to the president enjoy salaries of $100 a month. Government employees get regular pay rises.

Yet despite all this, it is the switch in foreign policy which might be Taya's downfall. The élite Bidan Moors are Arabs after all, and weren't entirely over the moon when the president decided to throw in his lot with Israel.

In June 2003, that displeasure was finally expressed when a real-live coup erupted in Nouakchott. Led, as all Mauritanian coups are, by an Army Colonel, Saleh Ould Hanena, it went on for about a day and a half. The presidential palace was shelled and the state radio station captured. For a while Taya himself had to go into hiding.

But eventually the rebels were crushed. Thirty-two Islamic leaders were arrested, along with a number of government officials (including the head of the Supreme Court) and 129 soldiers.

However, Saleh Ould Hanena was not captured. He later appeared on Al-Jazeera TV and threatened that he would 'open the gates of hell' if Taya didn't run a clean presidential election, scheduled for the following November.

As if: in the November poll, there were six candidates. One was a Black Moor. None were African. Taya received a rather surprising 66.7 per cent of the poll. It was particularly surprising to the BBC correspondent in the southern town of Selibaby. He heard the result over the radio while watching votes still being counted.

The following morning, energised by a new democratic

mandate, Taya announced yet another pay rise for government employees and then decided to arrest a few people. And top of his list was the man who had come second in the poll with 19 per cent: Khouna Ould Haidallah.

You remember him: he was the guy who banned slavery in 1981 and let them teach African languages in schools; the guy Taya ousted in the 1984 coup. With a completely straight face, Taya claimed he arrested him because Haidallah was now planning to do the same thing.

Perhaps he was. Certainly, Taya is starting to act like he's a bit worried. Suddenly he's starting to stress how Mauritania is an Islamic, rather than Arab, state. After the presidential election, he announced that his new Prime Minister was Sghair Ould M'Barek, a 49-year-old lawyer – and a Black Moor. He's even started talking again to neighbouring Senegal and Mali about repatriating the estimated 200 000 Africans he expelled.

It's quite likely that there are many more in the country who would like to see Taya go over his pro-western stance, while there are other potential leaders who might now be regarding Mauritania as a juicy little prize. In 2001, an Australian company found oil off the coast. They hope to start production by 2005. In international terms, it's not a huge find, but it could be worth $100 million a year to the Mauritanian government. Or whatever despot happens to be in charge at the time.

Of the long list of people who would like Ould Taya's job, there are, alas, few who want it for the right reasons. And Cheikhna Ould Beilil still won't be able to release his wife and children from their slavery, because it doesn't exist.

SENIOR GENERAL THAN SHWE, CHAIRMAN OF
THE STATE PEACE AND DEVELOPMENT COUNCIL
of The Union of Myanmar

It has been described as a Fascist Disneyland. All you need to know at this stage is that the history of Myanmar is a bit like a soap-opera, involving love, mysticism, madness, corruption, power and a sizable cast of characters.

Oh yes: and the fact that Myanmar used to be called Burma. You've got India on one side, China on the other, Laos and Thailand below. It's a Buddhist country. Most of the population are Burmese, with ancient links to the Chinese and Tibetans, though there are other ethnic groups in Myanmar, none of whom have had it easy. We'll get to that.

There have been kingdoms of one sort or another in the region since the fifth century, but let's not hang around there: in 1886, the British took full control of the country and named it Burma. You've seen the Merchant-Ivory films: white linen suits, perspiring Brits knocking back the gin and tonics, serene Burmese people.

Spin forward now to the 1930s and we meet our first two important characters: Shu Mang – meaning Apple of

One's Eye – (though he will change his name later; prepare to be confused), and Aung San, both members of Dobama Asiayone: the We Burma Association. The former a soldier, the latter a politician. The latter a legendary figure in Burmese politics, the former a total nutcase.

Of course, at the time they were just two young men agitating for Burmese independence: Aung San was already well-known as the leader of the independence movement. The campaigning had had some success – limited self-government was granted in 1937 – but what the nationalists wanted was a Burma completely free of colonial influence.

And an opportunity to achieve this arose in the form of World War II: one way to get rid of the Brits might be to throw in Burma's lot with the Japanese. Aung San, already wanted by the British authorities, left the country, eventually making his way to Tokyo.

In 1941, Aung San, Shu Mang and twenty-eight other nationalists – a group which became known as the Thirty Comrades – began their military training in Japan. Shu Mang changed his name to Ne Win, which means Brilliant as the Sun. Name-changing was all the rage at the time.

When the training was complete, the Thirty Comrades – now calling themselves the Burma Independence Army (told you about the name-changing) – returned to Burma, recruited more members and effectively acted as an advance force for the invading Japanese Army.

And very effective they were too. By early 1942, the British had been kicked out and the Japanese had established an administration. Aung San was made Minister for War while the re-named Ne Win became a General and Chief-of-Staff of the renamed-yet-again Burmese National Army.

But things change: especially when you start to realise that your Japanese liberators might not be too keen to vacate the country once the war is over; especially if the liberators might be on the losing side. So Aung San and his colleagues decided to switch sides. In 1945 he formed the Anti-Fascist People's Freedom League (AFPFL) and helped the Brits drive the Japs out of Burma. Just after the Japanese lost the capital, Rangoon, Colonel Ne Win made a national radio broadcast. "The Burmese Army is not only the hope of the country, but its very life and soul," he declared. That was going to become weirdly true.

Of course, there was a price for this switch of allegiance: Aung San wanted independence for his country, and in fairness to them, the British didn't welsh on the deal. In 1947, the AFPFL won an overwhelming majority in the Burmese Constitutional Assembly. It was a happy ending.

But some people hate happy endings. Some people knew that without the charismatic Aung San at the helm, Burma could descend into inter-ethnic conflict. Although two-thirds of the population are Burmese, there are several other indigenous minorities, each with their own language and culture: the Karen, the Shan, the Mon, the Chin and the Kachin.

So on July 19, 1947, Aung San and eight other members of his new cabinet were assassinated. Who did it? No one knows for sure. But it probably wasn't the British: it was probably the person who might have regarded Aung San as an obstacle to his own rise to power. Someone with access to guns and assassins.

See can you guess.

Aung San was replaced as Prime Minister by U Nu: a grand chap by all accounts, but no Aung San. In jig time, both the Karen and Shan peoples were agitating to be separate from the new Burmese state, which had officially declared independence on January 4, 1948. U Nu was finding it increasingly difficult to cope with the conflict, and increasingly had to turn to our old pal, Ne Win, for help. Ne Win was doing well for himself in the new state: not only was he Commander-in-Chief of the Armed Forces, renamed (yet again) the Tatmadaw, he was also Deputy Prime Minister, Home Minister and Minister for Defence.

In reality, he was already the most powerful man in Burma. Poor old U Nu simply didn't know it yet.

For the next ten years, Burma was relatively stable, mostly due to the army's ability to control the rebels. The economy grew. But in 1958, things started to look a little shaky again. Ne Win, possibly bored now with just being a soldier, led a split in the ruling AFPFL and set up his own group, the Burmese Socialist Party. Ethnic tensions re-emerged, so badly this time that Ne Win briefly formed a temporary military government.

In 1960 there were fresh elections. U Nu's AFPFL was returned to power. But Ne Win didn't like the look of this government: mostly because the Burmese Socialist Party wasn't part of it. The Shan and Kachin tribes both attempted fresh rebellions, and once Ne Win had crushed them, he had a rebellion of his own.

In early 1962, U Nu and most of the government were arrested. Parliament was dissolved and the constitution suspended. All opposition parties and independent media were closed down. A Revolutionary Council was established to rule the country.

It was the bog-standard communist revolution stuff. The economy was centralised and all private enterprise handed over to the state. Opposition was crushed. Ne Win made pals with Communist China and with the Khmer Rouge, the mass-murderers then ruling Cambodia.

In 1974, power was transferred from the Revolutionary Council to a single-party (the Burma Socialist Programme Party) People's Assembly. Ne Win resigned his military post and became President and Prime Minister. And there were more name changes: now it was the Socialist Republic of the Union of Burma.

The stony-broke Socialist Republic of the Union of Burma. Ten years of centralised economics had devastated the economy. Corruption and black-marketeering extended to all sections of the government. Burma was now one of the ten poorest nations on earth. The Ministry of Planning and Finance, tasked with seeking international economic aid, was in private known as the Ministry of Begging.

But it seems as if Ne Win didn't like being president very much. Just six years later, in 1981, he resigned the job. It was a surprise to the outside world, though what the outside world probably didn't realise was that while Ne Win may have given up the job, he certainly hadn't relinquished any power: he personally appointed his replacements as president and prime minister, while hanging on to his role as chairman of the Burma Socialist Programme Party. Burmese politics is a strange animal, depending more on patronage and personal loyalties than on titles or the results of elections. (*Definitely* not on the result of elections – we'll get to that.) For the next twenty years, nothing happened in government without Ne Win giving it the thumbs up: especially the appointment and purging of senior military officers, both of which happened on a regular basis.

Ne Win stayed in his palatial lakeside home and listened out for signs of dissent or disloyalty. He took an interest in numerology and Buddhist mysticism. He took policy advice from astrologers. Slowly, he became as crazy as a loon.

The first public manifestation of this came in 1988. Now convinced that nine was the best number out of any of them, he ordered that all bank notes be withdrawn from circulation – and be replaced with notes in multiples of nine.

Suddenly, people had to deal with nine-kyat and forty-five-kyat notes. The move caused rocketing inflation and riots.

A few months later, Ne Win also decided to step down as the head of the Burma Socialist Programme Party, though naturally he continued to wield total power. Appropriately, his replacement, Sein Lwin, was previously head of the riot police.

During the summer of 1988, the riots continued, building to a near insurrection in August. Universities were closed and remained so for the next two years. Around 3 000 demonstrators in the capital, Rangoon, were killed when the military fired on them.

And amidst all this turmoil, we now meet the third character in our soap. She is a young Burmese woman by the name of Aung San Suu Kyi: the daughter of Aung San, the assassinated independence leader.

Her name alone was enough to attract a following, but on top of that Suu Kyi was smart as a whip, with a family background in politics. She had lived with her mother – Burmese ambassador to India – before studying at St. Hugh's College, Oxford. Afterwards, she worked at the UN where she met her husband, Michael Aris, a PhD student in Tibetan Studies who later became an Oxford don. They had two children. She is also charismatic, beautiful and profoundly committed to the cause of democracy. In a letter to her husband, shortly before they married, she wrote: "I ask only one thing, that should my people need me, you would help me to do my duty by them." Later on, he did just that.

In August of 1988 Suu Kyi addressed a rally in Rangoon attended by half a million people.

The People's Assembly were now getting seriously worried, so there was nothing else for it: following a few phone calls from Ne Win, there was yet another military coup. Saw Maung, another of Ne Win's boys, established a

State Law and Order Restoration Council, composed of twenty-one military officers. The new SLORC (you just know it's going to change its name, don't you?) promised that once things calmed down, it would hold free and fair elections.

The opposition called itself the National League for Democracy and appointed Suu Kyi as General Secretary.

Hang on: free and fair elections? Is this a hard-line communist state suddenly giving in? Well, things were getting a bit hairy, so Ne Win was cunning enough to know he had to be seen to make some sort of concession. In the meantime, there was name-changing to be getting on with: in 1989, the country became the Union of Myanmar. (An attempt to include the non-Burmese populations.) The capital Rangoon became Yangon.

And there was arresting to do: in July 1989 Suu Kyi was placed under house arrest for 'endangering the state'. Under the catch-all military laws, she could be held for up to three years without charge or trial.

There was also all this ethnic nonsense to clear up: each tribal province was declared a military zone, in which the population was forcibly relocated to fenced compounds. It is estimated that 10 000 civilians have died *every year* since this decision was taken.

Finally, the economy to sort out. The answer? Force hundreds of thousands of people into slave labour, known officially as 'People's Contributions', mainly for construction projects. And as an extra little boost to the nation's coffers, the SLORC made peace with the United Wa State Army, the insurgent group representing the Shan tribe. This not only allowed the Wa State Army to rule their region with autonomy, but also enabled the unhindered wide-scale production of opium poppies for export. In addition to being the world's largest exporter of teak – a business which was devastating Burma's forests – it quickly became the world's largest producer of opium poppies. In effect, the government of Myanmar are international drug dealers.

And if you don't like drugs, there's always women. Criminal gangs based in the border regions also operate a large export business, kidnapping women and girls to work as prostitutes in Thailand. They are usually from the ethnic minorities, so the Burmese Government doesn't really care.

It was a busy year. And with the country now in such a terrific condition, definitely time to hold those free and fair elections. They took place in 1990.

Yet here is the thing: many despotic regimes stage elections, yet few of them think they will really win. Instead, they cheat: they exclude opposition candidates, they stuff ballot boxes, forge electoral roles. Yet bizarrely, the SLORC didn't do any of those things: they *actually had free and fair elections*.

Suu Kyi was still under house arrest. The state-controlled press called her a 'foreign stooge' and a 'genocidal prostitute'.

Her party, the NLD, won 82 per cent of the vote.

It would have been truly embarrassing, except that Ne Win and the SLORC were unembarrassable. They simply ignored the result, arguing that it couldn't hand over power until a new constitution was agreed. And to move this process along, they revoked Suu Kyi's rights to visits from her immediately family.

Another dumb move. Think about it: Suu Kyi is the daughter of a former leader, back to liberate her country. She's married to an Oxford professor, she's beautiful, she's committed, she advocates non-violence . . . it already read like a movie script. She was Burma's Gandhi. The western press jumped all over it like kids on a bouncy castle. The UN called for her release. The EU slapped an arms embargo on Myanmar.

In 1991, she was awarded the Nobel Peace Prize.

It was enough to put the regime under pressure, most of which rolled back onto Saw Maung, the head of the SLORC. Suddenly, he started to look decidedly dodgy. During public appearances he would slur his words and ramble incoherently. He claimed he was the reincarnation of an ancient Burmese king. In full view of the world, Saw Maung was having a major nervous breakdown.

In Myanmar, the treatment for such mental illness is the same as the treatment for everything else: have a military coup. In early 1992, after the usual meeting with Ne Win, two of his protégés, Than Shwe and Khin Nyunt were dispatched to take over. Than Shwe replaced the now-howling Saw Maung as Prime Minister, Commander-in-Chief and Chairman of the SLORC.

Here he is at last: our despot. Senior General Than Shwe is a short, portly man who likes to play golf. He was born in 1933, joined the army in 1953 and held various ranks, including one stint in the Psychological Warfare Department. Although a sullen, slow-moving individual, he rose quickly through the army ranks and quickly gained a reputation as someone vehemently opposed to reform.

Than Shwe is a guy who lives the communist dream. People who know describe him as modest and eerily calm, and not all that gone on the trappings of power. While a senior military officer he liked to travel in an army truck rather than the sedans which the other Generals favoured. His wife, Daw Kyaing Kyaing, is prone to distributing presents to soldiers and aides. They have seven children

He doesn't drink or smoke, he can speak English, reads *Time* magazine and has a habit of chewing betel, a local nut which provides a mild buzz. Not that Than is a buzzy guy. Truth is, he's dull. He can blather for hours and say nothing. He gets excited about building dams and organising agriculture projects, and apparently hasn't much of a sense of humour: senior officers have been fired for making jokes in his presence. No: none of your flash-Harry stuff from Than, who apart from the odd public appearance at a Buddhist temple is rarely seen by his own people. An official biography of him has never been released, and in his entire political career he has only ever given one interview.

But back to the story: Than wasn't ruling Myanmar yet. Just like before, the orders came from Ne Win and Than Shwe was happy to carry them out. To try and calm things down, they let out forty political prisoners. It was a tiny concession – there were still 2 000 locked up – yet still came as a shock. Rangoon was again swept with rumours: that an earthquake in the north of the country had spooked the superstitious generals; Ne Win's astrologer had told him that unless he stopped the human rights abuses he would pass into the next life as a cockroach. Not much of a change.

In 1993 the government organised a national convention to figure out the contents of Myanmar's proposed new constitution. The convention was supposed to reflect all shades of political opinion in the country, and it did: just not in the right proportions. Over 80 per cent of the delegates were appointed by the regime. However, Than Shwe did conduct secret talks with Suu Kyi.

And they must have got on. The following year, 1995, Suu Kyi was released from house arrest but forbidden from travelling outside the capital. A step forward. Then two steps back. Exasperated, the NLD finally withdrew from the constitutional convention, arguing that the regime really had no intention of making progress. What a surprise. On March 31 1995, the convention was completely suspended.

Now that all those NLD members had nowhere to go during the day, the ruling SLORC obviously worried that they might get into trouble. So they started arresting them. Around 800 were taken into custody.

Internationally, this drew the usual response: more sanctions from the US and the EU. But Myanmar completely ignored these protests: it could afford to now. In 1997 it was admitted to the Association of South-East Asian Nations, plus there was trade with China and Indonesia. Ne Win even visited Indonesia that year, though he was disturbed when President Suharto (himself no slouch when it comes to lining his pockets) complained that the level of corruption in Myanmar was affecting his investments.

Faced with such a problem, there was no other solution: yes, you guessed it, military coup time. Once again he summoned Than Shwe, Khin Nyunt and another follower, Maung Aye, and gave them their instructions. Several members of the SLORC were arrested and charged with corruption, while the SLORC itself was dissolved and replaced with the far more new-age-sounding State Peace and Development Council. (SPDC) Once again, Than Shwe was at the helm.

Things, however, weren't so sunny for the opposition. Since the breakdown of the constitutional convention in 1995, virtually no progress had been made, while hundreds of NLD members were still stuck in jail.

And it got even more grim in 1999 when Suu Kyi learned that her husband, Michael Aris, had been diagnosed with terminal prostate cancer. The problem was that he wasn't in Myanmar – he was in England. Yet despite repeated requests, the regime refused to allow him to come and visit his wife before he died. Suu Kyi, however, could travel to England – but in the full knowledge that she would never be allowed to return to Myanmar.

Even for a regime which regularly employed rape, murder

and slave labour as tools of oppression, this was a staggeringly cruel position to put her in. Suu Kyi stayed where she was. Her husband died on March 27th of that year.

There were more sanctions from the US and the EU. Germany and the World Bank withdrew aid programmes

Perhaps the death of her husband had made her more reckless, but Suu Kyi got a bit more uppity now. Despite the ban on her travelling outside the capital, she made repeated attempts to do just that. Eventually, in 2000, she was placed back under house arrest.

This time, however, the UN was a bit more proactive, and organised secret talks between Suu Kyi and the regime. It has been reported that Ne Win offered to hand over power to the NLD, in return for immunity from prosecution for the military and a commitment from Suu Kyi that she give up any personal political ambition. Don't want her getting in the way like the old man did. As far as is known, these negotiations took place through high-level proxies: Suu Kyi and Ne Win never met face to face. Even still, it must have been a strange experience for her, negotiating with the man who wouldn't let her see her dying husband; who probably murdered her father.

Yet it produced results: lots of them. In 2002, the NLD were allowed to re-open their branch offices in Rangoon. Hundreds of political prisoners were released – including Suu Kyi – and allowed to travel freely throughout the country.

Even better, Ne Win, now 90, had a heart attack and had to be fitted with a pacemaker.

And then he got arrested. Or overthrown. Call it what you like. On March 7, 2002, Ne Win, his daughter, son-in-law and three grandsons were all placed under house arrest for allegedly plotting a coup. There were reports that the plan involved kidnapping Ne Win's three protégés, Khin

Nyunt, Maung Aye and Than Shwe and holding them until they agreed to reorganise the government, (though what way he wanted them to reorganise isn't clear). Among the evidence produced to back up this theory were three voodoo dolls representing the three generals. Ne Win's astrologer was also arrested.

Ne Win remained under house arrest, while his co-conspirators – along with 80 soldiers – received life imprisonment.

In December, Ne Win dropped dead. He was cremated just hours later following a small ceremony. None of the military attended.

The era of Ne Win was finally, finally over – and the era of Than Shwe just about to begin.

Up until this point there had been rampant speculation as to who, after Ne Win, had the most power. Most attention had been focused on the tensions between General Khin Nyunt – apparently, a media-loving fop – and General Maung Aye, your archetypal hard-drinking tough guy.

But after the Ne Win arrest, Than Shwe emerged as the undisputed boss. There was the usual reshuffle. Khin Nyunt, (a relative liberal), lost some influence, being effectively demoted from his number two position on the SPDC.

Than also started pursuing some of his economic priorities: specifically, the industrial development of Kyaukse, a sleepy little town which just happens to be where Than Shwe was born. So far it has got a sewing machine factory, a bicycle factory, a slippers factory, a cement factory, a Government Technological College and an airport which is barely used. Many farmers in the area had to hand over land for these developments, except for members of Than Shwe's family.

Yet despite such 'developments', Myanmar swims in gruelling poverty. It is still one of the world's poorest nations, with most of its citizens still living in woven bamboo huts, without electricity or water. In the capital, there are daily power cuts. Slave labour is still widespread; child labour is becoming increasingly common. Because of the drug trade, it is estimated than two per cent of the Burmese population are HIV positive.

What enterprises there are tend to be run by the military. They personally own most of the tourist complexes, which were built by slave labour. One famous Burmese historical site, Bagan, has been almost completely destroyed by the building of touristy villas and shopping malls. The latest project for Bagan is a $3 million hotel complex which features a viewing tower which will dwarf the few ancient pagodas which remain. The idea for the tower apparently came to Than Shwe in a dream.

The ethnic minorities have it even worse. Most of them face restrictions on their movements. They are not allowed to own land and are barred from secondary education. Many are not even given citizenship. Thanks to the effectively-legalised opium trade, they are plagued with drug addiction. Their women are kidnapped and sent to Thailand to become prostitutes. The Burmese Armed Forces can kill, beat and rape people with total impunity. And given that their misery has been ongoing for forty years, it is now virtually impossible to estimate how many of them the regime has killed or sent into exile. But each figure is probably in the millions.

Naturally, the army live in splendour. Most of the remaining British colonial mansions are occupied by generals, usually with a brand-new golf course built outside. In the two cities, Yangon and Mandalay, traffic is routinely stopped by armed guards so a general can quickly get to his lunch appointment.

As for the NLD opposition, things haven't got much

better. Suu Kyi took full advantage of her new freedom to travel and toured the country, demonstrating that her support was as widespread as when the elections were held over ten years previously. So in May 2003, following an attack on one of her rallies in which 75 of her supporters were beaten to death with iron bars, Than Shwe had her placed under house arrest again: 'for her own protection'. The following month she was moved from her home at 56 University Avenue, Rangoon to Insein Prison, where she was not allowed contact with the outside world. Other NLD leaders have been arrested or disappeared. NLD branch offices have been shut up again.

The tiny glint of hope which existed in Myanmar during the 1990s was finally extinguished. However, in August 2003, following yet another purge, Khin Nyunt was bumped back up the pecking order again and made prime minister. Slightly less hard-line than Than Shwe, he got Suu Kyi moved back to her home, where she is still under arrest, and has held tentative talks with her.

But Khin has nowhere near enough power to institute any real change. That's up to Than Shwe, who rules absolutely. Still in his sixties, there is little sign of him retiring, though he says that when he does, he will devote himself to religion. God must be thrilled.

위대한 수령 김일성동지는 영원히 우리와 함께 계신다

KIM JONG II GENERAL SECRETARY OF THE KOREAN WORKERS' PARTY

of the Democratic People's Republic of Korea

Well, we all know North Korea, don't we? These are the guys the Yanks are *really* worried about when it comes to weapons of mass destruction. And not because North Korea has so many of them: it's because they might just be crazy enough to use them.

Or perhaps that's what they want us to think. The North Koreans are tricky to figure out. We've already met most of the remaining hard-line communist states, and North Korea is like a lot of them, but with its own distinct flavour: a dash of religiosity here, a sprinkling of cult brain-washing there. In North Korea, citizens aren't expected to serve the state: they are expected to *worship* it. By law, every day, every citizen is expected to wear a lapel pin depicting Kim Jong Il or his daddy, Kim Il Sung.

Royalty goes back a long way in Korea, where there has been a kingdom since at least the 11th century BC. China has invaded and retreated over the years, leaving behind a distinct cultural influence: Confucianism was made the official religion in the 1400s. Yet despite this occasional interference, Korea did well for itself. It established healthy trade links and was the first country in the world to use metal warships. And it was damned if it was going to become yet another European colony: when Christianity arrived in the 1800s the royal family were quick to suppress it.

But while trying to resist the West, it succumbed to the East. In 1910, Japan assassinated the Korean queen, then invaded and annexed the country. They remained in control right until the end of World War Two. It wasn't a happy time: Korean men were used as cannon fodder and Korean women as sex slaves. Understandably, Koreans, north and south, still aint too crazy about the Japanese.

(They aint too crazy about the Korean royal family either. The Yi Dynasty ruled the country for over 500 years before the Japs arrived. Most Koreans blame their incompetence and in-fighting for the ease with which the Japanese took over. Today, a few members of the Yi family survive, but without any trappings of power. One prince, a former singer (self-described as a cross between Pat Boone and Andy Williams) lives in the back of a van in Seoul).

When the war ended, there was the usual scramble for territory: the US took over the southern half of Korea and the Soviet Union took the north: dividing the country along cold war lines at the famous 38th parallel.

But in 1950 – thinking the US wasn't too pushed about it – North Korea invaded the South. A US-led, UN sanctioned force drove the North Koreans back to the 38th parallel. The success gave US forces chief General MacArthur a rush of blood to the head: he wanted to keep going into the North – possibly into China as well. But he was fired by President Truman just in time to prevent World War Three. Korea has remained divided ever since.

North Korea likes to think of itself as a unique place. And it is: it is the only country on the planet with a dead head of state. Kim Il Sung, the father of our despot, was appointed President in perpetuity. This happened in 1998, four years after he died. It is one of the many ways in which the short, fat Kim Senior and Junior (Dad is the *Great Leader*, son is the *Dear Leader*) have been portrayed as mystical, even religious figures to the Korean public. Unlike a lot of communist countries, religion (mostly Buddhism and Confucianism) is permitted, even encouraged here, while also being strictly controlled by the regime. There's God, and there's the Kims. And in North Korea, they are pretty much the same thing.

So: Daddy Kim. His family emigrated to Manchuria when he was a child, where Kim Senior became a founding member of the Communist Youth League. In 1930 he set up the Korean Revolutionary Army and spent the next ten years engaged in a guerrilla war to get rid of the Japanese. After the Japs put a price on his head, he fled to Soviet Union. There, he joined the Soviet Army.

When it was over, he returned with his family, Soviet backing and the personal money-back guarantee of Soviet dictator, Josef Stalin. The Democratic People's Republic of Korea was open for business, and was run according to a philosophy developed by Kim. It was called *Juche*, or self-reliance, and helped North Korea to become one of the most insular nations on earth.

As we already know, he passed away in 1994, apparently from a heart attack. According to one official government account, the attack was brought on by 'heavy mental strains'.

Still: he wasn't so strained mentally that he didn't know who would inherit the family business. In fact, *everyone* in North Korea knew: again, as part of this royalty-mystic-communist arrangement, Kim Junior was the only choice as leader, having been officially designated as such since 1980.

Kim Jong-il was born in Siberia in 1941 during Dad's period of exile in the former Soviet Union.

However, most North Koreans don't know this. What they have been taught is that Kim Jong Il emerged into the world in a modest log cabin atop North Korea's highest mountain: well, you couldn't have the *Dear Leader* being born in a foreign country. The log cabin, supposedly, was part of Daddy's guerrilla base.

But don't let the modest surroundings throw you. After all, wasn't Jesus born in a stable? And didn't a star appear at the moment of his birth?

Well, that's nothing. According to the official account, when Kim Jong Il popped out, a bright star *and* a *double* rainbow appeared in the sky. How a star could be seen during the day, or a rainbow at night, isn't explained.

Kim Jong Il was – and still is – a pampered brat. Yet there were some hardships: he lost a younger brother to a drowning accident, while his mother died when he was just seven years old. Shortly afterwards, in 1950, the Korean War broke out and he was sent to Manchuria, returning three years later when it ended. He studied politics (what else) at Kim Il Sung University (where else), and afterwards daddy fixed him up with a job in the party's propaganda department.

In his early days, Kim was a bit of a party animal, and something of a worry to Party bosses. But that all changed in 1980, when Kim Il Sung was formally designated as successor. He was given senior posts in the Politburo, the Military Commission and the Party Secretariat, while the great North Korean spin machine went flat-out to create a personality cult around him: the *Great Leader/Dear Leader* titles were introduced at this time, though since then, Kim

Junior has picked up a few more: *Heaven-sent Great General, World-renowned Literary Man, Guardian of Our Planet, Illustrious General of All Illustrious Generals, The Saint of All Saints, The Lodestar of the 21st Century, Philosophical Giant, Humankind's greatest genius of music, Greatest incarnation of human wisdom* and even *Present-day God.*

In total – and this is according to official sources – Kim has 1 200 different titles. Apparently, these were bestowed on him by dignitaries from 160 countries in five continents. In other words, pretty much all of them.

Today, every bookstore and library in North Korea stocks virtually nothing but pseudo-religious tracts about the two Kims. All public art consists of worshipful images of the two human deities, and when it isn't them, it's pictures of the holy Mount Paekdu – where Kim junior was 'born' and the rainbow/star miracle took place.

In 2003, to celebrate *Dear Leader's* 62nd birthday, (February 16th, if you want to send a card) the citizens of North Korea were treated to months of gushing tributes in the state press, in which young Kim was repeatedly referred to as the 'Sun of the 21st Century'. The official Korean news agency claimed that more than 50 countries had established committees to prepare for the birthday celebrations, set to go on for six months. Must have missed that one. (The Chinese, however, did give him a bottling plant. Thoughtful.)

When Kim Junior came to power, the President's job was already gone, so he took the titles of General Secretary of the Korean Workers' Party and Chairman of the National Defence Commission: a group of 10 men which includes the heads of the air force, army and navy; basically, the ten most powerful people in the country.

There was a settling-in period, of course: being late for

SEAN MONCRIEFF

work, forgetting to make phone calls, forgetting to have people killed; the usual stuff. Kim Jong-il took a few years to establish himself, but eventually he made his dead father proud, building a reputation for being completely ruthless. Over time, he developed a system of micro-managing every aspect of government business. Every day, a report of developments from all over North Korea is brought to his attention: even local authorities must report directly to *Dear Leader* if the issue is deemed serious enough. It's a system born out of paranoia as much as anything else: suspecting potential traitors everywhere, Kim wants to know about everyone.

Apart from crushing his own people, he's been suspected of a few pops at the South Koreans too: in 1983, a bomb killed 17 South Korean officials – including four cabinet members. Somewhat appropriately, they were all on a visit to Rangoon at the time. (See *Myanmar* to find out why.)

In 1987, another bomb killed all 115 on board a South Korean airliner.

These, however, are just suspicions – there is no direct evidence. Because Kim Junior is clever.

Actually, he's far more than that. According to official accounts, he is a *bone fide* genius: an author, film-maker, film critic and mystic. He is credited with writing six operas in two years, and with personally designing the huge *Juche* tower in the capital, Pyongyang. Naturally, he has churned out hundreds of books and theses, though there are only three known about in the West: *On the Art of Cinema*, *Kim Jong Il on the Art of Opera* and *Our Socialism Centred on the Masses Shall Not Perish*. You can buy them on the internet.

He is an accomplished jet fighter pilot, and on his first-ever game of golf, he shot eleven holes-in-one. Wow.

But even really clever blokes have their flaws, Kim Il

Jong's being that he doesn't like going out that much. He is a virtual recluse, rarely leaving his presidential palace. Perhaps he's shy, or he thinks people will laugh at his short stature: he's five foot three and wears shoes with lifts and has a huge mound of permed hair to maximise the illusion of height. It's also been claimed that Kim receives regular blood transfusions from young virgins to 'slow the ageing process': the Michael Jackson of Asian politics. Poor fella.

Still, unlike Michael Jackson, he's a dab hand with the women. His affairs with starlets, nurses, teachers – basically, anyone he fancies – have been too numerous to calculate. There are at least seven children outside the four which are officially recognised. Some of the affairs are said to have ended in suicide, while there have repeated reports of Kim arranging to have women kidnapped from abroad for use as his personal concubines.

Certainly, he does have a troupe of 100 women for his personal 'entertainment'. Known as The Pleasure Squad, they are often called upon to dance in one of Kim's many Banquet Halls, which are kitted out with elaborate sound and lighting systems. They often do it naked.

The official version is more restrained: four children by three different women. The first, Sung Hae Rim, was a North Korean movie star who lived with Kim for two decades. She was the mother of his eldest son. However Kim was terrified of revealing this relationship to his father, who wouldn't have approved. She died in exile in Moscow.

The second was Kim Young Sook, the daughter of a high-ranking military official. She was hand-picked by Kim Il Sung in the early 1970s to marry his son. She also produced a son, but they later divorced because of Kim Junior's extra-curricular activities.

The third, and current wife (though it is unclear if Kim was ever actually married to any of these women) is Ko

Young Hee, a former dancer. She has provided a son and a daughter.

The eldest son, Kim Jong-Nam, had previously been tipped as the one to take over the family dynasty. However in 2001, he was arrested in Japan for illegal entry (he had a false passport), apparently while on his way to visit Tokyo Disneyland. He has yet to return to North Korea.

Thus the youngest son, Kim Jong Chul, is now being viewed as the leader-in-waiting. To prepare the excited North Korean population for his ascension (though it will be many years away), an official campaign is now under way to glorify Chul's mother, – and the current wife – Ko.

In official documents, she is now being described as *The Esteemed Mother*, as well as being wheeled out for some official engagements. Before 2001, there was no official acknowledgement that Ko actually existed.

Kim is also known for his love of the odd tipple – he is reputed to be the world's largest buyer of Hennessy XO Cognac, and has a liquor cellar with 10 000 bottles. The cellar also has a karaoke set and a piano. This boy can party.

And then there's sports. Obviously, he's a natural at golf, but there's also jet skiing and horse riding. Kim Jong Il is an avid equestrian, and has even appeared in a TV movie atop a snow-white horse: all horses belonging to the Kim family are white.

However, the thing that pumps up Kim most of all are movies. He is an obsessive collector and owns a huge film library. Kim has founded a film school and written the aforementioned book on the art of the cinema. He is regularly quoted as saying that if he wasn't a deranged despot, he would have been a movie director. Or words to that effect.

And this is far more than a hobby: the Dear Leader takes

his flicks *very* seriously. In the opening scenes of *Die Another Day*, James Bond fights a North Korean who sells black-market nuclear weapons. When Kim witnessed this scene (in his private cinema, with various fawning government officials in attendance), he became apoplectic with rage: he grabbed a ball pen and repeatedly stabbed his Minister of Culture. He spat toward the screen, and when the movie ended made a half-hour speech about the falsity of Western propaganda.

No: Kim doesn't like propaganda. He's a bit of a softie, really. His favourites are westerns, anything with Elizabeth Taylor, *Titanic* (he was apparently so moved by Leonardo DiCaprio that he couldn't bear to see the film again) and the *Friday 13th* Series.

Indeed, so deep is Kim's commitment to the film industry that in 1978, he ordered his agents to abduct the famous South Korean movie director, Shin Sang Ok and his ex-wife, actress, Che Eun Hui. He kept them for eight years and forced them to produce propaganda films.

So while Kim hangs out with the Pleasure Squad, knocks back the cognac, gets his perms and blood transfusions and takes in a few films, what are the ordinary 22 million North Koreans doing?

Well, one thing they are not doing is changing channels. Apart from the dead president thing, North Korea is the only state on earth where television remote controls are illegal. All radio and television sets are pre-tuned to government stations which pump out a steady stream of propaganda. Foreign stations are jammed, there is no internet, and travel is forbidden. For the crime of listening to a foreign media broadcast, you'll get a few years in a labour camp.

But don't let the name fool you: in the Korean gulags they don't do that much labour. For the most part, people die. Hundreds of thousands have perished, though of course there are no exact figures: they are located in-country, away from the eyes of the few westerners allowed in. (And it is almost impossible to gain admittance: the makers of a documentary about the 1966 North Korean football team – who reached the quarter finals of the World Cup – spent *four years* negotiating to get into the country.)

It almost goes without saying that dissent of any sort is crushed: if you are viewed as an enemy of the state, then it's off to the gulags, or, if you're lucky, a quick execution. Your family and friends will be harassed and arrested also. If you flee the country, North Korean agents will attempt to hunt you down. One example: Kang Byong-sop, who in February 2004 was arrested by Chinese authorities, having fled North Korea. In all probability, Kang was handed over to Pyongyang. Several years ago, Kang's eldest son defected to Thailand. The North Korean authorities suspected Kang of leaking military secrets via the son, so they tortured Kang a bit: mostly, they dropped him on his head: *twice* breaking his back. Kang can no longer stand up straight.

But that didn't work, so they tried to kidnap the son in Thailand. Luckily, that didn't work either.

What had got Kim's secret police so excited was that Kang had documentary evidence that the North Korean regime was testing (or more precisely, killing) political prisoners with chemical and biological weapons – proof that had already been smuggled out of the country. No one knows what has happened to Kang Byong-sop.

Then again, it's tricky to say who is better off: those in prison or those outside it. A series of weather disasters, combined with the inefficient state-run agricultural system, has eroded the food supply, causing a famine in many rural areas. It has been on-going since the mid-90s. Aid agencies have estimated that up to two million people have died, not including those who were executed for stealing food. Officially, of course, the famine doesn't exist, though in recent times the regime has allowed in some limited foreign aid.

Not that everyone gets it: under Kim's 'military-first' policy (supposedly to counter the US threat), the army gets first pick on the grub. What's left is usually distributed to the most ardent supporters of the regime. Unsurprisingly, North Korea has refused to admit World Food Programme monitors.

Indeed, what seems to keep a huge number of North Koreans alive is the black market, mostly across the border into China. On the Chinese side, villages host open-air markets stuffed with contraband sourced in Korea: ginseng, dogmeat, bronzewear, timber and bear gallstones, a local delicacy. And if you're Chinese and want to buy a wife, North Korea is the place to go shopping for her. In return, the Koreans get whatever they can: food and consumer appliances.

This illegal trade is conducted quite openly, and with the tacit permission of both governments. Without it, millions of North Koreans would starve. It's also a handy bargaining chip for the Chinese. In September of 2003, following yet another unsuccessful series of talks over Kim's nuclear programme, Beijing quietly stationed 150 000 troops along the border with North Korea. The soldiers didn't do anything, but the threat was obvious: play ball, or we'll cut off your economic umbilical cord.

Yes, North Korea is surrounded with admiring friends, especially the South Koreans.

Three million people died in the Korean war so relations between the two halves aren't exactly congenial. There's lots of name-calling. Kim is a loopy dictator; the south is a US puppet.

However, things took a decided turn for the better in 2000 when South Korean President Kim Dae-jung came to visit. Kim even made a rare foray out of the house to meet him at the airport and threw on a huge welcoming ceremony. Afterwards, border liaison offices opened in the demilitarised zone between the two countries. North Korea released 3 000 political prisoners. The following year, a UN delegation visited Pyongyang to further the reconciliation process, while Kim himself even took a trip to Moscow. He travelled by land, because he hates flying: rather odd for an ace fighter pilot.

This change of tack largely came about due to the gentle encouragement of the Clinton administration. But when George W Bush took over the White House it all went belly-up.

Nuclear technology: that's the problem. If Kim didn't have the bomb, the West would happily ignore North Korea. Let 'em starve. But it's his supposed ability to nuke whitey that keeps them attentive. Not that he could do it very often: some estimates have it that he has only two warheads

During the Clinton administration the US addressed this problem by trying to charm North Korea into establishing more ties with the outside world. The then US secretary of state, Madeleine Albright, went to visit Kim and found him perfectly rational. Apparently she and Kim got on very well and they went to shows, dinners and movies. No more than that though. They are professionals.

As part of this new chumminess, Clinton offered supplies of oil and new light water nuclear reactors in return for access by inspectors to atomic facilities and a dismantling of its heavy water reactors – which produce weapons grade plutonium. North Korea agreed to suspend its heavy water nuclear programme, though it still denied that it had any nuclear weapons.

It was slow, tentative progress, but it was progress. But then Clinton finished his term, George W. Bush took over and made that speech in which he referred to Iraq, Iran and North Korea as an 'Axis of Evil'. Pyongyang claimed this was tantamount to a declaration of war. North and South Korean gunships fought a battle in the Yellow Sea. They haven't swapped Christmas cards since.

(Interesting aside: when Clinton offered the light water technology to Kim, ABB, a European engineering giant based in Zurich, won the $200 million contract to provide the design and key components for the reactors. From 1990 to 2001, one of the directors of ABB was Donald Rumsfeld, who went on to become George W. Bush's defence secretary and a fully signed-up member of the Axis of Evil Club. Funnily enough, no one can remember Donald strenuously objecting to this deal. ABB paid him around $200,000 a year.)

Not long later, the US halted the oil shipments, claiming North Korea had a secret nuclear weapons programme which was not halted. In response, Kim reactivated his Yongbyon nuclear reactor and kicked out the international inspectors. In 2003, North Korea withdrew from the Nuclear Non-Proliferation Treaty. There were last-ditch talks with US officials, during which Kim finally admitted that he did have nuclear weapons. Now he threatened to make more unless the US agreed to a 'non-aggression pact'. In other words, tonnes of cash.

George W huffed and puffed, publicly declaring that he wouldn't 'reward' North Korea for having nuclear bombs – that would only encourage other 'rogue' states. Yet privately, the White House administration was a wee bit rattled. At the international level, Kim Jong Il is notoriously difficult to deal with. He'll make agreements, then change his mind hours later. He can seem intelligent, then profoundly stupid, and it's impossible to tell if he is simply putting this on to spook the other side, or if he genuinely is a madman, prepared to let his own people starve rather than back down to the West.

When that madman has nuclear weapons – and has already expressed a willingness to do some sort of a deal – it's not really worth the risk.

So they came up with a new strategy: to gang up on North Korea. Together with China, Russia, Japan and South Korea, talks were held with a view to dismantling North Korea's nuclear threat. Many, many talks. The US offers financial aid and security guarantees. North Korea says it will freeze, but not dismantle, its nuclear weapons programme.

And thus it has remained. Some think Kim is simply holding out so as to squeeze as much as he can out of the Yanks: even he must see his people are starving. Yet it's difficult to be sure amidst all the bombast from the North Korean side.

It's also complicated by the attendance of the other countries: Russia and Japan are there because they want to be seen as international players, while South Korea's concern is obvious. However, China is at the talks not because it is worried about North Korea, but worried about the Americans. As the last large communist state, it is one of North Korea's few allies. Nonetheless, the last thing it wants is for the Yanks to get so exasperated with Kim that they decide to invade: a war which could end up with US troops on the Chinese border.

It is believed that in 2003 the Beijing government drew up a policy paper which looked at invading North Korea and bringing about a regime change. It would be a last resort for the Chinese, who normally don't do that sort of thing. But it would be better than the Americans doing it.

In a chilling counter-move, the US has withdrawn its troops from the border between North and South, the first time it has done so since the Korean war. The redeployment was clearly designed to move American soldiers out of range of any missile strikes from the north: attacks which could happen should the Yanks decide to bomb North Korea's nuclear facilities or invade. The poor old South Korean soldiers don't have that luxury.

Sadly, war might be the best the poor North Korean people might have to look forward to. Kim is still in his sixties, apparently quite healthy, no doubt thanks to all that virgin blood, and seemingly content to rule for as long as he is able. Then again, if he did get bored with being a despot, there's so much else he could do: movie director, architect, pilot, professional golfer . . .

SULTAN QABOOS BIN-SAID AL SAID

of the Sultanate of Oman

Now here's an unusual thing: a Muslim country without hangs-ups about women and sex; a country with oil, but not so much that it's gone mad with opulence; a Middle Eastern state that is friends with its neighbours and the West; a country without any democracy, but with well-fed, educated and happy citizens.

In Oman, we find that rare and almost mythical creature: a benign dictator. No, it's not a contradiction in terms. Oman is still an absolute monarchy. Qaboos Bin-Said could order everyone to wear funny hats if he felt like it. He just doesn't, because he's not a meany.

Now his dad was, but we'll get to that.

First, the usual history bit: Oman is the oldest independent state in the Arab world. Arabs migrated there from the 9th century B.C. onward, and conversion to Islam occurred in the 7th century A.D. Most of the population are members of the Muslim Ibadi sect, a situation which is unique to Oman. It has a relatively liberal interpretation of Islam: there is a tolerance of other religions, and women can pursue careers.

Being positioned at the toe of the boot-shaped piece of land sticking into the Arabian Sea, it has always had a strategic importance. Portugal occupied the capital, Muscat, in 1507 and did pretty well out of it: it soon became part of the highly profitable Indies spice route. And seeing there was money being made, it wasn't long before some other colonial powers starting sniffing around, particularly the Dutch and the British. It was the Brits, however, who managed to make those valuable contacts: in 1646 the British East India company signed a secret deal with some Omani tribes guaranteeing trading, religious and legal rights for British merchants operating in Oman. As a result of this new income, Imam Sultan Bin Saif was able to organise a rebellion against the Portuguese, and managed to kick them out in 1650.

The British, however, were more difficult to get rid of: mainly because they never attempted to colonise Oman. There was no need: the two countries did a roaring trade with each other over the next couple of hundred years. The Brits would provide the occasional bit of military muscle if there were any inter-tribal disputes (they had a permanent naval base there), leaving the Omanis free to develop their own empire: one that spread as far as Zanzibar and Mombassa in Africa. Oman has a long nautical tradition: by legend, this is where Sinbad the Sailor came from.

In 1749, the Al Bu Said family came to power and they have ruled Oman ever since. Under the Saids the prosperity continued.

Oman had its act together, and was clearly one of the most developed states in the region. But spin forward to the mid-1800s, and things started to go wrong. Following the death of Sultan Sa'id Ibn, there was a succession crisis (not uncommon in Arab states: see *Saudi Arabia*). As a result (and thanks to a lot of quiet British meddling), the Omani Empire was split in two: one based in Muscat, the other in Zanzibar. This further weakened the Omani economy, and made successive sultans more dependent on British protection to remain in power: effectively, the country was starting to split between tribes led by Idabite Imams based in the interior and the Sultan on the coast.

So spin forward again to 1932: Oman has shrunk back to one of the *least* developed countries in the region. This was the year that Qaboos' father, Said Bin Taimur, became Sultan.

The country he inherited was almost broke, and had something close to a civil war raging. Taimur had no option but to go to the British for help. Now if he was going to ask anyone, it was going to be the Brits: Taimur was a bit of an Anglophile. Nonetheless, the whole experience was thought to have been something of a humiliation, and perhaps *partly* explains his later parsimony. But only partly.

The British, however, were more than happy to help: they already knew there was oil in the interior and were rather keen to help the Sultan suppress the rebelling tribes in return for exploitation rights. Technically, the Omani forces were made up of seconded officers from Britain, Iran, Jordan and Pakistan, but in reality it was a British-organised army: an influence the Brits have maintained to this day.

The rebels were defeated and the oil started pumping. So you'd think it would be around this time that things started to improve for Oman: the majority of its citizens were now wretchedly poor.

But not a bit of it. There is an old Arab saying: 'Keep the dogs hungry, and they will follow you'. This, it turned out, was Taimur's political philosophy. Oh yes: and he was completely insane.

Although he was an Anglophile, he hated all things western: a contradiction, obviously, but the guy was crazy. He also hated his Arab neighbours, and broke off contact with all of them, then set about establishing what was essentially a feudal state.

Taimur was against, well, everything. The importation of evil 'western' goods such as radios, books, cigarettes, trousers or even eyeglasses was banned. Dancing and smoking on the street were forbidden. It was not allowed to build new houses, or to repair the old ones; forbidden to install a lavatory or a gas stove; forbidden to cultivate new land, or to buy a car without the Sultan's permission. There was no electricity.

Movies and newspapers were a total no-no, as was playing drums: the army used to have a band, but the Sultan had their instruments thrown into the sea. If someone appeared in one of the Sultan's dreams, he had them punished.

Travel was also out. The inhabitants of the coast were forbidden to travel inland, and those inland could not go to the coast. No one was allowed to go to Dhofar, in the extreme southwest. Visiting foreigners had to gain the Sultan's personal permission, while sailors on ships anchored at Muscat could not land. Any Omani who got out of the country usually wasn't allowed back in again.

By the 1960s, the only paved road in the country ran for six miles. In a nation of nearly a million people, there were only three (boys only) primary schools (if you wanted further education you had to leave the country and face exile), and one hospital; infant deaths and diseases such as malaria, leprosy, tuberculosis and trachoma were widespread. Taimur – now completely paranoid – was a virtual recluse in his palace in Salalah, apart from the odd trip to London. The British were the only foreigners he spoke to.

In short, he had refused to spend one penny of his oil income on improving the infrastructure of the country: he was convinced that if he bettered the lot of his citizens, they would revolt against him.

Which was true: in 1966, members of his personal guard tried to assassinate him, but failed. Not much of a personal guard. Marxist rebels were active in the south while Taimur's brother, Tariq, now in exile, had founded a democracy movement

Into this jolly set-up came Taimur's son, Qaboos. He had been born in 1940, but luckily for him, had been mostly shielded from his Dad's rampant craziness: the cunning British somehow managed to convince Taimur to allow Qaboos to be educated in England, thus making it much easier for the son to realise what a shambolic state his home was in.

So, quite understandably, when the education was over, Qaboos wasn't too keen to return. After school he went to Sandhurst and then joined the British army and served in Germany. At Sandhurst, Qaboos made friends with a man called Tim Landon. We'll come back to him. Then he left the army and studied local government, again in the UK. Then he went on a world tour – chaperoned by a British major.

He finally returned to Oman in 1964 – eight years later – whereupon he suggested to the old man that perhaps he might spend some of his petro-dollars on a few small tokens for the people: hospitals, schools, that sort of thing. Not surprisingly, Dad didn't take this suggestion too well and placed Qaboos – his own son – under house arrest: the royal equivalent of sending a cheeky teenager to his room. Qaboos remained isolated within the Salalah palace for the next six years. He was allowed books and records, but saw few people. Daddy rarely came around.

Enter the Brits again: the only visitors Qaboos was allowed were UK officials, who saw him regularly during his detention. Now, no one knows for sure, but most assume that these officials convinced Qaboos that if he was ever going to be allowed out of the house again, then he had to lead a coup against the old man.

This happened in 1970, by which time Qaboos hadn't seen his father for a year and a half. So how did he do it? Well, it was easy really. Qaboos had a bit of help from his old Sandhurst pal, Tim Landon, now a Brigadier and an 'intelligence officer': a phrase which some believe is code for 'member of the SAS'. Certainly, the Omani army did nothing: most of their senior officers were British and, it is suspected, were all warned in advance. There was a brief clash with Taimur's personal guard, during which the Sultan himself was injured, and then it was all over. Said senior had no option but to flee the country. He lived the rest of his life as a recluse in the Dorchester Hotel in London, where it is said he existed on a diet of Mars Bars. He died two years later, in 1972.

After Dad's departure, Qaboos found some residents in the palace: 500 African slaves. One of Qaboos' first acts was to set them free and ban slavery. Then he visited the capital, Muscat. Daddy hadn't been there since 1958.

Everyone was delighted. The people, the freed slaves, Qaboos, even his old chum, Tim Landon. The newly installed Sultan showed his gratitude by making Landon his equerry, special adviser, and chief military counsellor. It was a job he was to take very seriously indeed

Not only that: it looked like Qaboos was completely sane. When he first came to power he gave a speech now famous in Oman:

"I promise you to proceed forthwith in the process of creating a modern government. My first act will be the immediate abolition of all the unnecessary restrictions on your lives and activities.

"My people, I will proceed as quickly as possible to transform your life into a prosperous one with a bright future."

And amazingly, he did just that. He built roads, schools and hospitals, gave boats to fishermen and land to farmers. He set in place strict environmental laws covering architecture and litter.

When Qaboos came to power there were just six miles of road and three schools. Today there are over 6 000 kilometres of paved road, nearly 1 000 free co-educational schools. There are free health facilities in every village, town and city. Women can work and go to university: indeed, in Oman's main university they discriminate positively in favour of men in the medicine course because so many women are getting in.

Oman joined the Arab League and the United Nations in 1971, opened its borders and set up normal diplomatic relations with most countries in the world.

Due to the continuing British influence, Oman is probably the most pro-Western state in the Middle East. It was the only Arab country to support Egypt's peace deal with Israel in 1978 and during the same period allowed the SAS to use it as a base for secret operations into Afghanistan. It also provided support during both Gulf Wars and in the 'war on terror'. British troops are permanently based there.

Of course, there's influence, and taking the piss. Tim Landon's job was to build up the Omani military, and today it is one of the best-equipped small armies in the world. Not surprisingly, Landon, with a few old SAS chums, has done rather well out of it: he is reputed to be worth £300 million, and regularly appears in lists of Britain's richest people.

Naturally, the vast majority of these arms and equipment

were sourced in the UK. Landon, who became known in Oman as the White Sultan, had virtually unfettered access to Qaboos, continually encouraging him to buy more and more weapons. Qaboos, the soft dope, did what he was advised – despite objections from some Omani military commanders who argued that the country couldn't afford it. In 1974, after buying an integrated air-defence missile system from British aerospace, the country nearly went bankrupt. In 1980 alone, Oman spent £400 million on defence: in a country of just 1.6 million and with no great internal or external threats. (The threat from Marxist rebels was quashed relatively quickly in the 1970s.) It has oil, but not that much: and it may run out within the next twenty years.

During the 1970s and '80s, a small group of mostly British businessmen made fortunes for themselves, trading on the goodwill and naivety of Qaboos. And not just on arms: during this period Omani oil found its way to South Africa and Rhodesia, despite international sanctions, bringing in massive commissions to British business interests.

Even Maggie Thatcher jumped on the Omani gravy train: in 1981, a major scandal broke when the British PM (who also had links to Tim Landon) openly lobbied Qaboos to award the contract for the construction of a new university to a British company. The lobbying, (Thatcher later said she was 'battling for Britain') took place during an official visit to Oman. By sheer 'coincidence', her son Mark was also there. At the time he was a paid consultant for the construction company Cementation. Cementation won the contract.

Resentment over this waste of resources grew so intense in Oman that in 1994, 200 army officers conspired to assassinate Qaboos. But the plot was discovered and the conspirators jailed.

To this day, the Omani authorities are very touchy on the subject. In the mid-nineties, the *Financial Times* correspondent, Robin Allen, was banned from Oman for reporting the contents of a World Bank study which claimed that Oman was heading for a 'major economic upheaval' because of 'exceptionally high levels of defence and national security expenditure'. In 2002, the Omani-based British journalist John Beasant completed a book which outlined the various money-making schemes of Tim Landon and other British ex-military in Oman. He was offered a 'substantial' bribe not to publish, and when he refused, was expelled from the country.

Yes, even the nice despots have their weaknesses. But most Oman-watchers ascribe this to plain stupidity on Qaboos' part, rather than anything more sinister. Although his heart is in the right place, his brain doesn't always seem to be.

While various Brits were raking in the cash, Qaboos was bringing in even more reforms. In 1991, he established the Majlis Ash Shura, a Consultative Assembly, which in 2000 transformed into the Majlis: the Omani parliament, consisting of an upper and lower house. The first direct elections took place that year, with women winning seats: one was made a junior minister in the Omani government. (For an Arab nation, this is still a big deal.)

Hang on: elections? Isn't he a despot? Well, this is the odd thing. This is a man who kept his promises to the people. He modernised and united the country and he is still very popular. Yet Qaboos still rules Oman as a dictator. He is Prime Minister, Defence Minister, Foreign Affairs Minister and Minister for Finance. He appoints all the other ministers.

The members of the upper house of the legislature are all appointed by him. The members of the lower house were elected, but they had to be approved by Qaboos before they could run for office. And in that poll, only twenty-five per cent of the adult population were allowed to vote. Again, Qaboos chose who: Sheikhs, 'wise men', dignitaries, graduates and intellectuals was the official description

The legislature has no power anyway. It can only advise or ask questions, both of which are often ignored. The law is still made by decree and that's it.

You'd think that in such a go-ahead place that someone might suggest having a bit of democracy. But they don't. By law, they are not allowed to. Criticism of the Sultan is illegal and, even though censorship was abolished in 1985, Qaboos still controls all the media in Oman: journalists and publications have to be licensed by the Ministry of Information. If you publish something they don't like, you could get up to three years in prison. On the official Omani website, it's not even mentioned that Qaboos led a coup against his father – merely that his Daddy abdicated.

It's a popular, benign dictatorship (there are virtually no human rights abuses in Oman – or at least, no more than would take place in any western country), yet it is a dictatorship nonetheless. Qaboos seems to have developed the knack of being liberal while still retaining an absolute grip on the country.

In 1996 he introduced what they call the Basic Law: essentially a sort of constitution which guarantees human rights, provides for a legislature and a prime minister. However, the real reason he wrote the law was because he had had a serious car accident that year – in which two advisors were killed – and thus was prompted to think about who might rule after him: problems over succession had nearly torn Oman apart before. If Qaboos had popped his clogs in the car crash, it almost certainly would have caused a crisis because he has no children. He did marry a cousin, Kamilla, in the mid-seventies, but it is believed that the marriage was dissolved some time later. After that, no one expected him to marry again, though no one says why. Draw your own conclusions.

Anyway, the point here is that the Basic Law was hailed as a liberal step forward, but in fact was securing the future of the Sultanate system: it sets out in detail how Qaboos' successor should be chosen.

Similarly, while there is freedom of religion, there is no written statute guaranteeing it: non-Muslim places of worship are all on land donated by Qaboos and are not allowed to try and recruit members.

Women can travel and be elected but still need identity cards signed by the nearest male relative. Inheritance law also discriminates against them.

The Imams are kept a close eye on and not allowed to speak about politics.

It is generally assumed that the government routinely eavesdrops on phone-calls and letters. Anyone Qaboos doesn't like is quietly deported.

Yet at the same time Qaboos is said to routinely travel incognito around his country, looking for roadside eyesores that need to be removed and checking on how life is for his subjects.

But things will probably change. Qaboos doesn't say he is against voting for leaders, he just argues that it would have been a mistake for Oman to plunge straight into democracy as it would have de-stabilised the country too much. He points to the example of many African states where exactly that happened. "The man in the street often doesn't want or know how to deal with foreign governments or defend the country," he said in a 1997 interview. "He trusts me to do it. In this part of the world, giving too much power too fast can still be exploited . . . I'm against creating such situations when people aren't ready for them."

So instead he inches towards it: in 2003 Oman held its first parliamentary elections featuring universal suffrage for everyone aged over 21. The following year, in March 2004, Doctor Rawya bint Saud Al-Busaidi was appointed Minister for Education, the first time a woman has been given a cabinet portfolio.

Ironically, the turn-out for the 2003 vote was just twenty-five per cent, a little fact not reported in the Omani media.

The reason for the low turn-out was obvious: these were elections into a legislature than cannot legislate. It indicates a certain healthy cynicism within the Omani public, which now contains large numbers of young educated people. Sooner rather than later, they will want change, and they'll want to have a future. Despite all he has done, Qaboos still faces problems with poverty. Oman's relatively modest oil income isn't large enough to fix everything, especially if he keeps spending on defence. Attempts are being made to diversify the economy into areas like tourism – Oman is one of the beautiful countries in the Middle East. But time is short: as we've mentioned, the oil could run out within twenty years.

Yet the fact that Qaboos, who is still in his sixties, has already legislated as to how he will be succeeded indicates that democracy will come later rather than sooner. From a Western perspective, it's easy to say that this isn't good enough. Yet transforming a traditional Arab society into a democracy has never been done before: there is reason to tread warily. And in the meantime, Oman is still a damn sight better than some of its neighbours.

KING FAHD

of the Kingdom of Saudi Arabia

There are a lot of clichés about Saudi Arabia: all those coiffed Saudi princes, cruising between palaces in their Rolls Royces, whiling away the time by jetting to Paris to buy a few shirts and a half-dozen supermodels. And you know what? Every single one of those clichés is true. It takes but three words to describe Saudi Arabia: rich, rich, rich.

In Jeddah, the capital, there are some 300 palaces, squatting behind gates manned by red-bereted royal guards. Their gardens are fed by water desalinated and pumped 300 miles from the Persian Gulf. You don't get many hose-pipe bans in Jeddah.

For many (but not most) Saudis, Saudi Arabia isn't really a country at all: it's part oil refinery, part carpark for the fleet of Bentleys. It's where the cheques are signed but not spent; it's where the servants live. It's the only state on earth actually named after the family who run it – the Sa'uds. Imagine if the United States was re-named Bushland or France was called

La Mitterand, or – more appositely – New Jersey was called The Sopranos State: that's Saudi Arabia.

All the lolly, of course, is down to oil: but *so much* oil. Saudi Arabia is to oil what Ian Paisley is to bigotry.

The Kingdom has the largest confirmed reserves of the black stuff in the world: one-quarter of all the oil that we know about. It produces two million barrels a day and therefore controls the flow – and the price – of petrol on international markets. In effect, the Saudis keep the cost of oil cheap, so if anything unfortunate was to happen to that country – like, heaven forbid, a revolution or a war – the price of oil could more than treble.

The effect on the world economy would be calamitous, especially here in the West where we like to drive to the shops. In fact, if Saudi Arabia went belly-up, driving to the shops would be far too expensive to indulge in on a regular basis. Then again, a lot of the products in those shops would suddenly be too pricey to buy, certainly for those of us who had lost our jobs. Like it or not, cheap oil is what keeps most of us in the relative comfort we have grown accustomed to. When the President Bushes, senior and junior, launched wars against Iraq, securing future oil supplies was, of course, the big unadmitted motive. And quite understandably, many of us were outraged by this cynical trading of human lives for petrol. Yet the icky reality is that *we benefit* from it also: people died in the Middle East so our kids wouldn't do without.

But back to the Kingdom: the way things stand now, the economic nuts of planet Earth are gripped in a vice held by bejewelled Saudi hands – which is why we see so many Western leaders pucker up whenever King Fahd, his three wives, six sons and dozens of cronies come to visit.

At least for the moment: sooner or later, some Saudi will put the nuts-vice down and see what's on TV.

But before we speculate on the future, let's have a quick look at the past. Was there anything notable about Saudi Arabia before the oil? Well, not really. It's been part of the Ottoman Empire since the sixteenth century. In 1902, the Sa'ud family gained control. Following a few skirmishes with neighbouring states, Mecca, Islam's holiest city, was captured in 1924. In 1932 the Kingdom of Saudi Arabia was officially established. It was, and still is, largely desert. Apart from the cities and a few farms, a large proportion of the population are camel-rearing nomads. Before the oil arrived, its main income came from exporting dates and subsidies from Britain.

The current King – Fahd – took over in 1982 and immediately established himself as the ideal Saudi King: he changed absolutely nothing. But with more money than God, and the entire Western world sucking up to him, why should he?

Now this may sound a little critical, so let's be fair: Saudi Arabia is a fantastic place to live – as long as you are a Sunni Muslim and a member of the Sa'ud family. And not a woman.

Here's the set-up: there is no written constitution, no elected legislature and there are no political parties or trade unions. Saudi Arabia is an absolute monarchy, with King Fahd heading the government as Prime Minister and General Commander of the armed forces.

A few years back he did set up a Council of Ministers and then a consultative council: both to give the impression to the Yanks that he was keen on introducing democracy. But the ploy was so fake Barney the Dinosaur wouldn't have been fooled. Both councils have exactly zero power and are largely staffed by his relations.

About 92 per cent of the population is Sunni Muslim. Despite Islam's recognition of Christians and Jews as

'People of the Book', public adherence to other faiths is forbidden in the Kingdom. The possession of inflammatory non-Islamic religious objects such as Bibles, rosary beads and crosses is prohibited.

Then there's the legal system. Sharia law allows for corporal punishment, which is a posh way of saying that law-breakers in Saudi Arabia are routinely subjected to such treats as flogging and amputation. Trials are often held in secret.

But if you've done something really serious, there's always the death penalty – by beheading. It's the prescribed punishment for rape, murder, armed robbery, adultery, apostasy (i.e. being a non-Muslim in a public place), and drug trafficking. People sentenced to death are often unaware of the sentence and receive no advance notice of their execution; until they are asked to kneel in front of a basket, that is. Some are not even made aware of the charges against them. Every year there are about 100 lucky recipients of this justice, many of them foreigners.

However, there is a nifty appeals system, based on the sound jurisprudential principle that if you're rich, you can get away with it. The law enables heirs of a murder victim to demand money in exchange for sparing the life of the murderer. No cheques, please

Public demonstrations are banned. The government prohibits visits by international human rights groups or independent monitors. The media is strictly controlled and satellite dishes are forbidden. However, people rich enough to own a satellite dish (the Saudi Royal family) usually have one. In response to this law-breaking, the authorities (the Saudi Royal family) turn a blind eye.

There are donkeys in Kerry who enjoy better human rights than women in Saudi Arabia. They (the women) are segregated in the workplace, in schools, in restaurants, and on public transportation. Women are not allowed to drive, (a regulation, it must be said, secretly supported by some Western men). To keep from inflaming Saudi passions, they are required to wear the *abaya*, your basic big black sack garment covering the head, most of the face, and the body. Officers of the Mutawwai'in, or Committee for the Promotion of Virtue and the Prevention of Vice, merrily harass women for violating these dress codes and for, even more scandalously, appearing in public with unrelated males. Women may not travel within or outside the kingdom without a male relative. Although they make up half the student population, women account for less than six per cent of the workforce. They may not study engineering, law, or journalism.

At a recent business conference held in Saudi Arabia's second city, Jeddah, both men and women were allowed to attend, though they were separated by a large screen. However, a huge stink ensued when some of the men and women posed for a photograph which appeared the next morning in a Saudi newspaper. The men and women were *stranding together* while some of the ladies didn't even have their heads covered. Immediately, Grand Mufti Sheik Abdul Aziz al-Sheikh, Saudi's most senior cleric, condemned this activity, claiming that 'allowing women to mix with men is the root of every evil and catastrophe'. He warned of 'dire consequences'.

And in Saudi they take these kinds of rants very seriously indeed. Because of the segregation rules, many businesses simply don't bother hiring women because it costs too much to install all the screens and separate facilities. Many shopping malls get around the problem by having 'women-only' days, while it is even being suggested that a women-only industrial city be constructed.

Not that there are many pastimes to spend your wages on. There are no theatres or cinemas, no pubs or clubs or discos and even the importation of female dolls was recently banned. What a fun country. So it's no great surprise that King Fahd and many members of the Saudi Royal family spend a lot of their time out of it.

In the summer of 2002 Fahd went to Marbella for his holidays – where he owns a complex of villas with their own mosque, clinic and helicopter pad. He brought with him an entourage of 3 000 close relatives who landed in 12 Boeing planes. They were met by a convoy of 20 luxury limousines and seven trucks to carry the bags. (They were, by the way, coming from Switzerland where they had spent the previous three months.)

During his visit to Spain three years previously, Fahd is estimated to have spent some €55 million. So obviously, the Spanish are delighted to have him. Locals lined up at the palace gates in the hope of securing well-paid domestic work, (cleaning ladies reportedly get €3 000 a month); an entire aisle of the local hospital was reserved for Fahd, just in case; an aircraft was hired to fly above the city carrying a banner which welcomed His Majesty; while in town, Saudi limousines were allowed to park wherever they wanted, regardless of traffic rules; there was talk of naming a couple of boulevards after him. If Queen Elizabeth thinks the world smells of fresh paint, King Fahd thinks the world is full of people who want to kiss his ass.

Literally and metaphorically: there were also reports that a British agency provided a large group of women to 'accompany' the Saudi men during their vacation, on two conditions: the women must be young and blonde, and must be replaced every 15 days. Oh, classy.

But it's not just Fahd who likes to splash the cash around: when shopping in Europe or the US, these guys like to bulk buy. They think nothing of buying a dozen $10 000 watches; of handing out €600 tips to delighted shop staff.

In Saudi itself, they don't sell anything below 18 carat gold, considering it 'not real'. One Prince reportedly bought a new front door for his Jeddah home at a cost of $500 000; another, Prince Nawaf bin Faisal bin Fahd discovered that his son's boarding school in Somerset didn't have a swimming pool, so he gave them £6 million to build one; shortly after September 11th, Prince Alwaleed bin Talal made a pilgrimage to Ground Zero, and afterwards wrote a cheque for $10 million to the city's Twin Towers relief fund. (Somewhat indelicately, he then publicly blamed 9/11 on U.S. support for Israel, prompting the then-Mayor Rudy Giuliani to return the money.) A sister-in-law of Fahd's, Princess Hind Al Fassi, found herself in a Cairo court accused of spending the salaries of her fifty domestic staff. She got off because the employees didn't have proper contracts. They're rich, and a lot of them aren't very nice either.

So here's the punch line: while Fahd and his family boost the economies of the Costa del Sol, Park Lane and Park Avenue, ordinary Saudis are dirt poor. In the early 1980s, per capita income was €22 500. Now it's just €6 000. The population has exploded 300 per cent since 1973 to 23 million. More than 80 per cent live in the three cities, Riyadh, Jeddah and Dammam, packed into filthy slums. While Fahd lies by the pool and slaps on the factor twenty, his subjects have to live with water rationing and power cuts. On the United Nations Human Development index – which measures factors such as life expectancy, school enrolment and distribution of wealth – Saudi Arabia ranks just 71st out of 173 countries. Remember: this is the country with the biggest supply of oil on the planet.

Unemployment runs at 15-20 per cent – yet foreign migrants continue to account for 65 per cent of the workforce, causing intense resentment. The civil service, the educational system, in fact pretty much all arms of government, are riddled with corruption. In 2002, the Saudi budget deficit doubled to $12 billion.

Understandably, ordinary Saudis aren't exactly over the moon about the way things have worked out. In fact, it would be fair to say that they are hopping mad: and increasingly drawn to radical Islamic politics.

Pardon the pun, but Saudi Arabia is a bomb waiting to detonate, with the Saudi Royal family sitting on top.

So someone in authority is bound to do something – at least just to keep the lid on the country. If *we* know there's trouble brewing, surely the Saudi Royal family knows it too?

You'd think so. Yet any efforts at privatisation, structural reform, or economic diversification have been spoken about briefly, then abandoned. In fact, they seem to be working actively *against* changing the system, having recently issued an extensive 'negative list' of industries closed to foreign investment. These include the military, publishing, education, insurance, transportation, fishing, real estate, employment services, and 'poison control', whatever that is.

Bone idleness is part of the problem, as is the fact that it's really difficult to find the time to reform your country when you're constantly shopping for swimming pools. But the main reason is the old Turkeys-Voting-For-Christmas scenario: an inappropriate image for a Muslim country, but accurate nonetheless. Change would mean the Saudi Royals having to make do with a smaller slice of the gem-encrusted pie. And no one is going to volunteer for that.

At birth, Saudi princes are entitled to a six-figure allowance, free phone calls, free electricity and free first-class seats worldwide. They also own the entire country, pretty much. A generation ago, King Faisal registered state lands in the names of Sa'ud family members. The billions earned when they were generously sold back to the state for universities, airports and other projects established many family fortunes

In Jeddah and the other commercial centres, House of Sa'ud princes and close relatives sit, by one count, as chairmen of 520 Saudi corporations. In the capital, princes hold strategic cabinet posts – Defence, Interior, Intelligence – and others sit as junior ministers. Every provincial governor is a prince or an in-law, and family members control key military posts.

Young princes are imposed on Saudi companies as silent partners: so silent that the companies in question never see or hear from them again. Unless they stop sending out the cheques

To return to our earlier New Jersey reference: they are *The Sopranos* of the desert. Everything bought or sold there, they get a cut of: one estimate has it that a British Tornado jet fighter – $25 million on the open market – will cost the Saudis $65 to $75 million once the extra money gets distributed throughout the family.

All this activity, you must appreciate, costs the Saudi economy *billions* of dollars each year, because when we say the Royal family, we don't mean two sisters and a couple of cousins, we mean *thousands* of people. Thanks to the joys of polygamy and a high divorce rate, one estimate in the mid-1990s reckoned there were around 4 000 Saudi princes: all of them multi-millionaires; all of them on the payroll. It is also estimated that a new prince arrives at the rate of one a day. And that doesn't count daughters, cousins, in laws: one estimate puts the Saudi Royal family at 20 000 people. It's standing room only on the gravy train.

Time now for our plot twist. Another reason why Fahd doesn't do anything to reform the country is because he had a series of strokes in 1995 and can't do much about anything. The Saudis don't admit it, of course, but the *de facto* head of state is Crown Prince Abdullah, his half-brother. Brought up as a Bedouin, he is one of 37 sons – by 16 wives – of the founder of the state, the late King Abdul al-Aziz. Now there's a man in touch with his sexuality.

It's actually all down to Abdullah that Saudi Arabia hasn't already exploded in flames. Compared to some of his relations, he's Mahatma Ghandi. Granted, he does enjoy some small luxuries, (a Rolls Royce with 001 number plates; a customised tour bus with a small living room complete with satellite TV (isn't that illegal?); a ranch stuffed with some of the world's finest Arabian and thoroughbred horses). Yet his public image is one of relative piety. He speaks with a stutter, which probably helps. Abdullah has four wives, seven sons and some 15 daughters. Unlike Fahd, he doesn't travel much outside the Middle East. But given that he has twenty-two kids, he probably hasn't found the time.

And not only is Abdullah regarded as honest, he is seen as a relative liberal. He has even hinted that (gasp!) women should be allowed to work.

Not that Abdullah is going to do anything about it, of course. Remember, he's running the country, but he's not the king: he has some power, but never quite enough. When Fahd pops his clogs, Abdullah will officially take over, but by then it will probably be too late. In fact, it's too late right now.

While the Saudi princes stick their heads in the Kingdom's ample supply of sand, things are also unravelling internationally. Officially, the US and Saudi Arabia are still the best of chums, but the truth is that the US administration is backing away; very, very slowly: suddenly, the whole set-up is far too flaky to provide a reliable oil supply. The US – and the rest of the world – are looking with renewed fondness at oil-rich countries in Africa and central Asia. Many of them are run by genocidal maniacs. But hey: at least they're in charge.

Anyway, the US has other reasons to distance itself from the Kingdom: it doesn't look too clever if your ally in the War on Terror is the source of the terror itself. Apart from oil, Saudi Arabia is also the world's biggest exporter of Muslim fundamentalists: out of the nineteen highjackers on September 11th, fifteen were Saudis.

The exact relationship between the Saudi Royal family and fundamentalism has always been, well, unclear to put it kindly. It is a fact that up until relatively recently they were big fans of Osama Bin Laden (who is a Saudi), mostly due to his fight against the Soviets in Afghanistan: some reports have it that they paid him hundreds of millions of dollars. After 9/11 Saudi Arabia made all the right outraged noises, of course. Yet somehow it just wasn't *heartfelt* enough. Indeed, the FBI complained that Saudi authorities restricted access to suspects and evidence. It got even stickier when US-led air strikes on Afghanistan drew harsh criticism from Saudi clerics. The Royals remained conspicuously silent.

In the US, nearly all the senior Saudi royals have been named in a massive lawsuit, brought by victims of the September 11 attacks who believe the Saudis have been financing al-Qaeda. There's Prince Sultan, the deputy Prime Minister; Prince Naif, the interior Minister; Prince Abdullah al Faisal, a former Minister of Health; Prince Turki, a former intelligence chief and the Saudi ambassador in London. All deny the charges. But some of the poo-poo has already stuck. In legal papers, Prince Sultan admits giving huge donations to two Islamic charities accused of links to Islamic terrorism.

This did result in some action from the Sa'uds: Sheikh Aqil al-Aqil, the head of one the named charities was sacked from his job in January of 2004, while the charity, al-Haramain, has been ordered to close down all 50 of its overseas offices. (According to CIA claims, al-Haramain was distributing €40 million a year to various groups including al-Qaida, the Taliban and Chechan rebels.) Meanwhile, the Saudi interior ministry has finally admitted to the existence of several al-Qaeda training camps in remote parts of the Kingdom; all of which have now been closed down.

However, all this is probably far too little and far too late to get the Sa'uds back in the American's good books. And it certainly won't endear them to ordinary Saudis, who aren't at all shy about proclaiming their allegiances. Thanks to the poverty, the resentment against foreigners who they see as taking their jobs, the continuing US military presence, Palestine, the invasion of Iraq, plus the not unimportant fact that the Royal Family appear to be robbing them blind, ordinary Saudis have become intensely radicalised. Imams and Islamic teachers regularly preach sermons demanding all Westerners leave the country. They issue fatwas like parking tickets.

And a lot of these guys are seriously hard-line: as Sunni Muslims, they don't even have much time for the other branches of Islam, regarding them as idolaters: one senior Saudi Imam even recently said that a jihad against Shi`ite Muslims (who make up only four per cent of the population), would be justified if they continued practising their religion in public. Others talk of the Shi'ites conspiring with the United States to destroy Islam. It's that paranoid.

Even if they wished to, none of the Royal Family would dare oppose this mood: they know that the Imams give them what little legitimacy they have left.

But just when you think things couldn't get any more

complicated, they do. The whole sorry mess is turned into a really huge mess by the Saudi process of Royal succession. Which is messy.

King Fahd will die soon – everyone knows that – and he will be succeeded by Abdullah. However, Abdullah is hitting eighty and he's a chain smoker – so nobody is buying him any 4 000-piece jigsaw puzzles.

Concentrate now. The process of succession is supposed to work like this: the throne is passed from brother to brother through the line of sons fathered by the founder of the Kingdom, the aforementioned love machine, Abdul Aziz, who is Fahd and Abdullah's daddy. Thus after Abdullah puffs his last Rothmans, the throne is passed along to the next brother.

However, some in the Kingdom argue that Abdul didn't intend for it to work this way. And they may have a point. In 1992 Fahd (on behalf of his dead Dad) issued an edict recognising the claim of Abdul's grandsons on the Saudi throne. Alas, Abdul didn't take time out from impregnating his wives to tell Fahd which grandson he meant: there are several dozen of them.

Let's put it another way: after Abdullah joins Allah, there is a long line of brothers to take his place. A long line of doddery old brothers, the most sprightly of whom is in his sixties. If Saudi Arabia follows the 'brothers' succession rule, the Kingdom could find itself with a new king every two or three years – hardly a recipe for stability, and highly frustrating for the much younger (well: middle-aged) grandsons and 4 000 Saudi princes who all reckon they could do a much better job at running the place.

The jockeying for position has already begun. There are, apparently, lots of whispered conversations being conducted, nods and winks being exchanged, not to mention the recent spate of bomb attacks around the capital. In the more remote parts of the Kingdom, the grip of central government is slowly being loosened. Of course, Saudi Arabia being the paranoid, secretive country it is, no one really knows who is doing all the jockeying and loosening. (Though it is widely believed that there are tensions between the relatively-liberal Abdullah and his more hard-line half-brother, Prince Nayef, who controls the Saudi Secret Police and those jolly pranksters of the Commission for the Promotion of Virtue and Prevention of Vice.) A handful of princes could make a grab for power, or all 4 000 of them. We could have one winner or a new patchwork of tiny kingdoms.

What is certain is that any new King will need the support of the Imams, and to do that he will definitely need to burn all his Def Leppard CDs. There's only one way the Imams (and much of the population) want Saudi Arabia to go, and that's fundamental.

If you like a bet, and if you know of any bookies giving odds on 'countries likely to disintegrate in the next five years', stick a fiver on Saudi Arabia. You'll be grateful when the price of oil goes through the roof.

Better yet: if you have scribbled down designs for a cheap electric car, now's the time to take out a patent.

KING MSWATI III

of the Kingdom of Swaziland

It's amazing that Swaziland is a country at all. Not that it doesn't deserve to be: the Swazis are a distinct ethnic group and have been around for a long time. It's just that, apart from the little bit of border it shares with Mozambique, Swaziland is completely surrounded by South Africa. It's not a big place – about half the size of Ireland – with a population of just over one million.

Its survival is partly due to good luck, the protection of the British and the fact that Swaziland doesn't have any oil, and therefore wasn't worth invading. It has mountains though, loads of them, and has been referred to as the 'Switzerland of Africa': a phrase no doubt coined by someone who had never been to Switzerland. To paraphrase that big fat actor, Switzerland has 1 000 years of civilisation and cuckoo clocks. Swaziland has had 200 years of absolute monarchy and without doubt the most over-sexed heads of state in the history of this planet. In Swaziland, even the phrase 'Head of State' sounds suggestive. But we'll get to that.

First, where did the Swazis come from? Well, no one knows. The best that Swazi tradition can give us is that they travelled 'south' into what is now Mozambique, where they got their asses roundly kicked by the local inhabitants. So they went further south – into modern-day South Africa – where they ran into the Zulus. The Zulus weren't too hospitable either, so the Swazis turned around and settled in Swaziland in the early 1800s.

Under several able leaders, the Swazis established their territory, but, of course, it was impossible to escape any colonial influence. White settlers came, both from South Africa and the United Kingdom. From 1894 to 1902, the South Africans had administrative control over Swaziland. In 1902, following the Boer War, the Brits took over. They ruled the country through various councils and committees, while also allowing the Swazi royal family to continue their reign in a limited capacity.

The truth was that no one was too bothered about Swaziland. It was small and didn't have anything worth stealing, and most people assumed it would eventually be absorbed into South Africa. But after World War II – when just about every colonised country in the world sought a change of management – the Brits had a rush of conscience to the head. The South Africans were stepping up their apartheid policies, so perhaps independence would be better.

The Swazis wholeheartedly agreed, and by the early sixties the country was seeing a great deal of political activity. In 1964, the country saw its first elections to a legislative council on which Swazis would participate for the first time. Several political parties competed, but the overall winner was the Imbokodvo National Movement (INM) led by King Sobhuza II. Out of the twenty-four seats on offer, they won, er, twenty-four.

It wasn't a fix. Even today, the Swazis are a mainly rural people, fiercely protective of their traditional way of life – and the king is central to this. Sobhuza II was born in 1899, Sobhuza being his royal name. He was originally called Nkhotfotjeni (stone lizard), apparently because when he was conceived his parents were living among stones because of the Boer War raging around them. Sobhuza appreciated the importance of a stable, independent Swaziland.

Within three years, the INM and the Brits had agreed to establish Swaziland as a constitutional monarchy, an agreement which came into effect on September 6, 1968. In 1972, post-independence elections gave the INM 75 per cent of the popular vote.

Thus democratically mandated, the King decided to get rid of democracy, arguing that such notions were divisive and against the traditional Swazi way of life. He repealed the constitution, dissolved parliament and banned political parties and trades unions. A new parliament was eventually convened, but its members got there through indirect elections and direct appointments by the king – and most of them were relatives anyway. Sobhuza was in charge.

He ruled happily enough until 1982, when he dropped dead from pneumonia. He had ruled Swaziland for sixty-two years and was then the longest-ruling monarch in the world.

There was then the usual succession row. Because of a mixture of tradition grafted over a semblance of Western democracy, Swaziland has a highly complicated system of governance. There is the king, known as the Ngonyama or Lion, (Lion-King, geddit?), and all his advisors, the Queen Mother or Ndlovukazi, which translates rather unflatteringly as The She-Elephant, and all her advisors, various tribal councils, the aforementioned parliament, a cabinet and civil service.

And the situation certainly isn't helped by the fact that Swaziland practises polygamy on a world-class scale. The Swazis like their kings to have plenty of wives: it is regarded as a sign of virility. Indeed, there is an annual Reed Dance in Swaziland, one of the purposes of which is for the king to have a look at the young women and see who he fancies. If he has the energy and inclination, the King of Swaziland can get himself one or several new brides every twelve months.

And it seems as if Sobhuza was particularly keen on maintaining this tradition. He had so many wives that no one is sure how many wives he had: the estimates range from 60 to 120. He could have had as many as 200 children. Unhappily, Sobhuza didn't name a successor, leaving the field clear for his dozens of wives to argue that it was their son who was the favoured one, while also landing themselves the powerful She-Elephant gig in the process.

At first, Queen Regent Dzeliwe got the job, but kept squabbling with the Liqoqo, a supreme traditional advisory body. Two years later, she was replaced by another wife, Queen Regent Ntombi.

Ntombi was made of tougher stuff and managed to fire several of the leading members of the Liqoqo, while naming her son, Prince Makhosetive (King of Nations) as the heir to the throne. (She made such an impact that in 1985 Andy Warhol painted her portrait.)

In 1986, Makhosetive returned from school in England and was enthroned as King Mswati III. Mswati was just eighteen years of age.

Given his youth, there isn't a lot to tell about him. According to the official accounts, he joined the Swazi defence forces as a cadet when he was just five years of age, and afterwards was educated at Sherborne, a mega-posh public school in the south of England.

It's doubtful if Mswati had much of a vision of government at this time. One of his first acts was to abolish the Liqoqo and appoint a new parliament, but it was probably the mammy who was guiding these decisions. (As Queen Mother, Ntombi has a role in governing the state; her 'softness' balancing the King's 'hardness'.) However, Mswati did make one break with tradition in those early days. Having married and sired a son with satisfying haste, Mswati decided not to kill him: the custom had been that the first-born child of the first marriage was always put to death.

Mswati drew the line at infanticide, but that was pretty much the only idea he had. For the most part he took part in various rituals designed to increase his virility: in the Ncwala, a black bull is punched to the ground, slaughtered and then sat on by the naked king.

In truth, he probably didn't need the help. By all accounts, Mswati adores being King, and particularly enjoys the hunt for new wives. At the annual Reed Dance he is said to sit resplendent on his throne, covered in peacock feathers, a huge grin stapled to his face. A lot of the girls are rather keen too: hoping to escape their grinding poverty by getting to be a queen.

He knows what he likes, and in truth, a lot of men would agree with him. While the Reed Dance is ostensibly a mark of respect to the Queen Mother – a wall of reeds is built around her residence – it is more a chance of Mswait to ogle a few thousand topless thong-wearing virgins. In Swaziland, they call it tradition. In the West, we call it lap-dancing.

Not that the King's courtships have been without controversy. Eyebrows were raised when Mswati's first wife, Queen LaMbikiza, (she's actually his third wife, but the first he chose for himself) broke tradition by training as a lawyer. (LaMbikiza is also rather keen that their first-born son, Prince Lindani, be named as heir to the throne. Apparently she makes a habit of referring to him as 'His Majesty' in front of the King). In 1999 there was a huge stink when *The Times* of Swaziland published pictures of Mswati's eighth bride-to-be, Sentani Masango, claiming that she had been kicked out of two schools for absenteeism and disobedience. The story was condemned in parliament. The editor of *The Times* was fired from his job and arrested for criminal libel.

However, in October 2002, events took a far more sinister turn. Zena Mahlangu, an 18-year old A-level student, simply disappeared one morning on her way to school. Later on that day, Zena's mother, Lindiwe, was contacted by royal aides who informed her that Zena had been detained at the King's residence, the Kraal, for 'royal duties'.

Lindiwe then took the highly unusual step of going to the Swazi High Court and challenging Mswati's right to abduct her daughter. But before the hearing was over, Zena was officially named as a Liphovela (fiancée). As she was eighteen, Zena was not covered by the UN convention on the rights of the child. Lindiwe had no option but to withdraw the case. Shortly afterwards, Zena became wife number ten. Two other girls, also apparently abducted, have become wives eleven and twelve.

Such activities might be considered inconsequential when compared to the fates of nations, except in Swaziland it is exactly this behaviour which is helping tear the country apart. While Mswati marries anything he fancies, the still-large numbers of his citizens who support him try to follow this example – and are dying as a result. In March 2004, Swaziland overtook Botswana as having the highest HIV infection rate in the world: *40 per cent of the population.* Over 50 000 Swazis have died from AIDS.

Naturally, this has prompted many suggestions, both from inside and outside the country, that now might be a good time to re-consider the whole polygamy idea. Swazi society expects women to be subordinate and submissive, and even outside marriage it is difficult for them to say no to sex. Many claim that the Reed Dance – which is attended by 30 000 young Swazis – further promotes promiscuity. Dozens of studies, undertaken in Swaziland and elsewhere, have pointed to polygamy as a major cause of the spread of HIV.

King Mswati, however, doesn't agree: "HIV/AIDS is promoted by an individual in the manner he or she goes about with his or her life," he said in 2003. "Otherwise, polygamy is not a factor. So long as people stick to their HIV-negative partners, there is no risk of HIV and AIDS."

Easier said than done, especially as most Swazis avoid blood tests for fear they might prove HIV-positive.

Even if they are willing to get a test, they have to travel miles to do so: supplies of drugs and facilities to fight the epidemic are chronically insufficient. The King, however, is building a top-of-the-range hospital for exclusive use by the Royal Family.

In fairness, Mswati has made a few speeches about how terrible AIDS is. He even organised one of those various-artists do-gooder CDs (*Songs for Life*, it was called) to raise money for kids orphaned by AIDS. Had a nice junket around the US promoting that one. He decreed that teenagers should remain virgins (punishable by up to three months in prison), then broke his own law by marrying a 17-year old: for which he paid a fine of five cows

His efforts at fighting AIDS, and that of his government, remain criminally insipid, slyly predicated by the notion that if someone contracts HIV, they deserve what's coming.

Mswati's advisors make speeches hinting that the

government might in future stop 'wasting' medical support to HIV/Aids patients because they contracted the disease by choice. Others talk about setting up concentration camps for AIDS sufferers to isolate them from the rest of the population.

Mswati's apparent indifference to the suffering of his own people has also extended to the economy. Although Swaziland is the world's most efficient producer of sugar cane, agricultural production in general declined during the 1990s. The signs were that Swaziland would have to do something to reverse this trend or it wouldn't be able to feed itself.

So what did Mswati do? Virtually nothing. Four successive years of drought were more than enough to plunge the country into a crippling famine. Swaziland has foreign debts of €3.5 billion, one-third of its Gross Domestic Product. The unemployment rate is forty per cent, with sixty-six per cent of the population existing below the poverty line, most of them barely surviving on foreign aid. Thanks to the winning combination of AIDS and starvation, average life expectancy is 45. Infant mortality is one in ten. If things continue the way they are now, by 2010, life expectancy in Swaziland will be just 27 years.

To make things even more jolly, the World Food Programme, the EU and the IMF all withdrew their food aid in 2003 in protest over what they saw as the Swazi government's reckless spending.

Of course, what they failed to understand was that this wasn't reckless spending so much as maintaining tradition. You can't have members of the Royal Family riding bicycles around the place, which was why he had to spend €1.2 million on BMWs for his relatives. You can't have them working either: which is why the state has to financially maintain Mswati's 200 brothers and sisters. And you can't expect the queens to live in any old dump: which is why they are redecorating three palaces and building eleven new ones.

However, in 2003, in a moment of crushing meanness, the parliament opposed a proposal from the king to buy himself a brand-spanking-new €35 million executive jet, despite the fact that he had already put down a deposit. Poor baby.

Luckily, if Maswati needs a bit of pocket money, he can always turn to Tibiyo TakaNgwane, a multi-million dollar investment corporation set up by his Daddy in the 1960s. No one knows exactly how multi the millions are, because Tibiyo pays no tax, though it does own land, farms, diamond mines, newspapers and investments in every foreign business in the country, to name just a very few. Technically, the assets of Tibiyo TakaNgwane are held in trust by King Mswati for the starving, disease-ridden Swazi people, though they have yet to see any of the profits.

Indeed, thousands of Swazi subsistence farmers have been evicted from their land to make way for commercial farms run by Tibiyo; even land originally earmarked for distribution to Swazi peasants was suddenly gobbled up by the corporation.

Themba Dlamini, the current Swazi prime minister, was previously MD of Tibiyo TakaNgwane.

So with all this going on, you'd think the Swazi people would be going berserk. And some of them are: at least, the ones who aren't starving or dying from AIDS. In 1996, there were rumours of South African military intervention, prompting Mswati to promise that he would 'speed up' the democratisation process. Nothing happened.

A group called the Black Tigers were responsible for several bomb blasts in the capital, Mbabane, in 1999, though little has been heard from them since. Large trade union protests in 2001 were met with arrests. Many other opponents of the regime have been forced into exile. The press is rigidly controlled, and all political parties are still banned. Any criticism of the King is legally regarded as treason. Opponents have to say how much they love him, then respectfully suggest change.

In fact, the Swazi government appears to be attempting to increase its stranglehold on Swazi society, specifically the judiciary. In 2000, two local chieftains in Macetjeni and KaMkhweli were arbitrarily sacked and replaced with Mswtai's brother, Prince Maguga. Local people protested this decision, and for their trouble, 200 of them were evicted from their land. They went to the Swazi High Court, which ruled that the evictions were illegal.

So in 2001, Mswati signed what is now the infamous Decree 2, a law which effectively gave him the power to ignore court rulings. The Swazi Supreme Court hit back, ruling that the King's decree was illegal. The government said that the court ruling that the King's decree was illegal was itself illegal. Not only was it confusing, it was a major confrontation between the government and the judiciary. The six members of the Swazi Court of Appeal resigned in protest. Judges on the Hugh Court staged a sit-in strike.

Eventually, the decree was rescinded following threats from the US to withdraw aid.

Afterwards, Mswati said it wasn't his fault. "I must admit that when I signed this decree, I did not read it at all. I just signed it."

Perhaps, by appearing to be very, very dumb, Mswati was cunningly distancing himself from the mess created by his government. Or perhaps, even more horrifyingly, he is very very dumb: a grinning buffoon who is quite happy to let his people die as long as he gets his annual quota of women and palaces. Ntombi, his she-elephant mother, still has considerable influence. And even though she keeps a much lower profile, she is effectively co-monarch.

But it is impossible to tell. Some think Mswati is the conservative force; others that he is liberal but has no room for manoeuvre between his mother and the government. There have been promises about constitutional reform, but little has happened. There were direct elections to the Swazi parliament in 2003, but given that the House of Assembly has no power, the turnout was unsurprisingly low.

The antagonism between the King and the Courts is still to be resolved, especially after a 2002 ruling whereby Mario Masuku, leader of the opposition organisation, the People's United Democratic Movement, was acquitted on a charge of sedition.

In January 2004, Mswati condemned the 'cowardly messengers', citizens who expose the country's problems. They would, he said, live shortened lives because they had incurred the wrath of God and the ancestral spirits. The king was the spiritual head of the nation, and national prosperity, including good weather, was channelled through him by God and the country's ancestral spirits.

The problem is that Mswati can talk complete crap like this and the people still love him. There is a pro-democracy movement in Swaziland, yet it has been unable to muster sufficient support to mount any significant challenge to the government. It also lacks a leader of any great charisma to be pitted against Mswati.

Just like at the foundation of the state, most Swazis live a simple, rural life run along traditional lines. They don't know they are dying from AIDS because their King couldn't be bothered to help them; they are unaware that their poverty could be alleviated if he simply put his hand in his pocket.

At least in the short term, any political change in Swaziland is unlikely to come from popular dissent. As is often the case with despots, the only apparent threat may come from inside his own family. In April 2001, a massive scandal broke involving allegations that someone tried to poison the king.

Palace insiders alleged at the time that Mswati complained of stomach cramps immediately after eating a special breakfast prepared by his wife, Queen LaMbikiza, the one who trained as a lawyer. Shortly afterwards, LaMbikiza and her two children were detained at the airport.

She was reportedly driven to the Lozitha Palace and questioned, but then allowed to travel to London to visit her father, who is the Swazi ambassador there. According to witnesses, the atmosphere at the airport was 'extremely tense'.

Mswati, meanwhile, was rushed to a private clinic in Pretoria for a week before being flown home for treatment by a team of senior Libyan doctors. They had been flown in specially by Colonel Mu'ammar al-Qadhafi. (Swaziland and Libya are pals from way back: see *Libya*.)

So did Queen LaMbikiza try to poison her husband? It's impossible to tell for sure, but unlikely. She seems far too smart to try something so Shakespearean. A committed Christian, she has recorded a gospel album and hosts a weekly Gospel music show on radio. She also runs two charities full-time.

Then there's that law degree. LaMbikiza now has a Masters and is making lots of noises about practising at the Swazi High Court.

All this adds up to a major head-wreck for traditionalists within the Swazi court. Usually, Queens have babies, do a bit of waving and smiling and keep their mouths shut. They certainly don't, gasp, *work*.

But LaMbikiza – who is genuinely popular with Swazis – not only works (albeit in a charitable role), she singularly fails to keep her mouth shut: she has admitted that her lavish lifestyle 'bothers' her when so many of her fellow citizens are poor; which is why she runs the two charities. "I am as happy as I can be under the circumstances," she said, implying that this isn't very happy at all. One Western diplomat has described her as a 'peacock in a gilded cage'.

Only a few months before the poisoning scandal, LaMbikiza told a South African magazine, "I don't care what Mswati does with his life." The interview followed allegations that it was she who had leaked that information about another wife being a high-school drop-out. The controversy was followed by another impromptu trip to visit Daddy.

She has also been uncomfortably frank about her relationship with Mswati's other wives. When asked was she friends with the other women, she said: "Um, gee, friends. I do not think so. We get along, but what is a friend? We get along. We are very diplomatic towards one another."

Most shocking of all, LaMbikiza doesn't dodge questions about Swaziland's AIDS/poverty crisis. "It seems like we're losing our direction," she recently said. "We need to change our priorities. We have to think about our people and what they need. The king needs to be enlightened."

If any ordinary Swazi made such a statement, they would probably be in prison now for treason.

As for the poisoning allegations, LaMbikiza flatly denied them. After a month in London, she returned home and told the South African *Sunday Times*: "No, I didn't poison my husband. I'm not cruel enough to do that." (You'll note she doesn't say she loves her husband either.) Explaining her sudden flight to the UK, she said: "I needed to get away from it all. I needed to protect my children. I did consider that it would make me look guilty but it was more important for my peace of mind and for my children not to be entangled in all this."

La Mbikiza claimed that the allegations were little more than rumours started by dark palaces forces who want to get her 'out of the picture,' a claim which has been repeatedly reported before and since: there have been allegations of a whispering campaign designed to make the Queen appear insane.

Who would be behind such an operation is unknown – though La Mbikiza says it is not any of her fellow wives. However, it does make sense that a relative liberal such as she would be regarded as a major threat by the palace establishment. Apparently, she gives free legal advice to her dopey husband, but more significantly, she is the one who has campaigned most vigorously to have her son named as heir to the throne.

If that happened, that would make La Mbikiza the She-Elephant: and in a position to bring about radical change.

Of course, Mswati is still in his thirties, so it probably won't happen soon. Even still, he does complain about all the working and marrying and impregnating wives he has to do: and several of his ancestors saw early graves for precisely this reason.

And having to think occasionally is probably putting his nervous system under terrific strain also. At a recent meeting between the U.S. Ambassador, James McGee, and Mswati, the Ambassador took the bold step of showing the King photographs of starving Swazis.

According to witnesses, the King's response was: "Oh, that's nice."

KING TAUFA'AHAU TUPOU IV

of the Kingdom of Tonga

The thing about Tonga is that, on the face of it, it doesn't seem so bad. The people are relatively poor, yes, but they are not starving to death: if anything, they are a bit overweight, and they get free land from the government to farm. They seem happy; certainly friendly: there is a Tongan code of conduct called *nofo fiefie* which places a premium on hospitality. It was in the 1800s that Captain Cook dubbed the place 'The Friendly Islands' and – despite the fact that the Tongans were actually planning to kill him but never got around to it – he was right. The Tongans are a warm, good-looking lovable people, living on a tiny string of islands which offer tropical beaches, rainforests, active volcanoes and perfect diving conditions: it ticks all the boxes to fill the description 'tropical paradise'.

Yet with virtually no democracy, an absolute monarch ruling, a government made up of his relations, siblings helping themselves to national assets and regular suppression of the press, Tonga also ticks all the boxes for the description 'autocratic state'. It's just that the Tongans are so nice that they're too polite to complain. At least not that loudly. And it's sunny. Pretty much all the time.

Located a stone's throw from the international date line, Tonga is made up of 170 islands, but don't let that fool you: 134 of them are uninhabited and the rest barely inhabited at all. Tonga is tiny, with a population of just over 100 000 people.

Because of its location, Tonga was the first place on earth to celebrate the new millennium. This was partially helped by the fact that in 1999, Tonga observed western-style daylight saving by putting the clock forward an hour in summertime, which is our winter. However, because of its gorgeous, year-round climate, the move was completely cosmetic, so once the millennium was over, they abandoned it.

However, the government didn't bother informing anyone of this change, so for some weeks after the official start of summer the following year, no one was too sure what the time officially was. It's just that kind of place.

Still, it wasn't always so laid back. By legend, the Tongans came into existence when the sun-god Tangaloa raped a girl who was shell fishing. The resulting child of their unhappy union was the first Tongan. And the Tongans, at least the males, were all kick-ass types, adhering to the belief that war and carnage were proper pursuits for noble and worthy men. They raped and pillaged all over the area, spreading their empire to parts of Fiji and The Samoan Islands in the thirteenth century.

It was the 1600s before the first Europeans arrived. First the Dutch, who thought it was beautiful, but a bit far away from everywhere: Tonga means 'South' in Polynesian. Then the British, including the aforementioned Captain Cook, had a look around and left. The Spanish laid claim to one of the Tongan islands, Vava'u, but didn't do anything about colonising it. The French also had a look, but then went home.

Probably because of its remote location, Tonga was never properly colonised: by the start of the 1800s only a handful of Europeans lived there, and most of them were pirates and various dodgy types hiding from the cops back home.

The only Europeans to stay in any numbers were missionaries from the Wesleyan Methodist church, who did a top-class job. Today, Tonga is still a strict Wesleyan Methodist Country: even the mildest kissing scenes are edited out of imported videos and DVDs. On Sunday, everything closes down: planes don't land; there are no buses, taxis or cars. About the only thing to do is in the capital, Nuku'alofa, (Tongan for 'Abode of Love'), is see King Taufa'ahau Tupou attend services at Free Wesleyan Centenary Church, where he is a lay preacher. It's something of a tourist attraction.

Tonga experienced some minor upheavals: it wasn't until the mid-1800s that all the islands properly unified into a kingdom, while in 1896, the British coerced Tonga into a treaty placing the country under UK protection in foreign affairs: a situation which persisted until 1970, when Tonga regained full sovereignty

By this time, King Tupou was already on the throne, (he'd been there since 1965), while the Tongan system of governance had already been in place for over 100 years.

It's a small country, with a small parliament: a 30-seat Fale Alea, or Legislative Assembly. Nine of the seats are available to 'commoners' (yes, that's what they actually call them) through direct elections; another nine are voted in by 'nobles' and the rest are directly appointed by the King. Because it's such a small country, it's almost inevitable that some of those nobles and direct appointments occasionally turn out to be relatives of His Majesty. Well, most of them actually. Pretty much all the time.

Effectively, Tonga is still a feudal society, with heredity nobles living off the efforts of the commoners: by law, commoners are still required to salute passing members of the nobility, and can be fined for not doing so. (There are also laws against gossiping, though prostitution isn't illegal. Public whippings are still practised on a limited basis. There is no facility for youth offenders on Tonga, so they are sent to Ata, a nearby tropical island. Most of the inmates regard it as quite a nice holiday.)

Technically, the King *owns* Tonga: every single inch of it. But in fairness, there is a quite trendy-lefty land tenure system. On reaching the age of sixteen, every Tongan male is entitled to rent – for life and at a nominal fee – 8.25 acres to farm and about three-quarters of an acre on which to build a home. Two-thirds of Tongans raise pigs and poultry.

Of course, there's always a catch: if the King or any of the nobles are having a major knees-up banquet, they don't nip down to the Tonga branch of Tesco – they simply take if off the commoners.

However, it is this element of self-sufficiency which has probably saved the Tongan economy from catastrophic melt-down: in terms of natural resources, it doesn't have much. Tonga's main exports include pumpkins, coconut, vanilla and bananas, while the country is also heavily dependent on money sent home from emigrants. It's getting by, but by the year seems to slip behind its more prosperous neighbours like Fiji and New Zealand.

Tonga is a country desperately looking for an industry, both to increase its wealth and stem the ever-growing levels of emigration. And, by God, have they tried. But we'll get to that.

First let's have a look at the Tongan Royal Family. There

isn't much television in Tonga, but thanks to the Royals, no one really notices: they are a massive form of entertainment, both in Tonga and throughout the Pacific. Part *Dallas*, part *Monty Python*.

King Tupou was born in 1918. He was educated in Australia's Newington College and the University of Sydney, making him the first Tongan monarch to receive a university education. But as soon as that was over it was straight into the family business, where he was Minister for Health, then Education, then Prime Minister.

In 1947 he got married to Halaevalu Mata, his wife having been chosen by his mother, the then Queen, Salote. It was a double wedding: Tupou's younger brother, Prince Tu'ipelehake, also got hitched to a bride chosen by Mammy. After Mother died and Tupou became King, Tu'ipelehake became Prime Minister, a role in which he served until 1991. However, Tu'ipelehake was equally well-known in Tonga for being a musician. He was even in a group called Ko e Tau'ataina Talavou, or the Bachelors.

As a King, Tupou has been pretty unremarkable, his main policy drive being to keep things as they are. He likes to travel a lot. He likes having fancy titles bestowed on him by foreign governments. However, his main claim to international fame is that he is the fattest King in the world. In 1995, as part of a drive to coax Tongans into losing weight, Tupou went on a diet. At the public weigh-in, he clocked up 31 stone. (Obesity is a major problem on Tonga. Some scientists think that generations of feast and famine killed off the skinny Tongans, leaving only those who can store fat easily.) It's not known how much weight he lost, if any. He's in his mid-eighties now, and the health isn't great. Still, he's a pleasant enough chap. According to a former New Zealand High Commissioner stationed in Tonga: "It is a pleasure to spend time in their company and partake of their champagne and caviar." Hence the 31 stone.

What's more interesting about Tupou are the children he has produced. Mainly thanks to their adventures, Tonga has become a far less pleasant place to live. There are four of them: Crown Prince Tupouto'a, the heir to the throne and the only unmarried one, Princess Pilolevu, the only girl, Prince Ma'atu, and Prince Ulukalala Lavaka Ata.

Let's start with the youngest first:

Prince Ulukalala Lavaka: undoubtedly the most boring of the four, Prince Lavaka is the current Prime Minister, as well as Minister for Defence and Foreign Affairs. Lavaka got the PM job in 2000 and was a surprise appointment: everyone though that it should naturally go to the eldest son, and heir to the throne, Tupouto'a. But Tupouto'a had been making noises about reform and wanted to appoint his own cabinet. (Under the Tongan constitution, this is the King's job.) There's also the fact that Tupouto'a is a little weird.

In fact, many would privately like Lavaka to be the next King. He is well thought of in Tongan government circles: solid and cautious in his approach to issues. The sensible one of the family.

Prince Ma'atu: he died from a heart attack in February 2004, aged just 49. Told you these guys were fat. Yet in his short life, he managed to cause one major stink: in 1980, he fell in love with a commoner, Heimataura Anderson, the daughter of a Hawaiian millionaire. Knowing the relationship would not be tolerated at home, Ma'atu fled the kingdom and married her in Hawaii without Daddy's permission.

Somewhat miffed by this, King Tupou officially annulled

the marriage and stripped Ma'atu – and his heirs – of any royal rights.

However, five years later Heimataura Anderson died from cancer. Ma'atu returned home, where he was eventually reconciled with Dad and got back his Prince title. He re-married, to the granddaughter of Samoa's Head of State, (an approved union this time), and even took a Noble seat in the Tongan parliament. Some suggest that he secretly supported the growing pro-democracy movement in Tonga, though he never said this publicly.

Princess Pilolevu: not everyone thinks Lavaka would make a good king. Pilolevu thinks she would do a much better job, and already there is much speculation that she is the secret power behind the throne.

Not that Pilolevu has been that nice or sensible. Enter Josh Liava'a. A Tongan, Josh emigrated to Auckland where he became a detective sergeant in the police. There he met Princess Siuilikutapu, a niece of King Tupou. In 1969, they got married.

But it was that old you-can't-marry-a-commoner problem, so once again Tupou annulled the marriage. And this time it worked: the relationship with Siuilikutapu ended. Josh claimed he received death threats from Tongan officials.

In 1971, Josh married again. In 1986 he moved home to Tonga and set up a squash export business, which did very well until the Royal Family set up in direct competition. He was forced to return to New Zealand in 1989 without a penny. Shortly afterwards, he split with his second wife. However, the business failure probably wasn't the reason for this: turns out that while in Tonga he had embarked on an affair with Princess Pilolevu.

It became public some years later when the *Times of Tonga* published a rather poignant letter from Pilolevu to

Josh. Pilolevu, who was also married, wrote: "The purpose of such a marriage as mine is to beget a son to ensure the line of Tuita. I have as yet to fulfil this obligation.

"So, when you hear that I have become pregnant or given birth again, it's not that I have forgotten you (for I never will), it's just the normal performance of such duties that are expected of me." There were claims that their relationship continued until 1996.

Naturally, the Tongan Royal Family – who already weren't too keen on Josh Liava'a – went completely ballistic. They claimed to the New Zealand police that Josh was planning to assassinate King Tupou. Josh claimed King Tupou had put a contract out on his life. The row eventually died down, but it was probably one of the reasons why the government eventually got revenge on the *Times of Tonga*. More of that later.

With a broken heart to heal, Pilolevu threw herself into the world of business. Being on the equator, Tonga owns several slots in space in which to position geostationary satellites. Technically, these slots belong to the Tongan government, but Pilolevu just took them anyway and set up a company, Tongasat, which leases out those slots to other countries.

Thanks to her ability to help herself to national assets, she is now the richest women in the Pacific: worth $25 million, according to the US business magazine *Forbes*.

And she's been a dab hand at the politics too: in 1999, she convinced Daddy to establish diplomatic ties with China, despite the fact that Tonga had enjoyed years of diplomatic relations with China's arch-enemy, Taiwan. (See *China*.)

The Chinese were delighted, and gave King Tupou a statue of himself '25 per cent larger than life size', which must have been pretty big.

Pilolevu was also pleased. Her daughter, Salote Lupepeu'u Tuita, was installed as consul to China. Yet it seemed a bizarre change of policy, especially when Pilolevu unconvincingly claimed that they had only done it to get Christian evangelists into China.

However, shortly afterwards, Tongasat began leasing satellite slots to the Chinese government. *Aaah*. She's no dope.

Crown Prince Tupouto'a: it's difficult to know where to start with this one. Now in his fifties, and bothered by gout, he was in his early days a bit of a firebrand, giving out about his corrupt relations in government, about the waste and bureaucracy which was holding the country back.

Yet it doesn't seem as if this anger was prompted by care for the people. In a recent interview, Tupouto'a opined that ordinary Tongans were 'squatters who would urinate in elevators if there was nothing to stop them'. Ouch.

Tupouto'a has held some government posts – Minister for Defence, for Foreign Affairs – but in recent years seems to have lost his enthusiasm for politics. Now with no political role – at least until the old man kicks the bucket – Tupouto'a devotes his energies to various hobbies. Rather big hobbies. Think of a small boy with millions to spend.

Educated in Australia, Switzerland and Oxford, Tupouto'a is fluent in Tongan, English, French and German. Still unmarried, he's said to be something of a party animal, with regular trips abroad plus membership of an exclusive Tongan men-only club where they get up to all sorts.

He's bright, there's no doubt about that, but in a nerdy way: he has a huge collection of toy soldiers and used to stage Agatha Christie-type murder mysteries in his palace. Foreign actors were flown in to play the various parts. (The palace is a huge Italian-style villa with a half-mile driveway.

It is the only residence in Tonga to have a 110volt power supply, (everyone else has 220v), because Tupouto'a prefers to use American appliances.)

He fancies himself as a bit of singer, he collects Japanese art, he dances the Mambo, he founded a brewery and has written an (unpublished) 1 500 page novel set in Czarist Russia.

Yes, this guy has way too much time on his hands. In 2001, he spent the best part of a year shooting an expensive and as yet unscreened documentary about the lost tribes of Mongolia, during which an eagle attacked his Russian fur hat.

More recently, it's technology that's been turning him on. Thanks to a present from Daddy, he already owns Tonga's electricity system, and now plans to establish a high-tech communications system over the islands, delivering phone and broadband internet over a wireless link. He set up a centre to teach computer skills and also has ownership of the Tongan .to internet suffix, which he sells to foreigners.

But while Tupouto'a does have something of the visionary about him, he appears to be a completely crap businessman. Selling the .to suffix hasn't brought in the millions he'd hoped for, while – despite all the talk about the communications network – it still takes two years to get an ordinary phone installed in Tonga. And even if the high-tech system was completed, it seems highly unlikely that many Tongans would subscribe to it: these are mainly subsistence farmers with an average annual income of $1 000. The only obvious customer would be the Prince himself.

So they are the kids. It would be nice to report that Princess Tupouto'a inherited her business cunning from her father, but alas, that is not the case: King Tupou, just like his son Tupouto'a, has an eerie ability to get involved in bad business deals.

To give him the benefit of the doubt, the King's various ventures were probably motivated from the best intentions: to give his country some sort of economic future. Yet it seemed to leave him vulnerable to every snake-oil salesman and corrupt Tongan official who happened to passing by. Here's a selection:

* They loosened the banking laws, effectively making Tonga a tax haven. But this quickly led to accusations that the Kingdom was being used for money laundering. The Organisation for Economic Co-operation and Development (OECD) put Tonga on a blacklist, forcing the King to quickly reform the regulations.

* They tried selling passports in the 1980s: €15 000 for each one, no questions asked. But the scheme fell apart when it was reported that a lot of the buyers were Chinese 'businessmen' with extremely dodgy backgrounds.

* They searched for oil, despite geological reports indicating that there wasn't any.

* They considered making Tonga a nuclear waste disposal site.

* They began registering foreign ships, but the ships proved to be engaged in various illegal activities.

* They planned to build an airport hotel with casino, but their potential business partner turned out to be wanted by Interpol.

* They planned to import used tyres from the US and burn them to generate energy, a plan which fell down when Greenpeace intervened.

* To 'stimulate tourism', the government-owned Royal Tongan Airlines was made to charter a Royal Brunei Air Boeing 757 to fly daily between Tonga and Auckland. The plane is regularly out of service for repairs and the rest of the time is mostly empty. It is costing the government $17 million a year.

* In 1997 an obscure Korean Christian group bestowed a 'World Peace Prize' on King Tupou. A sucker for any sort of award, Tupou proclaimed a national holiday in Tonga and let the Koreans march down the main street of Nuku'alofa. And you can imagine his joy when the Koreans then announced that they were prepared to sell Tonga the world's first factory capable of converting seawater into natural gas. You can guess what happened. It is suspected that the elaborate hoax was part of a plan to dump unwanted nuclear waste in the kingdom. (In 2001, Sun Myung Moon, the head of Korea's Unification Church – or the Moonies – donated two naval patrol boats to the Tongan government. It's still not clear what they were up to.)

* Jesse Bogdonoff. Until it was closed down in 1991, the scheme to sell passports had brought in about $26 million, all of which was invested in a trust fund at the Bank of America in San Francisco. The Tongans' main contact at the bank was Jesse Bognonoff, who previously had run a business selling magnets to cure back pain.

Jesse and the Tongans got on well: so well that he began visiting the islands to provide first-hand financial advice. Jesse was obviously intelligent, but funny too, so King Tupou appointed Jesse as the Tongan official jester. He even gave him a three-pointed hat.

He also allowed Jesse to begin investing the $26 million. Jesse put the lot into a firm called Millennium Asset Management, which traded in the life insurance policies of the elderly and terminally ill. Shortly afterwards, Millennium Asset Management went bust. The money had evaporated.

You can imagine the stink: the Deputy Prime Minister and Education Minister both had to resign. The Tongan government sued Jesse in a US court, but ended up settling for $80 000. The jester's hat was never returned.

More recently, a Californian company called InterOrbital announced that it planned to use one of Tonga's uninhabited islands to launch week-long tourist trips into outer space.

They'll never learn.

What's truly amazing, however, is that the Tongan public let their Royal Family get away with it: in a country where the only real choices are emigration or poverty, the Royals enrich themselves on state assets and waste millions on nutty schemes.

It wasn't until 1992 that a pro-democracy movement sprang up in Tonga, forming itself into a proper political group, the People's Party, two years later. In the parliamentary elections of 1996, the PP won six of nine seats open to commoners.

However, King Tupou refused to appoint any of them to cabinet, claiming that they had only gone into politics because they couldn't get another job. The head of the PP, Akilisi Pohiva, has been jailed for contempt of parliamentary proceedings while he and other pro-democracy leaders are continually monitored and harassed by the Tongan police. In the 2002 elections, the PP won seven out of the nine seats, yet still are not in government.

King Tupou has also got sick of all this freedom of speech rubbish. Since 1989, the *Taimi 'o Tonga* or *Times of Tonga* has gleefully reported on the various Royal fiascos, in the process becoming the best-selling publication in the kingdom. For his trouble, the *Times*' editor, Filo Akau'ola, has been given an eighteen-month suspended sentence for 'provoking a civil servant to anger', then 30 days behind bars for reporting on a government impeachment proceeding. Naturally, the libel writs have fallen like snow, yet still the *Times* has survived.

In 1997 the government tried not to renew its trading licence, but a legal threat made it back down. In 2002, customs officers seized shipments of the paper (for practical reasons it is printed in New Zealand) and refused to allow it to be distributed. After a four-month legal battle, the *Times* was allowed back in the shops.

The King tried a different tack then, instituting legislation which banned foreign ownership of Tongan media. Simultaneously, he revoked the citizenship of the *Times* publisher, Kalafi Moala, thus making him a 'foreigner'. But given that the paper was printed in New Zealand, this was tricky to make stick.

So in 2003, the King went all the way and introduced a law giving him the power to ban any publication which 'went against Tongan culture': a definition so vague, it effectively meant he could ban anything he liked.

And finally, Tongans seemed to wake up to what has been happening in their country. More than 6 000 people – for Tonga, a huge crowd – marched on the Legislative Assembly demanding that the law be revoked. The King's nephew, Prince Uluvalu Tu'ipelehake, publicly supported their cause – and was threatened with being charged with treason.

But like any good despot, King Taufa'ahau Tupou IV didn't listen to a word of it, and in January 2004 refused a trading licence to the *Times of Tonga*. It is still published in New Zealand, Australia and the US, and along with the money they send home, Tongan emigrants now send clippings. But they have to be careful: anyone in Tonga now caught with the paper faces criminal charges.

A campaign of protests is on-going, yet it's difficult to see King Tupou backing down. And after he dies, his kids don't look too democracy-friendly either.

While they enjoy the caviar and champagne, their subjects will continue to scrape a living or leave the country altogether. Yet there is one business prospect which just might help the islands: in 2000, an Australian biotechnology firm struck a deal with the King which allowed it to construct a DNA database of the Tongans. Because of Tonga's isolation and ethnic homogeneity, there are fewer 'genetic distractions' there, and this information could help find the genetic cause of some common diseases.

Tonga will receive royalties, (pardon the pun), on any drugs which emerge from the study. Hopefully, this money will come while there are still any Tongans living there.

PRESIDENT SAPARMYRAT ATAYEVICH NIYAZOV
of the Republic of Turkmenistan

Ah yes, Turkmenistan: one of the jewels of central Asia. A land shrouded in so much exotic mystery that just the mere mention of its name prompts people to exclaim: where?

If you've never heard of Turkmenistan or, more probably, heard it mentioned in the news a few times recently but were too embarrassed to own up, fear not: no one else has either. Even the people who live there are but dimly aware of the place.

The main reason for this is that, until fairly recently, it was part of that huge oppressive blob fondly remembered as the Soviet Union. About half-way along and at the bottom: not a great location, it must be said. Let's try and put it kindly: if Turkmenistan was a house with a For Sale sign outside, it would be dark, tiny, damp and situated in between a brothel and a crack den. OK, that's not too kind, but look: the place shares borders with Iran and Afghanistan; huge swathes of it are uninhabitable as it possesses some of the hottest deserts on the planet; it was the poorest republic in the Soviet Union.

Still, mustn't grumble, and in large part the Turkmen don't. (Turkmen being what people from Turkmenistan call themselves. Yes, the women too). They are, and have been for centuries, a stoic race.

Except, of course, if you ask a Turkmen if they are from Turkey. They are distant cousins, both linguistically and culturally, but that's as far as it goes. The Turkmen were horse breeders who migrated around eastern Europe and central Asia generations ago, while the Turks, er, stayed in Turkey. There is, for instance, a Turkmen population in Northern Iraq which Turkey was concerned about 'protecting' (while in the process kicking some Kurd butt, but that's another story) during the second Gulf War. Yes: that's where you heard of the Turkmen before.

No one is too sure when the Turkmen arrived in Turkmenistan, though all agree that back then it wasn't called Turkmenistan. In fact it wasn't called anything: 'over there' was the best it aspired to. Yet even for unnamed countries there is a role, so Turkmenistan became a kind of ancient motorway service station: a place to pass through while you're on your way to invade somewhere else.

And by all accounts, it did a roaring trade: Alexander the Great, the Romans, the Arabs, the Turks, Genghis Khan; the guest book was jammed with famous signatures. Not that the Turkmen always came out to meet this celebrity traffic: as a tribal, nomadic people, the Turkmen were suspicious of outsiders and were more inclined to keep themselves to themselves. But if they were stuck for a few bob, they would hire themselves out as mercenaries. Hey: we've all done it.

And the experience the Turkmen picked up from fighting for others did pay dividends: after a few centuries of that they graduated to preying on caravans, stealing slaves and general pillaging. Oh yes: and by now the area had a name. Turkmenia. It even had a few towns, mostly established by the various armies which had passed through.

But you know what it's like: you're just going about your business, when next thing you realise that the people you kidnapped today are part of the strengthening Tsarist empire. And the Tsar wasn't too pleased. In 1881 Russians troops marched into Turkmenia and massacred an estimated 7 000 Turkmen. A further 8 000 were cut down as they fled across the desert.

The rest was easy. After all, Turkmenia didn't have any central government. Most Turkmen didn't even think of it as a country. So to show no hard feelings for the whole kidnap thing, the Tsar did it for them, christening their land, (pardon the pun: the Turkmen are Muslims) the Transcaspia Region of Russian Turkistan.

The Turkmen weren't entirely potty about this development. But like always, they kept themselves to themselves.

However, exciting times lay ahead for the TRRT – including even more snappy name changes. After the Russian revolution, it became the Turkistan Autonomous Soviet Socialist Republic, then in May 1925, the name changed again to the pithier Turkistan Soviet Socialist Republic.

Burdened with the unfortunate acronym TSSR, Turkmenistan didn't do particularly well under socialism. It didn't seem to produce much of anything, while its major import was Russians: sent there to run the country.

But let's whizz forward to happier times: the late 1980s. In Moscow, Gorbachev is dismantling state socialism while the Russian mafia are embarking on a major recruitment drive. The Soviet Union is falling apart.

In 1990, the Communist Party of the TSSR proclaimed sovereignty and quickly set about instituting massive democratic reform. Well: not massive. To be exact, there were two changes:

1) The Communist Party changed its name to the Democratic Party, though it remained the only legal political party in the state, and therefore, not even remotely democratic.
(They are not big on spotting irony in Turkmenistan.)

2) Presidential elections were held. As there was only one party, there was only one candidate: Saparmyrat Atayevich Niyazov, the head of the Democratic (née Communist) Party. Running against absolutely no one, his was a stunning victory, garnering 98 per cent of the vote.

How many people actually voted remains a mystery. Back to that nomadic, tribal thing: many Turkmen would have no interest in voting and maintain a deep distrust of central government. They would assume that those who go into politics only do so to benefit themselves.

Well, they weren't to be disappointed. Not only that: the Turkmen were about to start life with one of the classic despots of the twenty-first century and arguably, the maddest.

But this all lay in the future. Back in 1990, there may even have been some optimism lying around the place. After all, they were free of the communist yoke, they had a new president and yet another name for the country: Turkmenistan. And for the first time, perhaps even a future: the Turkmen learned that their country had natural resources which had lain unexplored and unexploited during the Soviet era: the world's fifth largest reserves of natural gas, and substantial deposits of oil.

Yes, the good times were going to roll for Turkmenistan and the new president wasted no time in promising that he would transform the country into a 'second Kuwait', (another country with no democracy). He decreed that electricity, gas and water should be free and that within a decade every adult citizen would receive their own car and house, completely gratis.

But before we detail how life became fantastic for the ordinary Turkmen, let's look at the humble beginnings of Saparmyrat Atayevich Niyazov.

Life wasn't easy for the young Saparmyrat. Born in 1940 in Ashgabat, the capital, his father died shortly afterwards during World War II. The Niyazovs struggled on, but then even more tragedy was visited upon them: in 1948, a massive earthquake rocked Ashgabat, killing Saparmyat's mother and the rest of his family.

This second loss had a profound effect upon the future president, and, eventually, everyone else in the country.

For a while, he lived in an orphanage and then was taken in by distant relatives. But like all great men, he didn't allow past tragedy to affect his future prospects. While working in a power station, he married and had a couple of kids, but more significantly, joined the Communist Party and slowly clambered up its ranks. He became Party Chairman in 1985, then Chairman of the Supreme Soviet in early 1990 – just in time for succession from the USSR. Like many Soviet-style politicians, he lacked charisma – even today, he's just a chubby guy in a cheap suit with badly dyed hair. But what he lacked in pizzazz he made up for with cunning, the ability to kiss ass and stab in the back. Often simultaneously.

Then again, this kind of experience is invaluable when you are president of a country and intend to remain so. Soon after his landslide election victory, Saparmyat had himself declared Prime Minister, Chairman of the Cabinet of Ministers (all of whom he appoints) and Chairman of the Democratic Party of Turkmenistan.

But that wasn't enough. Unlike a lot of former Soviet leaders, Saparmyat saw himself as having a 'significance' beyond politics. He was *culturally*, even *spiritually* important. After all, he was now leader of the first-ever Turkmen state. So he established the Association of Turkmens of the World, with himself as both founder and president

Then he gave himself an additional name: *Turkmenbashi*, which means Leader of all Turkmens. Everywhere. He likes people to call him Turkmenbashi. In a rather big way. The national slogan became *Halk. Watan. Turkmenbashi*: One Country, One People, One Leader.

It was around this time that many Turkmen probably had that *oh-uh* moment as they started to realise that not only was their president a power-hungry despot, but he was crazy to boot. Within five years, Turkmenistan had become a shrine to its leader.

Today the country is plastered with posters, portraits and statues of Turkmenbashi, including a 120-foot-high gold-plated monument in Ashgabat that actually rotates to follow the sun. Several towns, dozens of mosques, a meteorite (no, really) and a large Caspian City sea port have been named after him. So too have yoghurts, perfumes, a brand of vodka and various foodstuffs. Turkmen officials have tried to nominate Turkmenbashi for the Nobel Peace Prize on the basis of his 'contribution to world history'.

As planes begin their descent into Turkmenbashi airport, passengers aren't given the usual recommendations for hotels or car rentals, but instead have to listen to flight attendants recite the pledge of allegiance:

> *Turkmenistan, my beloved motherland,*
> *my beloved homeland!*
> *You are always with me*
> *in my thoughts and in my heart.*
> *For the slightest evil against you*
> *let my hand be lost.*
> *For the slightest slander about you*
> *let my tongue be lost.*
> *At the moment of my betrayal*
> *to my motherland, to her sacred banner,*
> *to Saparmurat Turkmenbashi let my breath stop.*

Then they are treated to a talk on the virtues of the leader. Of which there are many.

Some years back the collected speeches of Turkmenbashi were collected in a two-volume book – one of the few books widely available in Turkmenistan. *The Sayings of Turkmenbashi* are memorised in every school and university, every day. It includes gems such as: 'Anyone who complains about going without sausage or bread for a day is not a Turkmen'.

There aren't TV programmes in Turkmenistan, at least not in the way we understand them. Instead, the activities of the president are detailed for hours each day. And even when he's not on, a golden silhouette of the leader is superimposed on all TV pictures transmitted in Turkmenistan.

No, it's not a fun country. Telly is crap, books are hard to come by, while opera, ballet, the circus and classical music are all banned. Turkmenbashi doesn't like them.

What he does like, though, is a nice palace. He has many of them spread across the republic and two lavish estates on the edge of the capital. Recently, French architects designed him a vast new $100-million gold-domed, white marble presidential palace, described as post-modern Ottoman, with some Louis XV interiors, slap-bang in the centre of town.

Yet despite the opulence, he is modest to a fault, claiming that these riches are forced upon him by his adoring subjects. "All I wanted was a small, cosy house," he once said, claiming that Parliament overruled him.

In 1999 the country's supreme legislative body, the Mejlis, made him President-for-life. Of course, he didn't want the honour, but decided to accept it, not wishing to offend anyone.

Now, you may not be suitably impressed or appalled by this kind of carry-on: it is, after all, the standard personality cult stuff. (See *North Korea*.) But what makes Turkmenbashi special is his desire not just to be a towering political figure in his country, but also to be a kind of god.

A few years back Turkmenbashi wrote (or more exactly, got a team of scholars to write for him) a spiritual tract that the state media enthusiastically compares to the Koran or the Bible. It is taught in all schools. It's called *The Rukhnama* which means 'spiritual book'. On the leader's birthday in 2003, one minister said Turkmenbashi was 'a great personality who possesses the gift of a prophet'.

As Muslims, most Turkmen believe Mohammed was the last prophet. Therefore, Turkmenbashi's elevation to having prophet-like gifts is heresy. Yet in recent times the official Turkmen media have begun referring to their leader in quasi-religious language. The official website for Turkmenbashi's book, (www. Rukhnama.com) breathily declares that there are three great spiritual texts in history: the Bible, the Koran and the Rukhnama.

So obviously, once you're on the hotline from heaven, you're not going to be content to muck around with ordinary stuff of politics: increasing the old-age pension or banning the use of bicycles; you're going to want to use your superhuman powers to mould time and space itself.

Today, in Turkmenistan – by law – all the months of the year have different names. Most have been called after figures from Turkmen history, but January – surprise, surprise – is called Turkmenbashi. The last month of the year is Rukhnama and what was once April is now called Gurbansoltan-edzhe: the president's dead mother. The big man has also talked about renaming the days of the week and even opined that having twelve months is a bit extravagant when eight (forty-five day) months would be perfectly adequate.

If Niyazov wants his people to regard him as a Turkmen Jesus, then it follows that Gurbansoltan-edzhe should be Mary. Turkmenbashi idolises her memory, and expects all his fellow citizens to do the same. Not only do we have a month named after her, but also foodstuffs and publications: the Turkmen word for bread was officially changed to Gurbansoltan-edzhe, while Turkmenistan's only women's magazine is also named after her. Tricky if you want to buy some bread and the April issue of your favourite women's magazine. The Turkmenistan National Assembly also passed a resolution declaring 2003 as a year dedicated to the memory of Gurbansoltan-edzhe.

Some good news though: Turkmenistan might be a good place to retire to. By presidential decree, adolescence in Turkmenistan lasts until you are 25; old age does not arrive until you are 85; and the age range from 62 to 73 has been designated 'inspirational'. In 2003, Turkmenbashi was 63 years old. Or rather, 63 years inspirational.

Yet being inspirational doesn't put bread on the table. What about the ordinary Turkmen? How do they fare? What about all those early promises? What about that oil and gas?

You may be less than surprised to learn that so far, only

Ministers, committee heads, regional bosses and other senior bureaucrats receive a new car each year – a Mercedes. Electricity, water and gas are free for all, but strictly rationed. Hundreds of local schools and hospitals have been closed

The harsh reality is that ordinary Turkmen are poor and getting poorer. At the last estimate, the average Turkmen was living on an annual income of just €540. Unemployment runs at twenty-five per cent and drug addiction is rampant.

In fairness, Turkmenbashi has tried to sell his country's gas and oil, but until recently hasn't had that much interest. This is partly due to Turkmenistan's suspect foreign policy, (they were quite chummy with their former neighbours in Afghanistan, the Taliban), partly because Turkmenbashi is suspected of being involved in the drug trade (heroin and hashish into Russia), and partly because Turkmenbashi is viewed abroad as being, well, completely insane

But even nutters can do business, and in April of 2002 Russia finally signed a 25-year contract to buy natural gas from Turkmenistan. There were claims that one of the Russian companies buying the gas had connections to the Russian mafia, but everyone laughed off these ridiculous allegations. Corruption in big business? In Russia? Unthinkable.

There was some political advantages to the deal also. In exchange for the gas, President Putin agreed to end a 10-year-old dual citizenship agreement between the two countries, in place since independence. This gave Turkmenbashi the chance to send thousands of Russians back home: they were given a deadline by which they had to choose either Russian or Turkman nationality. Hmm, tough choice. The planes and trains to Moscow were thronged: a nifty piece of ethnic cleansing.

Whether the gas money will find its way down to the

ordinary Turkmen remains to be seen. But let's face it: no one's holding their breath. And it's not like anyone is going to complain. Turkmenistan remains a strict one-party state. Anyone opposing Turkmenbashi either leaves the country or faces jail/mental asylum. Elections there are viewed as so flawed that even the Organisation for Security and Cooperation in Europe (OSCE) refuses to send monitors.

In July of 1995, several hundred demonstrators marched down Ashgabat 's main avenue, handing out leaflets protesting food shortages. The leaders were arrested quickly.

At the time, President Niyazov declared that they were drug addicts who had lured teenage students to the rally with vodka and marijuana. Many of the protestors have never been seen since. But that's because it never happened. According to Turkmenbashi: "We have no political prisoners in this country."

One example of these non-existent political prisoners is Boris Shikhmuradov. A former Foreign Minister in Turkmenbashi's government, he resigned, fled to Turkey and became a leading light in the Turkmen opposition movement. But on a secret visit home he was arrested and named as the alleged mastermind of an attempt to kill President Niyazov.

And what an attempt it was: according to the official accounts, on November 25, 2002, a group of treacherous conspirators fired Kalashnikov submachine guns at the President's Mercedes in broad daylight while it moved through the centre of Ashgabat. Luckily, though, it was a bullet-proof Merc, so not only was Turkmenbashi unharmed, he didn't even notice the attack had taken place.

But, in what must be one of the greatest pieces of detective work in modern history, Turkmenbashi was able to appear on TV that night and name the masterminds behind the 'attack': chief among them being Boris Shikhmuradov, who had already been arrested.

The Ashgabat-based law weekly *Adalat* (Justice) quickly branded Shikhmuradov an enemy of the people, addressing him thus:

> *You are a son of a hangman capable of treading in his boots on corpses. Your blood is dirty, as are your soul, brains and mentality. Therefore, whatever your position, be it minister or ambassador, the filth within you comes from your ancestors, from your filthy father. Like father like son. You have not mended your ways, you traitor and offshoot of depravity. Your whole kin was bloodthirsty; the blood of a hangman runs in your veins. You are a rascal who does not hold anything sacred. If you hadn't been a man without conscience or honour, you would not have set foot, in the sacred month of Ramadan, on the land where our saints and protectors rest.*

Yet it would be churlish to keep such drama within the pages of a stuffy law review.

A year later, the book *Terrorist Act in Ashgabat* was published in Turkmenistan: a detailed account of the alleged attempt upon Niyazov's life, complete with pictures of all the conspirators. It was penned by one Leonid Komarovsky who was in an excellent position to know about the 'plot': as he admits in the foreword, "I was a witness and for some time a suspect . . .in one of the most absurd and stupid crimes in modern history."

Komarovsky, a Russian-born former journalist (but with a

US passport), happened to be in Turkmenistan on a business trip when he was arrested, drugged and forced to confess on national TV. He wrote *Terrorist Act in Ashgabat* while in prison. As coincidence would have it, once he had finished the book, and once the Turkmen chief prosecutor declared himself satisfied with all its 'facts', the charges against Leonid were dropped and he was allowed to leave the country.

Back home in the US and – surprise, surprise – Leonid promptly disowned the book and revealed that he only wrote it as part of a deal to get himself out of jail. More gob-smacking though was Leonid's claim that the Turkmenistan leadership actually believed that he would try to get *Terrorist Act in Ashgabat* published in the US. Either Turkmenbashi is a bit naive or Leonid is seriously good at sucking up.

Instead, Leonid published *Archipelago Turkmenistan*, an account of his five months in a Turkmen prison and what he had to do to get out of it.

Still, it's difficult to be entirely sympathetic to Leonid: the November 25 'terrorist attack' was of course nothing more than an elaborate ruse to stitch up Boris Shikhmuradov, the aforementioned former foreign minister and now leading light of the Turkmen opposition. *Terrorist Act in Ashgabat* – which put all the blame on Shikhmuradov – was a key part of that stitch-up.

After a Stalinist-style show trial, Boris Shikhmuradov received life, meaning life, imprisonment. He currently rots in a Turkmen jail where it is believed he has been extensively tortured. It is not thought he will live much longer. So far, fifty-six other 'conspirators' have received sentences ranging from five years to life.

So what are the international community doing about this? Well, the usual. Reports. Statements: the diplomatic equivalent of making the *tsk* sound. Turkmenistan simply isn't important enough for the US or the EU to put any effort into changing the regime there. Unless Turkmenbashi declares himself immortal, his presidency will end when he chooses.

Yet there are signs that this may happen sooner rather than later, because the presidential health hasn't been great: there was a bout with cancer in the mid-nineties, after which Turkmenbashi ordered his cabinet to give up smoking (he has fined government ministers caught with a ciggie), and banned smoking in public places. The cancer treatment also caused him to lose his hair, so he resorted to Chinese herbal remedies to spare his people from the 'unpleasantness' of having a bald leader. In 2002 there was a further tussle with kidney disease, though this didn't prompt the big man to give more thought to health care: in 2003 he savagely cut back spending on the Turkmen national health service, such as it is, while proudly announcing that he had spent $200 million on armaments

Instead, Turkmenbashi's brush with mortality has brought him to consider his legacy: as soon as he was well again, he announced that he would probably step down in 2007 or 2008 and make way for a new 'elected' leader. (Though the Turkmen parliament called on their beloved leader to reject this plan and stay in power until his death.) Then he engaged in some most un-despotic activity: a few (but by no means all) political prisoners (not that they have any) were given amnesty. While in his inspirational years, Turkmenbashi wants to be regarded as a democrat; a Nice Guy.

Well: not that nice. 2003 also saw the introduction of a jolly new law where all religions have to be registered, the catch being that only Sunni Muslims and Russian Orthodox groups are allowed do any registering. Since then, virtually all other (mostly Christian) groups have been raided, beaten, fined, sacked from their jobs, had their homes confiscated or sent for 'corrective labour'. If you ain't a Muslim or part of the Russian Orthodox church, now might be a good time to leave Turkmenistan, except you can't do that either: in January 2004, Turkmenbashi signed a decree which makes it virtually impossible for citizens to get an exit visa.

Not that he wanted to get all tough, no: he was forced to because of 'security concerns brought about by – yes, you guessed it – that 'assassination attempt' in November 2002'.

Still: the warm, caring cuddly personality which sometimes inhabits Turkmenbashi's brain did abolish the death penalty in 2003, calling it 'unworthy of a civilized society'.

In March 2004, having no doubt given the matter long and careful thought, President Niyazov passed a decree forbidding young men to wear long hair, beards or moustaches. The logic behind the new law is that too much Turkmen hair gave outsiders the 'wrong impression' of the country. You can see his point: as we all know, most foreigners have an irrational fear of hairiness.

Hairiness is also unhygienic, decreed Turkmenbashi, who for no apparent reason ordered that the Turkmen Education Ministry should police the ban.

With the regulations in place, Turkmenistan is becoming one of the best groomed countries on the planet, giving that all-important Good First Impression to visitors. However, the law also applies to visitors: *legally, you can't enter Turkmenistan in possession of a beard*; can't even get a special permit or leave it in some sort of Beard Kennel while you are visiting. If you want to visit Turkmenistan, the beard goes. State-funded barbers have now been set up at all airports and border crossings into the country.

It's not much to ask. In the presence of a god, we should look our best.

PRESIDENT ISLAM ABDUGANIEVICH KARIMOV

of the Republic of Uzbekistan

We've done two other countries ending in 'stan' already, so there's not as much to explain. But there are differences: the respective despots of Turkmenistan and Kazakhstan are jolly and colourful characters when compared to the dour, thunderous Karimov: a man who probably wouldn't appreciate the irony that his first name – Islam – is the thing he seems to hate the most; even though Uzbekistan is a Muslim country. Islam would probably have you boiled for making a joke like that.

Really: he would.

Just like many of its neighbours, Uzbekistan is a former Soviet Republic that didn't really want to let the old system go. So it made a few noises about human rights and market reform, changed a few job titles and then proceeded pretty much as it had before.

Only difference here is that while the West might be more cautious towards most of the other Central Asian republics, Uzbekistan is now a firm friend: at least with Britain and the US. As part of the War on Terror, Uzbekistan became the first former Eastern bloc country to have a US base on its territory. Thus blessed, Islam Karimov has been free to conduct a terror war all of his own.

So let's do the history bit: the Uzbeks are a Turkic people, which means they are related to the Turks, but very distantly. The Turkic tribes are thought to have originated in central Asia, then roamed all over the continent. Some of them ended up as far away as modern Turkey, some of them stayed where they are, in Uzbekistan. It was part of the Mongol empire for a few hundred years, but when that fell apart, the nomadic Uzbeks had established three Khanates in Uzbekistan. Those tribal divisions still have a subtle influence on Uzbek politics.

The Russians took over in the mid 1800s and you can guess the rest: the Russian revolution and the establishment of Uzbekistan as a 'Republic' within the USSR. As was the policy at the time, places like Uzbekistan were not so much countries as means of production: while neighbouring Kazakhstan was designated as a place to dump nuclear waste and fire off a few rockets, Uzbekistan was chosen as a huge cotton farm. Without coastline (it is surrounded by all the other 'stan' countries) and any apparent natural resources, this was all it was good for.

But, by God, if it was cotton they wanted, the Uzbeks were gonna give it to them. To boost production, they constructed vast irrigation systems, seriously reducing the country's water levels, and creating severe ecological problems later on. Uzbekistan became a huge, cotton-growing monster, so huge that in the mid-1980s thousands of Uzbek officials were arrested after it became apparent that cotton yield figures were being doctored and millions of roubles had gone missing. In a nice piece of revisionism, President Islam's official biography claims that at the time he bravely fought these Moscow-inspired 'criminal myths'. Yeah, right.

Then came 1991 and the break-up of the USSR. In Uzbekistan, just like every other former Republic, the head of the Supreme Soviet became President of the newly independent country. In Uzbekistan they did have an election to decide this, and Islam Karimov did get 85 per cent of the vote. But thanks to a lot of harassment, media manipulation and vote-rigging, most Uzbeks weren't even aware there was another candidate. Islam took his presidential oath with one hand on the new Uzbek constitution and another on the Koran. It's probably the last time he has seen either book.

So what's he like? Oh: dull, dull, dull. Except when he's angry. Then he's dull and really scary. He was born in the Silk Road City of Samarkand in 1938. His parents – his mother Tajik, his father Uzbek – were civil servants, but both died when he was still a child. The young Islam did most of his growing up in the dreary surroundings of a Soviet orphanage. After school he studied engineering in the Polytechnic Institute in Tashkent, the capital.

He was a bright young man, by all accounts, with a particular gift for mathematics. He could have pursued post-graduate studies, but instead opted to work as an engineer at the Chalov Tashkent aviation production complex. In 1966 he moved to the State Planning Office, did an economics degree at night, and began the slow, laborious climb up the party hierarchy: Chief Specialist, then First Deputy Chairman, then Minister for Finance, then Deputy Chairman of the Council of Ministers . . . finally, in 1989, he was appointed First Secretary of the Central Committee of the Communist Party of Uzbekistan.

Two years later, the whole Soviet Project had gone belly-up, and like most good communists of the time, Islam didn't think twice about dumping the old ideology: it was all Uzbek nationalism now. Islam, who spoke better Russian than

Uzbek, had to take secret language classes. The Communist Party became the People's Democratic Party. The new constitution guaranteed multi-party democracy.

Well, sort of: what the constitution didn't mention was that the Uzbek government would choose who the opposition parties were. Real opposition groups, such as Unity, the Islamic Renaissance Party, Freedom and the Erk Democratic Party were all banned. Their leaders either 'disappeared' or hurriedly left the country.

Instead, the opposition consists of the snappily-titled Homeland Progress Party, the Social Democratic Party, the National Rebirth Democratic Party, and the National Unity Social Movement. They are officially known as the 'loyal' opposition, to go along with the 'loyal' Prime Minister and cabinet, appointed by Islam, and the 'loyal' judiciary, appointed by Islam.

According to the constitution, the president is allowed a maximum of two five-year terms. But in 1995, Islam decided he was doing such a wonderful job, he should extend his first term in office until the year 2000. They had a referendum to decide the matter, and quite wonderfully, no one disagreed.

It's not known if this particular vote was rigged or not. Islam Karimov does have a measure of genuine support in Uzbekistan: like a lot of Eastern European countries, there is a tradition of admiring a strong leader, while any who opposed him probably didn't bother voting at all. Although the government wasn't promoting a personality cult like neighbouring Turkmenbashi's (see *Turkmenistan*), Islam had stamped his authority: his picture was and still is everywhere, while his ten books of speeches (with sexy titles like *Uzbekistan: Its Own Road of Renovation and Progress*) had become mandatory reading in schools and colleges.

Although freedom of speech is guaranteed in the Uzbek

constitution, the press were far too terrified to report anything negative. If anything, they were instrumental in touting the myth that a political future without President Islam at the helm was unthinkable.

It's a situation which has been maintained for so long that Islam seems to have begun to believe that journalists genuinely love him: in June 2003 the President accused the Uzbek press of lacking courage. "The authorities never come in for criticism," he said, adding that journalists were prone to the "stereotypical habit of taking officials' words as gospel."

So why are the press so craven? Probably because most of it is state-owned. There are some privately owned papers, but if they step out of line they can face massive libel actions. Foreign news bureaus have been subject to mysterious 'robberies'.

But these things happen only if dissenting journalists are really, really lucky. For the most part, they get thrown in jail, often on trumped-up charges of paedophilia or homosexuality (illegal in Uzbekistan). Sometimes, in classic Soviet style, they get shipped off to psychiatric hospitals and stuffed with drugs.

Then it's party time: Uzbekistan is the torture capital of the world. And they don't just do it to extract confessions: they regularly torture people to death. Hey: we all have to be good at something. If you're squeamish, avoid the next two paragraphs.

The most favoured methods include beating on the soles of the feet; breaking fingers, then ribs, then skulls with a hammer; stabbing with a screwdriver, sometimes for weeks, until the victim is dead; systematically ripping off flesh with a pliers; driving needles under the fingernails; leaving prisoners up to their knees in freezing water for weeks at a time. However, the most spectacular technique was only discovered when the dead bodies of prisoners were handed back to their families for burial: some of them had a red 'tidemark' around the middle of the torso.

They had been boiled to death. There are repeated reports of this happening.

Given such methods, would you write anything bad about this guy?

Not that journalists are the particular focus of Islam's attention; if anything, they are treated with relative leniency. It's the 'enemies of the state' he doesn't like: bogeymen with which to terrify his own people, justify his brutal oppression and even win some brownie points with the West. Luckily for him, he has an almost inexhaustible supply.

It's more than a decade since Uzbekistan achieved independence, yet it's still the same old post-Soviet story: there has been little reform of the economy, with most industry still resting in state hands. What is privatised has gone to party hacks and members of Islam's family: more of that later. Despite rich reserves of precious metals and natural gas, virtually nothing has been done to exploit them. The Uzbek currency, the Sum, is worthless: you can buy over 1 200 of them for €1. In the cities, there are daily power and water shortages; in rural areas, most Uzbeks survive on as little as $1 a day: unemployment in some areas is 80 per cent, while large tracts of land are polluted or have been turned into deserts due to the irrigation projects – which used salt water from the Aral Sea. Organised crime, drug addiction and human trafficking for prostitution are rife. Police arbitrarily stop citizens and extract 'fines'. Schoolchildren are annually used as slave labour to pick the cotton crops: still Uzbekistan's main export.

Into such a void of misery, there's usually someone ready to come in and provide an alternative: and it's come over the border from Afghanistan in the shape of Muslim fundamentalism.

Let's keep this in context: Uzbekistan is 88 per cent Muslim, and the vast majority of them are not radicalised. Yet there is a small, active and vocal minority, particularly in the dirt-poor Fergana Valley, into which a sizable proportion of the Uzbek population are stuffed. There are two groups: the Islamic Movement of Uzbekistan (IMU), which has links to the Taliban, and Hizb ut-Tahrir (Party of Liberation), which is legal in most western countries. Both advocate the usual stuff: the establishment of a strict Muslim state. The IMU wouldn't say no to a violent overthrow of the government, while Hizb ut-Tahrir seems to prefer abuse: it called Karimov a 'Jew' for establishing diplomatic links with Israel.

Then again, they could have called themselves Allah's All-Giggling Schoolgirl Party for all President Islam cares: in crushing dissent, he has made no distinction between 'radical' Islamists and ordinary Muslims. They provided the excuse Karimov was looking for to control the day-to-day lives of his citizens; to sell the idea to Uzbekistan that there was something even worse than him.

Declaring that religious or political pluralism does not suit an 'oriental' people like the Uzbeks, President Islam began instituting regulations to control how ordinary Muslims worship and live. By law, Uzbeks need a permit to move between towns, while the practice of Islam must now only take place within approved government mosques: an impossible demand, given that most Muslims pray five times a day. The definition of what 'practising Islam' means was also left deliberately vague: fasting during Ramadan, worshipping at home or failing to praise the president during prayer are just some of the reasons used for arresting Muslims. As you'd expect, they are routinely tortured and forced to sign confessions. In court, they often have no defence counsel. A wide variety of Islamic groups – most of them completely peaceful – have been banned. Even carrying a leaflet produced by any of these groups is punishable by up to twenty years' hard labour, the charge being 'misguided membership in terrorist groups'. In prison, they are again tortured and forced to renounce their religion. Those who don't, die.

And this isn't happening to just a handful of people: *tens of thousands* have been arrested or 'disappeared' since the mid-90s: so many that Uzbek jails are stuffed to overflowing and Karimov is forced to announce regular 'amnesties' to make room. In truth, a large proportion of those let out are ordinary criminals. As a result, the capital Tashkent is an extremely dangerous place at night.

Now anyone with a brain in their head would know that such policies will almost certainly make the problem worse: by oppressing ordinary Muslims, he is driving them into the arms – in both sense of that word – of groups like the Islamic Movement of Uzbekistan. But you don't argue with President Islam on this one. During a 1998 parliamentary debate on the issue, Karimov ranted: "Such people must be shot in the head. If necessary, I'll shoot them myself if you lack the resolve."

Inevitably, someone hit back: in February of 1999, six bombs went off in Tashkent, killing seventeen people. One narrowly missed Karimov himself. At first, the government tried to pass it off as a gas explosion, but even they couldn't keep this one quiet. Karimov went on television and appealed for calm. He made the crowd-pleasing announcement that he would give $300 (a fortune in Uzbekistan) to each affected family and would re-build destroyed homes. He added that once the perpetrators were caught, he would personally chop off their hands.

But who the perpetrators were remains a mystery: it could have been Muslims, but it could just as easily have been democratic activists, separatist groups from the Khanates of Bukhara or Samarkand, Karimov's home town, or even Tajikistan, with whom Uzbekistan has long-running territorial disputes. There's a long list of people the President has pissed off.

So they opted for the old reliable: Islamic fundamentalists, from either Afghanistan or Pakistan. In parliament, President Islam declared: "I'm prepared to rip off the heads of 200 people, to sacrifice their lives, in order to save peace and calm in the republic . . . If my child chose such a path, I myself would rip off his head." Every school, university, hospital and factory held mandatory meetings to inform citizens of the evil foreigners attacking them. Mosques were temporarily closed. There was another wave of arrests.

So to recap: you've got poverty, driving the young towards crime or fundamentalist Islam. You've got the government oppressing Muslims, driving them towards fundamentalist Islam. You've got routine torture and jails so full of religious and political prisoners that they have to let out all the rapists and murderers, thus increasing the crime.

On top of that, there are occasional bizarre changes in the law: in October 2002, for instance, Karimov decide to abolish the sport of billiards. Overnight, all billiard halls in Uzbekistan were closed. The national team was banned from travelling to tournaments and the Uzbek Billiard Federation was abolished. No explanation was ever given.

Naturally, the combination of torture and no billiards made Karimov somewhat unpopular with the international community. Sometimes he proclaimed that he didn't care, but on other occasions he made attempts to charm Europe and the US, including his deeply hilarious decision in 1995 to establish a human rights commission in Uzbekistan. Like many Uzbeks, it too has disappeared.

Still, you can't fault the guy for being a genius at elections:

after another dodgy parliamentary poll in 1999, once again criticised as flawed by the OSCE, President Islam responded with this baffling quote: "The OSCE focuses only on the establishment of democracy, the protection of human rights and the freedom of the press. I am now questioning these values."

The following year, 2000, Islam romped home with 91.9 per cent of the popular vote in the Presidential elections. This time the OSCE didn't even bother sending monitors, claiming there was no chance of a genuine contest. Perhaps, from focusing too much on human rights and freedom of the press, the OSCE failed to notice what a hugely popular chap Islam is: afterwards, Karimov's 'opponent' in the election, Abdulhasiz Dzhalalov (he got 4.1 per cent) admitted that even he had voted for Karimov. There's a guy with self-esteem issues.

But you can't have too much of a good thing: in 2002, another referendum (approved by over 90 per cent of the voters) extended Islam's term of office, leaving him in power until 2007.

Now you may be wondering how President Islam continues to get away with it. Uzbekistan, after all, is a poor country: it doesn't have oil – the usual reason why western governments turn a blind eye to human rights abuses – and it doesn't have powerful friends: relations with Russia have been at best lukewarm, while the US and Europe have continually complained about the torture and rigged elections.

President Karimov is still in power because in September 2001, he had a tremendous stroke of luck: the attacks on New York and Washington. In the resulting War on Terror, Uzbekistan suddenly became the must-have military ally: a country which shared a border with Afghanistan and shared the US' hatred for radical Muslims. Suddenly, Karimov went from being a pariah to a close friend of the Bush administration. Sure, there were a few human rights problems, but they could be resolved by 'engagement'.

And did the Americans engage: US aid to Uzbekistan currently stands at around $500 million a year, $79 million of which goes to the police and the Uzbek intelligence service, the SNB: an amount which could buy a fair few human-sized boiling pots. Uzbekistan became the first post-Soviet country to allow US troops to be stationed on its soil. The 10th Mountain Division are still there, 250 miles south of Tashkent. No reporters have ever been inside or even close to the Khanabad military base, but it's believed to be massive, with roads named after New York Avenues. There are claims that US Special Forces are also based there, and train Uzbek troops. Both countries deny that it is a permanent base, yet few expect that the Yanks will have left within the next decade.

The UK has also done its part, signing a deal in 2003 to allow Uzbekistan to import arms from Britain. The same year, the European Bank for Reconstruction and Development controversially decided to hold its annual meeting in Tashkent: the logic being that it would use the occasion to coax Karimov into condemning torture.

He didn't.

'Engagement' doesn't seem to be doing much good either. In 2003 the US claimed that it had donated $26 million towards 'democracy programmes', whatever they are. However, the only progress on human rights it could report was that average sentencing for members of peaceful religious organisations had gone down from 12-19 years to 7-12 years. Wow.

In effect, the Engagement 'policy' was little more than a distraction to get military funding around the US congress' ethics rules. Yet even for some in the normally cynical world of international diplomacy, it was all a bit too much.

Craig Murray, the United Kingdom's Ambassador in Tashkent, finally lost patience. Having sent home repeated reports to London on the dismal human rights situation in Uzbekistan (all of which were apparently ignored), he went public.

Addressing an audience in Tashkent, he said: "Uzbekistan has made very disappointing progress in moving away from the dictatorship of the Soviet period . . . The major political parties are banned; Parliament is not subject to democratic election, and checks and balances on the authority of the electorate are lacking . . . many have been falsely convicted of crimes with which there appears to be no credible evidence they had any connection . . . the intense repression here combined with the inequality of wealth and absence of reform will create the Islamic fundamentalism that the regime is trying to quash."

For a diplomat, it was a highly undiplomatic thing to say. Murray was threatened with the sack, then subject to an internal Foreign Office enquiry: the strain proved so great that he ended up in a psychiatric ward. Quite appropriate, given that so many Uzbek have had the same experience.

But at least the plucky Murray got to leave hospital at a time of his choosing, and with his ambassador's job still secure: his speech and subsequent treatment by the British Foreign Office caused such a row in the UK media that Tony Blair didn't dare sack him. The news even crossed the Atlantic and began to generate some serious discomfort in Washington. Curiously, the engagement-with-Uzbekistan 'policy' hasn't brought about any change: but the row about it just might.

Embarrassment at being bedfellows with Karimov has reached such a pitch in the US capital that Uzbekistan is now threatened with decreased levels of US aid: around

$100 million of the annual cash giveaway has to be approved by the State Department, contingent upon Uzbekistan being 'sufficiently supportive of human rights'. The speech by Craig Murray has made such approval politically impossible.

Fewer dollars coming into the Uzbek coffers won't bring the regime crashing to the ground, but it does make it more difficult for President Islam to argue at home that his 'anti-terrorist' policies are tacitly supported by America. Certainly, the last thing he wants is to be cast back into international wilderness: that would finally destroy his thinly-concealed dream of transforming Uzbekistan into the major power of central Asia. And economically, Uzbekistan couldn't survive any more isolation.

So he's made a few concessions: the 'amnesties' have been stepped up – the government claims it has released 200 000 prisoners since 1997, a figure which few believe. The best guesses are that there are still between six and ten thousand political/religious prisoners rotting in Uzbek jails. Some citizens of the country, perhaps sensing this mood, have even been brave enough to stage a few small demonstrations in Tashkent.

But let's not get too excited: Islam isn't about to loosen his grip; certainly not after the bomb attacks in late March 2004. For the first time, there were suicide bombers in Tashkent: part of a series of attacks over a twenty-four hour period which left nineteen people dead. No prizes for guessing who the government blamed. But given the style of attack, they were probably correct.

Yet fundamentalists do not pose the only threat to Uzbekistan. Those old tribal divisions from the time of the Khanates still exact a strong force in Uzbek society. President Islam has to be careful, allowing various clans to control certain sections of the Army, the National Security

Committee and the Ministry of the Interior. Few of them trust each other, which is exactly as Karimov wants it.

Because while they squabble and jostle for power, he thinks about the future. Islam is in his mid-sixties, and there are rumours that he suffers from poor health: rumours which became even more widespread when the Uzbek government recently passed a law granting him and his family lifelong immunity from prosecution.

In some ways, despots are predictable souls. Inevitably, they reach a point where killing and oppressing their subjects just isn't enough: they want to leave a legacy. They want their work to continue. Just like many other dictators around the world, President Islam Karimov may be thinking about who will take over after he is gone. And much of these thoughts may be resting with his eldest daughter, Gulnara.

In general, the Karimov family have kept a low profile. Islam is married to an economist, has two daughters and lives modestly enough. However, in 2001, the world's press was treated to a long look at what some of the Karimovs have been getting up to, following the rather nasty divorce of Gulnara.

Nicknamed the Uzbeck Princess, Gulnara seems to have Heir Apparent written all over her: she has a PhD in Politics from Harvard, a black belt in martial arts, she's loaded and she's gorgeous. When she was just nineteen, she got hitched to Mansur Maqsudi, an Uzbek-American businessman who, among other concerns, owned the Coca-Cola bottling plant in Tashkent. They lived between Uzbekistan and New Jersey, but in 2001 the marriage disintegrated. Gulnara went back to Tashkent with the two kids, saying that she was penniless. She refused to return for a custody hearing in New Jersey, claiming she didn't have the resources to fight her husband.

As a result, a US arrest warrant was issued for Gulnara which is still outstanding. In 2002, Mansur was awarded sole custody of the children. Gulnara still refused to give them up and hasn't been back since. Initially, it was something of an embarrassment for Uzbek and American diplomats. But they decided not to talk about it.

Yet during the divorce proceedings, it emerged that Gulnara owned $4.5 million worth of jewellery, 20 per cent of Uzbekistan's Uzdunrobita wireless telephone company, worth $15 million, $11 million in bank and investment holdings in Geneva and Dubai, a house in Tashkent, a $10 million retail complex, a $13 million resort in Uzbekistan, Tashkent nightclubs worth $4 million, a TV station and a recording studio.

And that was just the stuff the husband knew about: other journalistic snoopings have turned up a 44.5 per cent stake in the Quvasay Cement Factory, one of Uzbekistan's prime industrial assets, various offshore accounts with millions stashed away and a company in the United Arab Emirates called Unitrend Travel, which has a monopoly on travel between Uzbekistan and UAE.

You wouldn't think there would be a lot of tourism between Tashkent and Dubai, and you'd be right for thinking so. However, it's been estimated that between 30 and 35 per cent of all prostitutes working in UAE are Uzbek. Guess who helped get them there.

How Gulnara managed to amass such a fortune has never been revealed: up until the divorce she had claimed to be a civil servant, working mostly at the Uzbek mission in the United Nations. But it wouldn't take a genius to figure out that Daddy has been allowing her to help herself to state assets. As it is, she is enormously wealthy, and along with the family name, extremely powerful.

For proof of that, look no further than what happened

to poor old Mansur: a month after the separation, there was a series of raids on his Coca-Cola plant in Tashkent. Tax inspectors, fire inspectors, customs inspectors, and even an anti-narcotics squad queued up to kick in his front door.

The plant was shut down for four months, and then the Uzbek attorney general issued an arrest warrant for Mansur and other members of his family. They are accused of tax evasion, corruption and, most imaginatively of all, secretly selling oil for Saddam Hussein. You just don't mess with the Karimovs.

Since then (and with Daddy's full support), Gulnara has worked at the Uzbeck mission at the UN in Geneva and is currently attached to the embassy in Moscow, (where she bought an apartment for more than $1 million). Thanks to diplomatic immunity, she can't be extradited to the US. Lately, she's even begun to give interviews to the western press. Though supportive of the old man, she hints that mistakes have been made, that perhaps some things could be done differently in future.

Telling the truth, however, doesn't seem to be one of them. She still claims to be broke: "All this stuff about a fortune, with hotels, complexes, etc is rubbish," she said recently. "Yes, I have a lot of friends who have things like restaurants and hotels and who restore buildings. But that does not mean that these things are mine."

Yet in a country becoming progressively more impoverished, Gulnara is one of the few Uzbeks lucky enough to have all these wealthy 'friends' and no visible means of support. Oh, she's a cunning chip off the old block. Another reason for Islam Abduganievich Karimov to be very, very proud.

PRESIDENT ROBERT GABRIEL MUGABE
of the Republic of Zimbabwe

This is a sad story. Ten years ago, even five years ago, Robert Mugabe was still able to vaguely cling to his early reputation as potentially one of the great African leaders: intelligent and visionary and ready to bust apart the old saw about tinpot African dictators running their countries into the ground. Robert had it going on: he made speeches about building schools and moving past racism, and he knew how to do it, because he had education, lots of education. The man has – count 'em – *seven* separate university degrees.

But what happened instead? Instead, Robert got himself a motorcade. When he travels around Zimbabwe now, it is in the company of no fewer than nine vehicles: four police bikes, an ambulance, two Land Cruiser trucks stuffed with troops and heavy weaponry. The rest are Mercedes, the president's own being a custom-made Merc imported from Germany at a cost of $2.5 million and complete with a mobile office with internet access. It's comfortable, it's safe and once inside, Robert can happily travel down Cliché Avenue.

While his people starve, Robert lords it up and blames everyone else.

Then again, the history of Rhodesia, as Zimbabwe used to be known, is the history of colonialism itself. Folks have been living there for the last half a million years, though it was probably around the 12th century that the Shona, the largest ethnic group in the country, founded their dynasty. They built a large structure known as the Great Zimbabwe, which in Bantu means 'sacred house'. The ruins are still there.

The Shona ruled the area for the next few hundred years, until the Portuguese came, then the Ndebele tribes from the south. By the late 1800s, what would become Zimbabwe was largely occupied by Shona and Ndebele, but with the Ndebele now in the ascendant.

Which is when our first character enters the story: Cecil Rhodes. You've probably heard of him. You may even have seen those drawings in history books of Cecil astride Africa like a colossus, yet pointing back towards Britain. Cecil loved Africa, the way a lot of people love their dogs: especially a dog that has made you a millionaire and saved your life, but a dog nonetheless.

Born in Hertfordshire, Cecil first went to South Africa in 1870 where he and his brother got into diamond mining. And he did pretty well: ten years later he formed the De Beers Mining Company, which is still in business today. He had made his first million before he reached 30, which in those days would be the modern equivalent of owning Australia.

He went back and forth to England a bit to finish his Oxford degree, but finally settled back in Africa, the climate suiting his often frail health. But being a zillionaire wasn't enough for him: he had a vision. He became convinced that the only hope for Africa – and for Britain –

was for the UK to colonise as much of the continent as humanly possible. In other words, all of it: 'from the Cape to Cairo' as he said himself. The reasons for this were twofold:

1) If the British didn't do it, then other colonial powers would: like those annoying Boers in the neighbouring Transvaal Republic.

2) The poor old Africans were far too dumb to rule themselves.

Plus there was all this lolly to be made. In 1888, Cecil took a trip up to Zimbabwe to have a chat with the then Ndebele King, Lobengula, about mining rights. Back then the area was absolutely bursting with gold and diamonds. Lobengula got some arms, cash and a riverboat. Cecil got access to millions of pounds worth of free precious jewels and metals.

The deal was for Cecil to be allowed to mine the land. He obviously forgot to mention to Lobengula that he planned to steal it as well. As soon as the boat was delivered, Cecil started offering free 3 000-acre farms to white settlers, who came in their greedy droves. Lobengula might not have liked it, but what he probably didn't realise was that Cecil was doing this for his own good: Cecil Rhodes was creating a 'corridor of civilisation'. Well, obviously he didn't realise it: just five years later the ungrateful Ndebele attempted a rebellion against the increasing colonisation. They were slaughtered.

His civilising work done, Cecil then turned his attention to politics. In 1890, he became Prime Minister of the Cape Colony, modern-day South Africa. He made lots of speeches about expanding British influence, squabbled with the Boers in the Transvaal and restricted voting rights to white people. For a while, he was virtual dictator of the Cape. But when an attempted coup in the Transvaal had his fingerprint all over it, Cecil was forced to resign. He turned his attention back to Zimbabwe: now so civilised that they had named it after him. It was called Rhodesia.

Cecil died in 1902, leaving behind a fortune of £6 million and the Rhodes Scholarships: a scheme where students from all the (now former) British colonies, along with the US and Germany are given the chance to study at Oxford. It's how Bill Clinton got the chance not to inhale dope.

What he left behind in Rhodesia, however, were 12 500 white settlers, a figure which rose to 23 600 by 1911. Rhodesia was now exporting £2.5 million worth of gold each year, along with £35 000 in tobacco. Free fags and gold: literally and metaphorically, an addictive combination.

For the next few years, nothing of any great interest took place. The (white) rich got richer: by the 1950s there were over 150 000 Europeans living in Rhodesia. Out of a population of over 12 million, it's not a huge proportion. However, they owned *everything*: virtually every scrap of land was in white hands. The £28 million a year revenue was going into white pockets. And although Rhodesia was self-governing by this time, there was nothing the blacks could do to change the situation. Election laws had made sure that only a tiny minority of 'domesticated' blacks were allowed to vote.

Basically, Rhodesia was pursuing the same racist policies as South Africa, so in 1957, a group of Rhodesian blacks – who had all sorts of crazy ideas like universal suffrage – set up the African National Congress. (There was already an ANC in South Africa). Its first president was Joshua Nkomo, a member of the minority Ndebele tribe. Within two years, protests, riots and some minor insurgency organized by the ANC forced the Rhodesian government to declare a state of emergency.

Not surprisingly, the ANC was banned. So Nkomo set up a new organisation, the National Democratic Party. All its leaders were arrested, so in 1960, a third body came into existence: the Zimbabwe African People's Union, Zapu.

And it's here that Robert Mugabe enters the story. Born in 1924, he was educated in missionary schools by Jesuits, (Mugabe is a committed Catholic), and did the first of his degrees in South Africa's Fort Hare University, where he trained as a primary school teacher. He taught in Zambia and Ghana, but returned to Rhodesia in 1960 to join Zapu.

Although an introverted, studious type (his idea of a holiday is to travel alone and study for university exams), Bob rose quickly through the organisation. But there were tensions: Mugabe was a Shona, while Nkomo was Ndebele.

Eventually, these strains proved so great that Mugabe broke away and set up his own group, the Zimbabwe African National Union, Zanu.

Not that it did him much good. The following year, 1964, Ian Smith became Prime Minister of Rhodesia. Smith had no time for this being-nice-to-the–blacks nonsense: indeed, he wanted a white-only Rhodesia, with perhaps just a few blacks around to do the cleaning. The entire leadership of Zapu and Zanu were arrested. Without trial, Robert Mugabe spent the next ten years in jail. Meanwhile, Smith declared '1 000 years' of white rule.

In his cell, Mugabe studied for more degrees and refined his Marxist thinking. Outside, Ian Smith's attempts to create a white-only state prompted UN sanctions. A guerrilla war against the Smith regime began in earnest.

However, the war didn't really take off until Robert's release in 1974. He moved to neighbouring Mozambique and built a large – and often vicious – rebel army. By 1979, the Rhodesian regime was ready to give up. Talks were held in London at which a ceasefire and a new constitution were agreed. Even Mugabe and Nkomo made up, merging their respective organisations into the Patriotic Front, known as Zanu-PF.

In 1980, Rhodesia became Zimbabwe and Robert Mugabe became Prime Minister: feted by the west as a non-racist, intellectual moderate. Certainly, he talked the talk: "The wrongs of the past must be forgiven and forgotten. It could never be a correct justification that because the whites oppressed us when they had power, the blacks must oppress them today because they have power."

The largely ceremonial post of President was awarded to the festively named Canaan Banana, a former VP of the ANC. Ian Smith simply retired to his huge ranch, where he still lives (one of the few in Zimbabwe today owned by a white person.) Joshua Nkomo was offered the vice-presidency, but declined. He was already in a huff following Bob's decision to yet again split from Zanu-PF and run independently in that year's elections. Mugabe won 57 of the 100 seats on offer; Joshua only managed 20.

There were many changes under the new government, the most notable being the expansion of education. Today, Zimbabwe has a literacy rate of 85 per cent, the highest in Africa. However, first thing on the agenda was the land problem: re-allocating it from whites to blacks. Robert declared that this was his number one priority, while also stressing that white citizens were welcome to stay: after all, the whites still controlled the economy, and under the terms of the 1979 peace agreement, land could be purchased only from willing sellers.

It was a tricky problem, so Bob did virtually nothing about it. Perhaps it was the decade in jail, or all those years fighting a nasty guerrilla war, but Robert had become a bit paranoid (even after independence, a free press was not tolerated in Zimbabwe), and began to invest far too much energy into suspecting plots and treachery.

And he was right: people were out to get him. There was a bomb attempt on his life shortly afterwards. It could have been white farmers, but Bob preferred Nkomo and his Ndebele/Zapu supporters as the prime suspects. He did have a point. Nkomo had always regarded Mugabe as an upstart, and the discovery of arms at the home of an Nkomo supporter certainly didn't help. Mugabe fired Nkomo from the government, prompting protests and riots in Ndebele parts of the country – prompting the deployment of troops. Because he still distrusted the national army, Bob had engaged the North Koreans to train his own military unit known as the Fifth Brigade – made up entirely of Shona.

More than 20 000 civilians were killed. It was around this time that Bob revealed that he has eight, not seven degrees. He told supporters: "I have a degree in violence."

Robert Mugabe was now the boss of Zimbabwe, a position which was reinforced in elections in 1985. Despite the now on-going oppression of the Ndebele, the Shona still gave Bob their whole-hearted support. For his part, Bob organised as much political power as possible around himself, establishing a patronage system for government contracts that led to extensive corruption. What little land that was re-distributed, invariably went to Mugabe supporters.

But even Robert knew he wouldn't survive unless he resolved the land issue. And that couldn't happen while he was engaged in costly actions to suppress part of the population. So in 1987, Robert and Joshua Nkomo again kissed and made up, re-starting their merged political party, Zanu-PF. The Ndebele were back in government.

As part of the deal, Robert became President, but this time with executive powers: he could appoint the cabinet and propose legislation. Joshua Nkomo, already in declining health, became Vice-President. (From this point on, his political influence waned. He died ten years later.)

The deal did come as something of a shock to poor old Canaan Banana, the sitting president, who hadn't been consulted. Canaan took a job in the Organisation of African Unity. Canaan, however, had a secret. Later on, that secret, and Robert Mugabe, would destroy his life.

This deal made the power of Zanu-PF – and ultimately Robert Mugabe – completely unassailable, winning elections in 1990, '95 and '96. Zanu-PF has 147 of the 150 seats in the Zimbabwean parliament, effectively making Zimbabwe a one-party state.

In the meantime, there was *still* this annoying land problem to solve. 1989 saw the tenth anniversary of the 1979 peace deal – and the expiry of the clause that stated landowners had to be willing to sell. The Zimbabwean parliament passed legislation empowering Bob to make compulsory purchases as long as full compensation was paid.

Yet still Bob did little about it. Why? No one knows for sure. It could have been simple corruption or political cowardice or paranoia. Unless Robert Mugabe goes in for an intensive session of psychotherapy and writes a book about it afterwards, we probably never will.

The simple fact was that Bob wasn't doing what he said he would, and eventually people started kicking up: specifically a group known as the War Veterans' Association, who as the name implies, had taken part in the independence struggle. They were led by a charming individual by the name of Chenjerai 'Hitler' Hunzvi, a wife-beating nutcase who wasn't a war veteran at all: Hunzvi was a doctor, and from his practice in the capital, Harare, had handed out thousands of declarations of disability, with which the war veterans claimed payments from the government. It made him extremely popular with the veterans. A self-confessed admirer of Hitler, Hunzvi liked to compare himself to the likes of Napoleon, Che Guevara and even Jesus Christ. So under his sane and reasonable guidance, the war veterans began staging a series of often violent, protests. The upheavals lasted six years, and were enough to frighten the life out of Robert. In 1997, he finally compiled a list of 1 503 farms for acquisition. He also granted one-off payments of US $2 500 to the association's 50 000 members and monthly pensions of US $100. In a country where the average wage at the time was less that $30 a month, this was a huge sum of money, further crippling the economy. A couple of years later, Hunzvi was imprisoned for embezzling War Veteran funds. He died in 2001 and isn't missed much.

But let's leave the land question aside for a moment. What had been happening to Robert on the home front? Well, it wasn't too rosy. After assuming the presidency, Bob had built two enormous presidential palaces: not for himself you understand, but to please his wife Sally who had something of a taste for the good life. Sally, however, contracted cancer. But while she lay dying in hospital, Bob managed to find some comfort in the arms of his secretary Grace, forty-three years his junior. Before Sally died, they had had two kids. Not bad for a man in his seventies who, according to Grace, rises every morning at 4a.m. to do his exercises. And no, that's not a *double-entendre*.

Normally, such goings-on wouldn't be anyone's business: certainly, this is never reported in Zimbabwe, and even off-the-cuff remarks about Bob's domestic arrangements have led to people 'disappearing'.

What's curious about it is that Mugabe repeatedly makes

much of his staunch Catholicism. He is virulently homophobic, saying that gays are "worse than pigs and dogs". Even during his 80thieth birthday party in 2004, Bob told his guests: "I'm morally repulsed by homosexuality. It's Adam and Eve, not Adam and Adam, Eve and Eve. Let us never entertain the theory that man and man can form a family."

Indeed, so strict are his views that homosexuality is a crime in Zimbabwe, punishable by up to ten years in prison. Which is where Canaan Banana comes back into our story. Canaan's secret was that he was gay. It was one of those secrets that a lot of people knew about, including his wife, Janet, and several of his bodyguards. Perhaps his name was a bit of a give away. Yet they had managed to keep it quiet enough all through his presidency, and afterwards when Canaan worked for the Organisation for African Unity. But in 1996, when one of those bodyguards was taunted by a Zimbabwean police officer as 'Banana's Wife', the bodyguard became so angry he shot and killed the cop.

The bodyguard got ten years, but during the trial claimed that Canaan had sexually assaulted him. Canaan denied it, but was subsequently found guilty on eleven charges of sodomy. Before sentencing, Canaan fled to South Africa, having received a tip-off that Mugabe planned to have him killed. Following the intervention of Nelson Mandela, Canaan returned to Zimbabwe and received two years in prison.

Canaan's wife, Janet, was followed by police and harassed until she moved to London. She now lives in a one-roomed flat and exists on state benefits.

So, let's get back to the land reform. Exasperated by all the talk of buying land from the white farmers, black families began occupying farms by force. There were demonstrations about food and fuel shortages, brought on by floods that had left 250 000 people homeless. So what did Bob do? He ignored them, and – for no apparent reason – decided to waste even more money by dispatching troops to the Democratic Republic of Congo to help prop up the sleazy government of Laurent Kabila. That operation is still on-going, and costing the starving Zimbabwean tax-payer £1 million a day.

So in 2000, to settle the issue, Bob held a referendum to change the constitution. The changes would have allowed the government to seize lands without compensation, and would also have allowed Bob to remain on as president for another twelve years. It was a campaign marked by wild statements from Bob, alleging all sorts of international racist conspiracies to bring Zimbabwe to its knees For the first time in his political career, Robert Mugabe lost the vote. This was partially due to voter frustration, but also because there was now a viable alternative to Zanu-PF, in the form of the recently minted Movement for Democratic change. Led by former union rep, Morgan Tsvangirai, the MDC represented a younger, more educated generation of Zimbabweans, less interested in the land reform and more interested in Bob's mismanagement of the economy. Ironically, those who had benefited most from Mugabe's expanded education programme were those who wanted to see the back of him.

So Bob ignored the result of the referendum and began seizing farms anyway, mainly through his new friends in the War Veterans' Association. The police did nothing. In 2001, he agreed to cease the illegal occupations in return for the UK funding the purchase of the farms. Then he continued seizing farms as if it hadn't happened. There was a presidential election scheduled for 2002, with Tsvangirai, already preparing to run against him. Chastened by his defeat in the 2000 referendum, Bob decided to leave nothing to chance: he introduced new laws outlawing criticism of the president, and gave sweeping powers to the police to maintain public order.

And he rigged the election, mainly through the use of widespread voter intimidation (provided by the War Veterans' Association), though he also brought in new regulations forcing voters to prove their residency with utility bills: something most of the young, unemployed MDC supporters were unlikely to have.

He was now a fully-fledged despot.

Afterwards, he proclaimed that he would only step down when the 'revolution is complete'. Whatever that means. The EU imposed a travel ban, Zimbabwe was expelled from the British Commonwealth and Mugabe's own Swiss bank accounts were frozen.

In response, Bob had Morgan Tsvangirai charged with treason. The case was based upon an unbelievably dodgy video tape made in 2001. In that year, Tsvangirai travelled to Canada for a meeting with the Montreal-based consulting firm, Dickens and Madsen. Tsvangirai claims he hired the firm to lobby for the MDC in Washington.

However, the owners of Dickens and Madson say Tsvangirai wanted them to engineer a coup in Zimbabwe and to kill Robert Mugabe. As proof, they provided a secretly-made videotape of their Montreal meeting, during which Tsvangirai certainly relishes the prospect of a post-Mugabe Zimbabwe. However, he makes no reference to killing or coups. One of the men from Dickens and Madson does mention the 'elimination' of Bob, but that could mean anything. The tape is of very poor quality. Around thirty per cent of it is inaudible.

In his defence, Morgan Tsvangirai claims the whole thing was a 'sting'. And it's difficult to disagree with this. The two men he met had just bought Dickens and Madsen.

The first, Alexandre Legault, subsequently fled Montreal after being sought for extradition to the US. He is accused of masterminding a $13 million swindle in Florida. The second man, Ari Ben-Menashe, is a former Israeli Intelligence Agent who was described by a 1980s US congressional report as a 'talented liar'.

The court records also show that around the time of the videotaped meeting, the Zimbabwean government gave Legault and Ben-Menashe $615,000. The trial finished hearing evidence in February 2004 and is yet to deliver a verdict. But if found guilty, Morgan Tsvangirai could be executed.

How long Bob can go on like this is anyone's guess. In the past twenty years, Zimbabwe has travelled from being poor to devastated: inflation is running at 620 per cent. More than half the country are unemployed and survive on international food aid: though this is slowing due to a wariness from foreign governments of appearing to assist Mugabe. And what aid does get through usually ends up in areas which support the president. Nine in ten urban households survive on a dollar a day per person. One in four children are stunted from malnourishment. *One quarter* of the population is HIV positive.

Around ninety-five per cent of the white farmers have been evicted, but most of the land lies idle: much has been poisoned, while over 300 000 acres are now in the possession of senior military officers and government officials. And few blacks have the resources to buy cattle or grain anyway. Zimbabwe's once-famous national beef herd is on the verge of extinction.

Shops have begun refusing cheques from Zimbabwe's six commercial banks, which teeter on the verge of insolvency due to the skyrocketing interest rates, as well as unsecured loans to Mugabe followers which will never be repaid. Some banks are so desperate they are offering 650% interest rates for a ten-day deposit.

Political opponents and journalists are routinely arrested and tortured. Thousands of Zimbabwean youths are now 'recruited' into training camps for Mugabe's Green Bombers Youth Brigades, where they are brainwashed into becoming rapists and killers: a new generation to continue the repression

It is believed that a majority of his cabinet now oppose Bob. (There has been talk of Zimbabwean ministers holding secret talks with South African president, Thabo Mbeki.) But if they did attempt to oust him there is no guarantee that the army or Zanu-PF would support such a move: too many have benefited from Bob's gravy train. Recent in-fighting in the MDC has also helped to make Bob's position more secure.

But nature might do the job for them. In early 2004 there were (denied) reports that Mugabe had to be rushed to hospital in South Africa after he collapsed. The following month there was talk of chest pains.

There were also claims that glass had been found in his food. Who would want Robert Mugabe dead? Form an orderly queue.

Then again, the guy is a survivor, mainly due to his stunning powers of self-delusion. At that 80th birthday party when he ranted against homosexuals, he also bemoaned the fact that there were some who did not appreciate that Zimbabwe is 'precious, like an egg'. If Bob handed out a few more eggs rather than talking about them, more of his fellow citizens might agree.

ONE THING YOU CAN DO . . .

It's a big, horrible world. If powerful Western governments can't or won't stop these guys, then there's little you or I can do. And anyway, you simply haven't the time to be handing out leaflets or chaining yourself to the US embassy: there's work, kids, traffic jams . . . the irony of our relative opulence is that we are too busy maintaining it to help anyone else.

So here is one small suggestion: it doesn't take much time, and, if you're at work, won't cost you a penny.

Get on the internet and go to *www.amnesty.org*. Click on the 'Act Now' button at the top of the page. There, you'll find details of people detained without trial, possibly facing torture or execution. There will be instructions on how to send a fax or email to the relevant government. You don't even have to write the letter: Amnesty provides the script. And if enough people fax and email, lives can be saved. It's happened before, and it takes five minutes. Even we can afford that.